The Atlantic Economy
and Colonial Maryland's
Eastern Shore

The Atlantic Economy and Colonial Maryland's Eastern Shore

FROM TOBACCO TO GRAIN

Paul G. E. Clemens

CORNELL UNIVERSITY PRESS
Ithaca and London

First published 1980 by Cornell University Press.
Published in the United Kingdom by Cornell University Press Ltd.,
2–4 Brook Street, London W1Y 1AA.

International Standard Book Number 0-8014-1251-X
Library of Congress Catalog Card Number 79-26181
Printed in the United States of America
*Librarians: Library of Congress cataloging information appears
on the last page of the book.*

*To Roberta
and the memory of
Gilbert Chinard
and
Eli Winston Clemens*

Contents

MAPS

ILLUSTRATIONS

GENEALOGICAL CHART

TABLES

GRAPHS

Abbreviations

AM	William Hand Browne et al., eds. *Archives of Maryland*, 72 vols. (Baltimore, 1883–).
CSPCS	W. N. Sainsbury et al., eds., *Calendar of State Papers, Colonial Series, America and West Indies*, 44 vols. (London, 1860–).
EHR	*Economic History Review*, 2d series (unless otherwise noted).
JEH	*Journal of Economic History*.
MHM	*Maryland Historical Magazine*.
MHR	Maryland Hall of Records, Annapolis.
MHS	Maryland Historical Society, Baltimore.
PRO	Public Record Office, London.
Southern Studies	*Southern Studies: An Interdisciplinary Journal of the South*.
USDA	United States Department of Agriculture.
VMHB	*Virginia Magazine of History and Biography*.
WMQ	*William and Mary Quarterly*, 3d series.

References to prices are in pounds (£). In most cases I have used the decimal system to record fractions of a pound (thus £10 15s 0d = £10.75). Generally, the current Eastern Shore price is given. When sterling or deflated prices are used, this fact is clearly noted.

Preface

I began this work with a discovery. While reading court records from the colonial Eastern Shore of Maryland in the hope of turning up information about the everyday life of Chesapeake tobacco planters, I uncovered evidence of an unprecedented burst of economic activity during the years 1697–1701. My attempt to unravel the story behind what occurred in this brief period in the history of Talbot and Kent counties forced me to enlarge my vision to take into account the place in the Atlantic economy of these seemingly isolated counties. That perspective is central to the portrait I have tried to present here of how the evolution of white society in one of the more prosperous areas of the colonial Chesapeake was shaped by the gradual switch of the region's planters from tobacco to grain.

My debts are many. The years spent at the Maryland Hall of Records working alongside Lois Green Carr, Russell R. Menard, and Lorena S. Walsh were among the most intellectually stimulating of my life. Their generosity in making their unpublished work available to me and their continuing criticism of my ideas have done much to shape my analysis. While at the Hall of Records, I found invaluable the assistance of Phebe Jacobsen, Patricia Vanorny, and Diane Frese. Many other historians working on the colonial Chesapeake were in Annapolis and Baltimore when I was, and I was fortunate in being able to discuss my research with Gregory A. Stiverson, Edward C. Papenfuse, Ronald Hoffman, Carville J. Earle, Gloria Lund Main, Allan Kulikoff, and P. M. G. Harris. Jacob M. Price deserves special thanks for his close reading of my chapters on the tobacco trade and his willingness to share his research with me. To Helen Roe and Herman Belz I owe especial thanks for introducing me to serious historical inquiry. David S. Lovejoy initiated my enthusiasm for colonial history; he gave me the freedom to ask my own questions and the direction that made me answer each question carefully. Thomas Archdeacon and Allan Bogue of the University of Wisconsin criticized drafts of the work. Diane Lindstrom provided especially useful comments on two versions of the manuscript. At Rutgers University, I have been rewarded by the willingness of my colleagues to give me their time and assistance. I am indebted in particular to Rudolph M. Bell, Philip J. Greven, Jr., Herbert H. Rowen, Donald Weinstein, Richard H. Kohn, Ivan E. Brick, and Hugh Rockoff. Richard L. McCormick provided me with an exceptionally valuable and detailed critique of each chapter while I was engaged in the final stages of preparing this book; Warren I. Susman's constant encouragement contributed immeasurably to my efforts. Charles Ogrosky of the Rutgers Geography Department designed the maps and graphs. The painstaking review of the manuscript and the personal support offered by Bernhard Kendler at Cornell University Press have been everything for which an author could ask. My work was facilitated by a Rovensky Fellowship in Business and Economic History and by several generous grants from the Rutgers University Research Council. My parents, Eli and Lucienne Chinard Clemens, helped through their interest and love. Most important, my wife, Roberta, had the patience to live with me while I was absorbed in this book, and took time from her own work for critical readings of its various drafts.

PAUL G. E. CLEMENS

New Brunswick, New Jersey

The Atlantic Economy
and Colonial Maryland's
Eastern Shore

Introduction

Market agriculture was not new to the English settlers of the American colonies. They came from a world in which rural cultivators had long been accustomed to selling food surpluses and lived in a century during which market considerations increasingly affected the way families used their land and labor. Money and credit were replacing the last vestiges of a barter economy in England. Wage labor and contractual responsibilities had taken the place of traditional obligations. Communal landholdings were being broken up, land was given over to individual proprietorship, and improvements were introduced to increase the productivity and profit of farming. The English gentry led the way, by engrossing large estates and carefully supervising their use, but humbler rural folk as well found themselves thrust into commercial agriculture. Others were thrown off the land and forced to travel to the industrial and trading towns on the English coast in search of employment or passage to the New World. We need not claim that the market dominated the seventeenth-century English countryside in order to assert that most white settlers of the American colonies had already learned, if sometimes unwillingly, to balance the demands of family and community and those of a commercial economy.[1]

1. Of the vast literature on the way attitudes in seventeenth-century England affected and were affected by economic change, I found the discerning and subtle analysis in Joyce Oldham Appleby, *Economic Thought and Ideology in Seventeenth-Century England* (Princeton, 1978), the most useful, but see as well Edmund S. Morgan, "The Labor Problem at Jamestown," *American Historical Review* 76 (1971): 595–611, and Michael Greenberg, "William Byrd II and the World of the Market," *Southern Studies* 16 (1977): 429–456.

Initially these English settlers moved to the foreboding wilderness of New England, the fertile tidewater peninsulas of the Chesapeake, and the lush isles of the Caribbean. They shared at the outset membership in an Anglo-American world and reliance on Atlantic trade. But facing dissimilar environments and driven by contrasting cultural imperatives, the first English inhabitants of Massachusetts, Virginia, and Barbados resolved quite differently the questions of whether and what to produce for the Atlantic market. In New England, neither the harsh climate and rocky soil nor the intensity of the Puritans' religious errand encouraged immigrants to live by market agriculture. Instead, they settled in small, self-contained farming villages, and except for a select but thriving merchant community in the coastal towns, got by relatively independently of the Atlantic economy. To the south, a more humid climate, richer soil, and a longer growing season invited colonists to plant crops no English farmer had previously grown, and when the market for these new products proved profitable, settlers quickly adopted staple agriculture. In doing so, they turned away from the simpler life of English arable farmers, though to quite different degrees in Virginia and Barbados, and committed themselves instead to dependence on Atlantic trade and slave labor. From the foundations of self-sufficiency farming in New England, tobacco planting in the Chesapeake, and sugar cultivation in the West Indies arose distinct rural social orders.

This study is an attempt to analyze the way the Atlantic market economy shaped the development of a single region of colonial America: Maryland's Eastern Shore. The story begins in the mid-seventeenth century, when a booming tobacco economy pulled wave after wave of English immigrants to the Chesapeake Bay colonies. In the late 1650s, settlement spread to the Eastern Shore of Maryland, where Lord Baltimore's proprietary government soon established three new counties, Dorchester, Talbot, and Kent. The English people who came to this area brought with them, to be sure, conventional notions—about renting and buying land, hiring and using labor, dividing household tasks by age and sex, selling produce, and willing property to heirs —that suited them equally well for market agriculture and subsistence farming; but the relative ease with which tobacco could

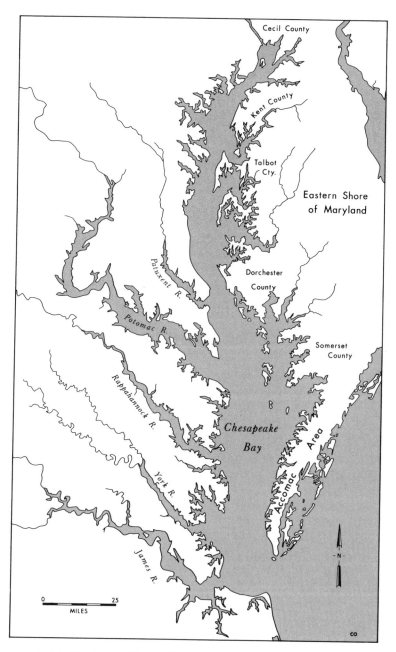

Map 1. The Eastern Shore of Maryland and the colonial Chesapeake.

be grown, the ready market for the crop provided by London, Bristol, and Liverpool shippers whose vessels frequented the northern Chesapeake, and the value of this "weed" in terms of the English goods for which it could be exchanged all helped involve these immigrants in commercial agriculture. For the next three decades, despite the growth of production throughout the Chesapeake and the gradual decline in the price of the staple, the tobacco economy thrived and settlers filled the Eastern Shore. Some came with money to buy land; others came as servants, in the hope that when freed they could join the planter class. In the closing years of the seventeenth century, however, trade conditions turned decidedly against these immigrant tobacco planters. Recession gripped the Chesapeake. Clogged and closed markets in Europe pushed down crop prices to new low levels and ended the period of rapid growth of the Eastern Shore's economy. English immigration virtually stopped. More wealthy planters, unable to get servants, turned increasingly to slave labor, while other residents cut back on market production; more and more whites left the region. Yet the tobacco economy endured, and by the second decade of the eighteenth century, improved conditions in the Atlantic market returned prosperity to the Eastern Shore. Tobacco remained a viable cash crop through the 1770s, and many inhabitants of the region continued to derive a substantial part of their income from supplying the crop to English merchants.[2]

Over the course of the eighteenth century, however, Atlantic market conditions effected a decisive reorganization of the Eastern Shore's economy. As the demand for corn and flour in New England, the Caribbean, and Southern Europe grew, merchants began looking to the northern Chesapeake for grain supplies and local planters had the opportunity profitably to increase production of crops previously grown only for local consumption. Wheat and corn farming first complemented tobacco planting and then, in Kent, replaced production of the traditional staple entirely. By the 1760s the grain trade had acquired the

2. My understanding of the tobacco trade owes much to the work of Jacob M. Price. See, in particular, his *France and the Chesapeake: A History of the French Tobacco Monopoly, 1674–1791, and of Its Relationship to the British and American Tobacco Trades*, 2 vols. (Ann Arbor, 1973).

same importance as commerce in tobacco. As the economic base of the society changed, Philadelphia merchants pulled the region into their commercial orbit and assumed many of the financial and marketing functions previously performed by English shippers. This sequence—the rapid growth of the Eastern Shore's economy through the 1680s and its subsequent stagnation, the renewed prosperity of tobacco planting after the first years of the new century, and the gradual diversification of agriculture and reorientation of trade over the course of the eighteenth century—forms the economic backdrop of my study and provides the structure for this book.[3]

We can chart the development of colonial settlements not only by the course of Atlantic trade but also by the changing relationship of land, population, and family. In no colony was the supply of land really unlimited. Whether in the Caribbean, where plantation acreage was relatively scarce; or in the Chesapeake, where settlers had to remain close to navigable waterways in order to participate in the Atlantic economy; or in New England, where ties to place and kin, once established, restricted movement elsewhere to take up land, colonists soon learned that as the number of inhabitants increased, the amount of land available to support each member of society diminished. For those with land, the situation was manageable: each generation of landowners simply found itself farming a somewhat greater proportion of its acreage and a little less able to provide for the next generation. For those, in the Chesapeake and the Caribbean, who controlled the labor of others, the falling land–labor ratio reflected their increasing use of slave labor and meant ever higher levels of output and income. But for poor whites, the pressure of population on land translated into higher costs for buying a farm and a contraction of opportunity. Emigration generally followed. At the same time, population growth ensured that as property was passed from the members of one generation to their children, the number of landowners would increase. This new landed generation of farmers soon married and thereby

---

3. The diversification of economic activity in the eighteenth-century Chesapeake first received careful attention in Lewis C. Gray, *History of Agriculture in the Southern United States to 1860*, 2 vols. (Washington, D.C., 1933).

strengthened the kinship networks that bound together a region's established families. Population growth thus made certain the increasing size and stability of the landowning class while it accentuated the inequality that separated the landless from the great landowners.[4]

On the Eastern Shore of Maryland, the gradual growth of population and the major shifts in Atlantic market conditions brought about a fundamental transformation of society. When the boom years ended in the 1680s, a fluid, essentially male immigrant society gave way to a more static, family-oriented, and native-born social order. Marriage among second- and third-generation residents, steadily rising land prices, and lower returns from tobacco all worked to shut new settlers and freed servants out of the planter class, while at the other end of the social spectrum, the fortuitous accumulation of inherited wealth, the introduction of slave labor, the careful management of plantations, sustained investment in commerce, and appointment to offices of power and profit advanced a small number of men to a dominant position in the economy. This four-tiered social order—a growing class of enslaved laborers; a large, geographically mobile, and rootless stratum of poor whites; an ever more numerous class of modestly well-off householders and their families; and a small elite of merchant-planters—was well in place by 1700 and endured through the 1770s. The revitalization of Atlantic trade in the eighteenth century neither dislodged the elite nor provided abundant opportunity for the poor, but it did usher in a new era for the established landowners and tenants of the region. Better tobacco prices and the spread of diversified agriculture improved the planters' material life and opened avenues of advancement for their children.[5]

4. The theme outlined here is more fully discussed in the Conclusion, but note Jan de Vries, *The Dutch Rural Economy in the Golden Age, 1500–1700* (New Haven, 1974), p. 1–21; Robert Brenner, "Agrarian Class Structure and Economic Development in Pre-Industrial Europe," *Past & Present*, no. 70 (1976), pp. 30–75; and Kenneth A. Lockridge, "Land, Population, and the Evolution of New England Society, 1630–1790," *Past & Present*, no. 39 (1968), pp. 62–81.

5. On Maryland, see Aubrey C. Land, "Economic Base and Social Structure: The Northern Chesapeake in the Eighteenth Century," *JEH* 25 (1965): 639–654; and on Virginia, Edmund S. Morgan, *American Slavery, American Freedom: The Ordeal of Colonial Virginia* (New York, 1975).

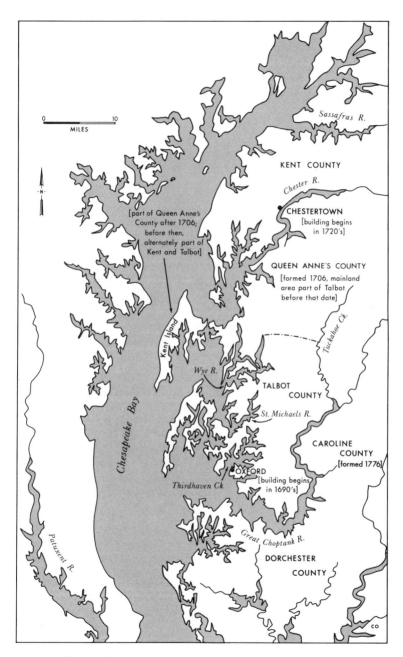

Map 2. The eighteenth-century Eastern Shore of Maryland.

In recounting this history, I hope to demonstrate how decisively the Atlantic market shaped the development of Maryland's Eastern Shore. Because my starting point is the Atlantic economy, I have focused on the development of an entire region of the Chesapeake rather than a single county. During the seventeenth century, the Eastern Shore, as defined here, encompassed Dorchester, Talbot, and Kent Counties. Then in 1706 the provincial government established Queen Anne's County out of sections of Talbot and Kent. Bounded on the west and north by the Chesapeake Bay, on the east by the uninhabited areas of Delaware, and on the south by swamps that transversed Dorchester County, the Eastern Shore was isolated from the rest of the Chesapeake, while two major river systems, the Great Choptank and the Chester, which cut through the heart of Talbot and Kent respectively, tied the region together and integrated the inhabitants of distant plantations into the Atlantic market.[6]

From an Atlantic perspective, we shall discover that just as the life that Eastern Shore settlers made for themselves in the New World followed closely patterns in the Old, so the society these planters fashioned around commercial agriculture and family farming set them apart from the inhabitants of New England and the Caribbean.

6. My study excludes the three southern Eastern Shore counties: Somerset in Maryland and Accomack and Northampton in Virginia. Settlers in all three planted little tobacco and derived their income chiefly from shipping lumber and livestock products to the West Indies. The swamps in Dorchester County separated the northern and southern Eastern Shore. For an excellent introduction to the history of this region, see Susie M. Ames, *Studies of the Virginia Eastern Shore in the Seventeenth Century* (Richmond, 1940).

PART I

From Boom Economy to Stagnation, 1620s–1713

Wherein we shall cover the history of Maryland's Eastern Shore from the hectic, prosperous years of settlement through the period of intensifying economic stagnation and social stratification. Following a brief discussion of the operation of the Anglo-Chesapeake tobacco trade, the analysis focuses in Chapters 2 and 3 on the market's effects on economic life and social organization on the Eastern Shore.

Chapter 1

The Atlantic Economy
to 1713

The Eastern Shore of Maryland developed as part of a commercial and agricultural system spanning the Atlantic Ocean and linking economic life in the Old World and the New. The place of English inhabitants of the Chesapeake in that system depended primarily on their ability to plant tobacco and market the crop with the aid of English merchants. In regions—such as the Eastern Shore—settled relatively late in the seventeenth century, bad times rapidly followed good. Through the 1680s, high but falling crop prices kept production booming. But from 1689 to 1713, war frequently disrupted Atlantic trade, and the inability of merchants to open new markets left Chesapeake prices low and production stagnant. The transformation from a boom to a recession economy shaped the initial development of the Eastern Shore. Only in 1713, with the end of hostilities between France and England, did prosperity return.

AN OVERVIEW

The task of colonizing the Chesapeake fell first to the Virginia Company of London. The settlers the company dispatched to the New World during the first decades of the seventeenth century shared little except the hope of improving the life they had known in England. If some were yeomen, most had only rudimentary familiarity with arable farming. A few were gentlemen, a number were artisans, some were adventurers of modest fortune and middling status, and many more were from the laboring poor. For all, settlement was fraught with immense hardships and tragic miscalculations. They expected that they could live with little effort off the bounty of the land; that complaisant Indians would labor for them; and that the animal and mineral wealth of Virginia would supply the way to an easy life. Blunders, epidemics, Indian attacks, and famine rapidly shattered their dreams. While struggling to save themselves, however, Virginians began to shape their region's economic development. In 1618 the Virginia Company abandoned its attempt to operate the colony as a corporate economic venture controlled from England and allowed settlers to pursue whatever private economic endeavors they wished. The Company also abandoned all commitment to the native population of Virginia and let the colonists subjugate and exploit the Indian inhabitants of the region. Most important for our purpose, this early period witnessed the introduction of tobacco cultivation. By the end of the 1620s, with the Virginia Company dissolved and royal government established, the rapid spread of tobacco planting tied the future development of the Chesapeake to market agriculture and the Anglo-American commercial system.[1]

Boom and bust characterized the economic lives of Chesapeake tobacco planters. These cycles of prosperity and recession depended on the relationship among immigration, the price of tobacco, the production of the staple, and the consumption of the crop in England (see Graph 1). Booms began with an upswing in the price of tobacco. At times, successive crop failures in the Chesapeake initiated the price increase. On other occasions, planters received better returns for their crop because of falling shipping costs or the growth of European demand. Generally, production increases followed soon after a rise in the price of tobacco, as English merchants, encouraged by favorable market conditions, shipped large numbers of laborers to Maryland and Virginia. Because tobacco cultivation required little land, planters quickly cleared new fields and set immigrant laborers to work. The supply of the staple grew, and the price of

1. On the early history of Virginia, Wesley Frank Craven, *The Dissolution of the Virginia Company* (New York, 1932), is outstanding, but of equal importance is Edmund S. Morgan, *American Slavery, American Freedom: The Ordeal of Colonial Virginia* (New York, 1975), p. 44–130.

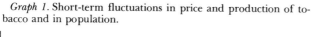

Graph 1. Short-term fluctuations in price and production of tobacco and in population.

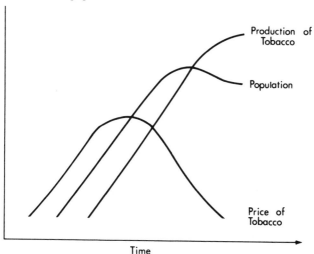

Production of Tobacco

Population

Price of Tobacco

Time

the crop, because the demand for tobacco was inelastic, began to falter. Planters might, of course, have curtailed production, but after they had readied land and purchased labor, this solution had little appeal. Instead, they grew as much as they and their servants and slaves could, often plunging the economy into a recession. But the process was self-correcting: as the price for tobacco fell, English merchants stopped supplying planters with laborers, and production gradually leveled off. Price then stabilized (though at a point below where it had been when the cycle began), and it would not again rise until demand once more inched its way past the existing level of supply.[2]

Over the long run, the growth of production drove down price. At first, decreasing costs—best attributable to improvements in the organization of trade and changes in the plant-

2. The discussion in this and the next two paragraphs is based on an analysis of data presented and documented below. Particularly useful for background information were Ralph Davis, "English Foreign Trade, 1660-1700," *EHR* 6 (1954): 150-166, and Gary M. Walton and James F. Shepherd, *Shipping, Maritime Trade, and the Economic Development of Colonial North America* (Cambridge, England, 1972), p. 6-26.

ing process that increased productivity—balanced falling prices somewhat and helped maintain profit margins, but once these efficiencies had been realized, the rate of increase in tobacco production dropped rapidly as the price of the staple fell and approached the cost of cultivating and shipping the crop (see Graph 2). By the late 1680s, a crisis point had been reached. In England, neither inelastic demand nor the slow growth of population promised greatly improved sales. Overseas, English merchants attempted to penetrate the continental market. Their efforts met with some success but in 1689 war disrupted this trade. In consequence, the Atlantic tobacco economy stagnated, not to recover until after the first decade of the eighteenth century.[3]

THE BOOM PERIOD, 1620s–1680s

As early as 1619, one Virginia settler claimed that "all our riches for the present doe consiste in tobacco." With tobacco commanding a luxury price on the London market and with rich tidewater soil available in Virginia almost for the asking, a planter in the 1620s could easily clear £50 on his crop. Aided by servant labor, he could multiply his income considerably, and the servants, when freed, might become independent proprietors and follow their former master's footsteps. In return for consignments of tobacco, merchants willingly shipped more laborers to Virginia and Maryland and helped sustain the growth process. Even as tobacco prices fell, they remained high long enough to encourage investment and settlement, and while falling prices dimmed the prospects of poorer immigrants, others maintained their profits by obtaining more laborers and increasing output. Moreover, an apparent increase in productivity, from less than 300 pounds of tobacco per worker in the 1620s to over 1,000 pounds per worker in the 1670s, balanced much of the fall in price.[4]

---

3. In "Secular Trends in the Chesapeake Tobacco Industry, 1617–1710," *Working Papers from the Regional Economic History Research Center* 1, no. 3 (1978): 1–34, Russell R. Menard has carefully presented a supply model of the economic growth of the early colonial Chesapeake.

4. The quote is from John Pory to Sir Dudley Carleton, September 30, 1619, in *Narratives of Early Virginia, 1606–1625: Original Narratives of Early American History,* ed. Lyon Gardiner Tyler (New York, 1907), p. 284. Tobacco

Graph 2. The boom period of the tobacco economy: long-term movements of price, production, and population.

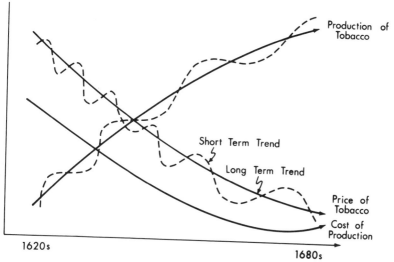

Production of Tobacco

Short Term Trend

Long Term Trend

Price of Tobacco

Cost of Production

1620s

1680s

Under these circumstances, population grew from about 1,300 people in Virginia in 1625 to almost 4,900 in 1634 (on the eve of the colonization of Maryland). By 1640, Virginia had 8,100 English settlers and Maryland an additional 400. Neither treaties with the Indians nor the admonitions of royal officials deterred land-hungry colonists, who pushed north up the York, Rappahannock, and Patuxent rivers in the 1640s and 1650s and then followed their tributaries in search of virgin tobacco soil. In 1653 the population of the Chesapeake reached 16,800 people, and by 1674 it had climbed to 47,000 souls. At the outbreak of King William's War in 1689, perhaps 74,000 settlers lived in Maryland and Virginia.[5]

---

export and population figures were used to estimate productivity in the 1620s. See Morgan, *American Slavery, American Freedom,* pp. 108–110, 397, 402–404, for population totals. Export figures were calculated from the English Port Books, E.190, PRO (microfilm at the Alderman Library, University of Virginia). For the 1670s, productivity estimates are based on crop reports in the Inventories and Accounts, MHR.

5. For Virginia, the best data come from Morgan, *American Slavery, American Freedom,* p. 404; but see also the figures given in Evarts B. Greene and Virginia

In contrast, the tobacco trade initially grew rather slowly. In 1627–28, three years after the dissolution of the Virginia Company, 366,000 pounds of tobacco reached England from the Chesapeake (55 percent of total English imports), 184,000 pounds from Bermuda, and 69,000 pounds from Spain. Seven years later, in 1634, London alone received imports of 388,000 pounds of tobacco from the Chesapeake, 81,000 from the Caribbean, and 89,000 from Spain—figures that suggest a lethargic growth rate for the entire English trade. By the late 1630s, however, this situation had changed. In 1640, Virginia and Maryland planters sent 1,024,000 pounds of tobacco to London. Caribbean producers added 139,000 pounds, while virtually no tobacco arrived from Spain. The Chesapeake boom was on.[6]

For the next half century, prices fell and production grew. Between the early 1640s and the mid-1660s, the farm price of Chesapeake tobacco dropped from around 3.0 pence per pound to about 1.5 pence per pound. In 1666 the price sank for the first time to less than a penny a pound, but over the next decade, Chesapeake crop tobacco generally brought between 1.0 and 1.2 pence per pound. In 1681 prices again tumbled below a penny a pound, and then, in 1688–89, dropped to 0.7 pence per pound. For the next twenty-five years, Chesapeake tobacco prices showed little tendency to rise.[7]

Harrington, *American Population before the Federal Census of 1790* (New York, 1932), p. 144–151. I relied for Maryland figures on Russell R. Menard, "The Growth of Population in Early Colonial Maryland, 1634–1712" (unpublished, 1972), pp. 12–29. A copy is available at MHR. Some of Menard's findings are in his article "Immigrants and Their Increase: The Process of Population Growth in Early Colonial Maryland," in *Law, Society, and Politics in Early Maryland,* ed. Aubrey C. Land, Lois Green Carr, and Edward C. Papenfuse (Baltimore, 1977), p. 88–110.

6. London Port Books, E.190/38/5 (1634), E.190/43/5 (1640), give import totals. The 1627–28 figures come from Neville Williams, "England's Tobacco Trade in the Reign of Charles I," *VMHB* 65 (1957): 403–449. A comprehensive tabulation of pre-1640 port book data is given in A. M. Millard, "Analysis of Port Books Recording Merchandises Imported into the Port of London by English and Alien and Denizen Merchants for Certain Years between 1558 and 1640" (unpublished, 1950–59). Copies are available at PRO and the Harvard University Library.

7. Unless otherwise noted, all references to tobacco prices pertain to the local, or Maryland, price. Eastern Shore prices are given in the Appendix, but the reader should also consult L. C. Gray, *History of Agriculture in the Southern*

At least through the early 1680s, however, the price of tobacco remained strong enough to drive up the level of production. Chesapeake tobacco exports to London grew from around 1.0 million pounds in 1640 to about 7.3 million in 1663. As prices continued to fall, the pressure to increase farm production and maintain profit levels intensified. In 1673, London imports had grown to 10.5 million pounds of tobacco, and by 1688 approached 15 million. Total English imports, while less well documented, probably increased from about 2 million pounds in the 1640s to 28 million pounds in the late 1680s. Such was the boom: initially high but gradually falling tobacco prices, spiraling population growth, spreading settlement, and expanding production.[8]

By the late 1680s, however, falling prices had confronted both merchants and planters with an agricultural-commercial crisis. Demand had not grown as quickly as supply, and profits had evaporated. For the next two decades, the tobacco economy stagnated. Population continued to grow, primarily because natural increase made up for the drop in immigration, and reached 130,000 people by 1713, but planters no longer devoted all their attention to tobacco; as a result market production did not keep pace with population growth. With the trade already weakened in the early 1680s, three events sped deceleration and delayed recovery: the passage of a tobacco duty act, the outbreak of King William's War in 1689, and the renewal of hostilities between France and England in 1702.[9]

United States to 1860, 2 vols. (Washington, D.C., 1932), vol. 1, pp. 218–219; Russell R. Menard, "Farm Price of Maryland Tobacco, 1659–1710," *MHM* 68 (1973): 80–85; and "A Note on Chesapeake Tobacco Prices, 1618–1660," *VMHB* (forthcoming); and Lorena S. Walsh, "Charles County, Maryland, 1658–1705: A Study of Chesapeake Social and Political Structure," Ph.D. dissertation, Michigan State University, 1977, p. 214.

8. U.S. Department of Commerce, Bureau of the Census, *Historical Statistics of the United States, Colonial Times to 1957* (Washington, D.C., 1957), Series Z223-Z240, pp. 765–766.

9. After growing at an annual rate of 5.4 percent during the period 1640–78, Chesapeake tobacco exports grew at a yearly rate of 1.5 percent in 1678–1721 and 1.1 percent in 1686–1709. These rates are calculated from the following tobacco export figures (in million of pounds): 3 (in 1640), 22 (1678), 28 (1686), 36 (1709), and 41 (1721). The 1640 figure was set above the 2-million-pound level given in the text because in 1638, London imports apparently soared to an extraordinary total of 3.8 million pounds. See note 7 for sources, and D. W.

New Tobacco Duties and Wartime Trade, 1685–1713

In 1685, new tobacco duties went into effect. Before that year the duty on each pound of Virginia tobacco imported into England had been 2.0 pence. The new law gave merchants two options: if they paid the duty promptly and in cash, they received a substantial discount; if they posted bond for the duty, they secured a smaller discount. The posting of bond allowed merchants to sell the tobacco and use the proceeds to meet their obligations without drawing on cash reserves. In effect, the bonded rate corresponded to the cash rate plus an interest penalty for late payment. By the mid-1660s, the regular duty on a pound of tobacco was already twice the Maryland purchase price. The 1685 act raised this duty from 2.0 to 5.0 pence, and the bonded duty from 1.60 to 4.15 pence. As a result, English merchants paid five to six times more to import tobacco than to buy it.[10]

While London and Bristol merchants complained about the new duties, they had little to fear. Because demand was inelastic, the price change did not substantially reduce the size of the home market. Moreover, consignment merchants, who made their living by selling the tobacco of Chesapeake planters and taking a percentage of the sale price as a commission, actually increased their profits because the act raised the price of the crop. At the same time, the large price differential the act created between what it cost to buy tobacco in Maryland or Virginia and what it had to be sold for after duties were paid in England invited merchants to purchase tobacco outright, rather than accept it on consignment, and then smuggle it ashore or

---

Jones, "London Merchants and the Crisis of the 1690s," in *Crisis and Order in English Towns: Essays in Urban History*, ed. Peter Clark and Paul Slack (Toronto, 1972), pp. 311–355; and Jacob M. Price, *The Tobacco Adventure to Russia: Enterprise, Politics, and Diplomacy in the Quest for a Northern Market for English Colonial Tobacco, 1673–1722*, Transactions of the American Philosophical Society, n.s., vol. 51, pt. 1 (Philadelphia, 1961), pp. 5–17.

10. Reports of the Committees of the House of Commons (London, 1803), vol. 1. pp. 603–634. A comprehensive survey of the revenue problem is to be found in Jacob M. Price, "The Tobacco Trade and the Treasury, 1685–1733: British Mercantilism in its Fiscal Aspects," Ph.D. dissertation, Harvard University, 1954.

bribe port officials to permit it to enter without payment of customs duties.[11]

But where the merchant gained, the planter often lost. A tidewater staple grower's remuneration, as Table 1 illustrates, was the residual after fees, duties, and freight were subtracted from the sale price. When the bonded duty jumped from 1.60 to 4.15 pence per pound, English tobacco prices increased somewhat less, and as a result the planter's residual shrank. In turn, falling profit margins sucked up investment capital and adversely affected the growth of supply. Possibly more important, the new import duties went into effect at a time when the tobacco trade had already begun to decelerate. By raising the English price of tobacco, the act ensured that it would be at least several decades before the home market might again expand and stimulate recovery in the Chesapeake.[12]

Merchants also reexported tobacco. The organization of this trade had been shaped by three imperial wars fought by the Dutch and English during the mid-seventeenth century. From these wars had emerged a fundamental rapprochement between the century's greatest naval powers. The Dutch had been unwillingly dislodged from direct participation in the development of the English colonies, while retaining a stranglehold on much of the European market for colonial crops. Amsterdam and Rotterdam wholesalers transshipped Virginia tobacco to almost every port in Europe after mixing it with cheaper European varieties, thus gaining a hearty profit. The scale of this reexport business made the expansion of continental markets of critical importance to the growth of the Anglo-Chesapeake economy. London's reexports went from perhaps 2 million pounds of tobacco a year in 1668–69 to 5 million in 1679–80, to 12 million annually in 1697–1702. Imports over these same years grew from 9 million to 13 and then to 21 million pounds of tobacco. In other words, the reexport trade accounted for three-fourths of the expansion of the London tobacco market in the 1670s and almost all the expansion during the next two decades.[13]

11. Price, "Tobacco Trade and the Treasury."
12. See Table 1.
13. Price, *The Tobacco Adventure to Russia,* and Jones, "London Merchants and the Crisis of the 1690s," cover this period. On the Dutch, the best material

Table 1. The effect of importation duties on the English price of tobacco: component costs in the sale of a pound of Oronoco tobacco at 7.5 pence per pound, c. 1710

Cost	Pence	Percent
Money returned to planter	1.12	14.9
Freight and handling	.89	11.9
Duties secured by bond	5.28	70.7
Commission (2.5% of sale price)	.19	2.5
Total	7.48	100.0

NOTE: Between 1704 and 1748, a duty of 5.28 pence per pound applied. If paid in cash, the duty amounted to 4.75 pence per pound.

SOURCE: *Report of the Committees of the House of Commons* (London, 1803), vol. 1, pp. 620-621.

Most of the reexported tobacco passed through Dutch hands and then went to northern European consumers. In 1680 the principal outlets for tobacco reexported from London were Rotterdam (617,000 pounds), Hamburg (481,000 pounds), Amsterdam (374,000 pounds), the Baltic (343,000 pounds), and Spanish Flanders (208,000 pounds). London merchants directed their efforts to expand the reexport trade in the 1680s and 1690s chiefly at Amsterdam and Rotterdam, although there was some growth in reexports to other ports. Outport reexporters traded primarily with Ireland.[14]

In 1689 the outbreak of war between England and France upset the reexport market. Men, money, and ships were drawn out of the tobacco trade; risk multiplied and shipping costs rose; European ports of call were closed to English merchantmen. While sea captains invariably developed ways of shipping tobacco to belligerents via neutral countries and obtained passes that allowed direct shipments to hostile nations, the wars dampened efforts to increase their share of the continental market.

includes Charles Wilson, *Profit and Power: A Study of England and the Dutch Wars* (London, 1957); and J. E. Farnell, "The Navigation Act of 1651, the First Dutch War, and the London Merchant Community," *EHR* 16 (1964): 439-454. The 1679-80 figure is from the London Port Books, E.190/91/1, PRO. The 1697-1702 figure comes from Customs 3, Import-Export Ledgers, PRO (microfilm at the University of Maryland library). The 1660s figure is an estimate, but see L. M. Cullen, *Anglo-Irish Trade, 1660-1800* (Manchester, 1968), p. 38.

14. London Port Books, E.190/91/1, and Customs 3, Import-Export Ledgers, PRO.

During Queen Anne's War, which began in 1702—shortly after King William's War ended—and lasted until 1713, reexports fell from a peacetime boom level of 23 million pounds of tobacco annually in 1697–1701 to an annual average of 15 million pounds of tobacco over the years 1702–13. Surprisingly, the French trade benefited from the wars. Before 1689, no headway had been made in dealing with the French company, created in 1674, which held a royal monopoly on the buying and distribution of tobacco; but the capture by French privateers of English prizes returning from the Chesapeake alerted businessmen on both sides of the Channel to a previously untapped trading potential. Elsewhere, however, the wars intensified the impact of the long-term deceleration of the tobacco trade.[15]

While anemic prices and reduced profits discouraged both merchants and planters, these conditions also had a less obvious consequence. The state of the market drove from the tobacco trade many smaller merchants, and left most Chesapeake planters less bargaining power over the terms at which they would ship their crops. The increasing importance of the costly and risky reexport business further intensified the pressures to consolidate control over Anglo-Chesapeake commerce. Prominent merchants built their reputations in Maryland and Virginia by establishing working relationships with the wealthiest planters and by creating credit networks that more or less assured that certain settlers would trade with them year after year. From these credit and trade arrangements, large planters gained economic leverage denied their neighbors. In both England and the Chesapeake, the wealthy weathered the slowdown in Atlantic trade better than others.[16]

The history of English settlement of the Eastern Shore of Maryland consequently begins with a coincidence: the first Eng-

15. Jacob M. Price, *France and the Chesapeake: A History of the French Tobacco Monopoly, 1674–1791, and of Its Relationship to the British and American Tobacco Trades*, 2 vols. (Ann Arbor, 1973), vol. 1, pp. 509–543, and "The Map of Commerce, 1683–1721," in *The Rise of Great Britain and Russia, 1688–1715/25*, ed. J. S. Bromley, vol. 6 of *The New Cambridge Modern History* (Cambridge, England, 1970), pp. 834–901. For trade statistics, see Customs 3, PRO.

16. Evidence of the changing scale of commercial enterprise in the tobacco trade is best obtained from the English Port Books, E.190, PRO. I used records from London, Bristol, and Liverpool. These records allow one to work out the

lish people to establish permanent residency in the region came in 1658, while the Anglo-Chesapeake economy was still very prosperous. If settlers had come three decades earlier, they would have had neither the experience nor the wealth that tobacco planting had already provided those people who in the 1660s left Virginia and the western shore of Maryland to relocate in Talbot and Kent. If English colonization had begun thirty years later, commercial agriculture would have paid far less well. As it was, in 1658, a healthy tobacco market invariably committed English immigrants and migrants from other parts of the Chesapeake to staple agriculture. Each boom in the economy, each success English merchants had at expanding the market, brought new settlers to the region and assured good returns to those who bought land and controlled labor; as long as English ships cleared for the continent, no recession pushed the price of the crop so low or held it down so long that tobacco planting became unprofitable. Through the 1680s, high staple prices encouraged immigration and provided avenues for rapid advancement. In the subsequent war years, however, less favorable market conditions changed the options facing Eastern Shore whites and altered the structure of society in Kent and Talbot. As deteriorating market conditions made it increasingly difficult for the free inhabitants of the region to live by tobacco planting alone, control of the economy gradually passed from the hands of immigrant colonists to their children. This new generation would preserve the heritage of commercial agriculture and family farming that dominated rural England.[17]

---

relationship between the reexport business and large-scale import operations. On commercial organization, the outstanding study is Robert Paul Brenner, "Commercial Change and Political Conflict: The Merchant Community in Civil War London," Ph.D. dissertation, Princeton University, 1970.

17. Before 1658, English settlers had lived on Kent Island (see Erich Isaac, "Kent Island," *MHM* 52 (1957): 93–119, 210–232), and some 1,500 Indians on the mainland of the Eastern Shore. The Indian population is discussed in Raphael Semmes, "Aboriginal Maryland, 1608–1689. Part I: The Eastern Shore," *MHM* 24 (1929): 157–172; and Jane Henry, "The Choptank Indians of Maryland under the Proprietary Government," *MHM* 65 (1970): 171–180. After English settlers appeared, the Indian population retreated to the Nanticoke-Choptank region of Dorchester County. The history of these Indians is currently being studied systematically by several scholars.

Chapter 2

The Settlement of Maryland's Eastern Shore: The Market

When in the 1660s the first English settlers in Talbot and Kent counties began clearing farmland to plant tobacco, they left behind a simpler way of life. Many had come from stable rural communities. For generation after generation the routine of day-to-day existence had changed little. The English farmer knew his land, its soil and topography and what the climate allowed him to grow; he knew the market, for he bartered and exchanged on a face-to-face basis in a nearby town; and he practiced a form of husbandry, whether stock breeding, corn growing, or dairying, which had been common to the community for as far back as memory reached.

Yet in the decades preceding the colonization of the Eastern Shore, English life had changed. From Elizabethan times, the enormous expansion of England's overseas trade, not only in the Atlantic but also with northern Europe and the Mediterranean, and the concomitant rise of London pulled ever more farmers into new market activity. In response to the spread of regional marketing networks, landowners introduced new crops and adopted new methods of cultivation; yields rose. Forests were cut and fens drained to clear land for growing and grazing. Pasture was converted to arable, and elsewhere arable back to pasture, as the ideal of self-sufficiency was abandoned and cultivators increasingly based their decisions on price and profit. Simultaneously, the sustained growth of population put pressures on England's landed resources and created an ever burgeoning class of mobile, propertyless poor. Many moved into the textile trade, where their well-being was defined by a wage relationship and determined by market conditions in distant nations. If much of the old order remained, a new commercial society was emerging.[1]

The transformation of the late-sixteenth- and early-seventeenth-century English economy had well prepared people for adventure and enterprise in the New World. England had an abundance of restless, rootless people. Few found it impossible to abandon the community of their birth to seek sustenance and employment elsewhere. Nor were men and women unwilling to leave behind the fragile security of subsistence farming for the hazards and rewards of specializing in the production of crops and commodities demanded by the rapidly increasing population of England's trading cities. Just as certainly, many English people already had to chart their economic outlook according to the little-understood vicissitudes of an intra-European trading system. Yet ready as many English men and women were to go to the Chesapeake and seek opportunity in a new market economy, there was much they would find distinctive about the economic life that awaited them on the early colonial Eastern Shore.

Chesapeake settlers, of course, planted tobacco, and tobacco, unlike the produce from English villages, had only exchange value. English farmers raised corn and cattle, used what they needed, and sold their surplus. Chesapeake planters, in contrast, grew tobacco, sold as much as they could, and bought from English merchants most of the household goods they needed. They stopped thinking in terms of supply and now calculated in terms of demand, and their reliance on European demand for tobacco forced them to consider land and labor in new ways. Both land and labor became preeminently market commodities. Planters bought and sold both regularly for profit. Thus in the

---

1. On English agriculture, see Joan Thirsk, ed., *The Agrarian History of England and Wales, 1500–1640,* vol. 4 (Cambridge, 1967); E. L. Jones, "Agriculture and Economic Growth in England, 1660–1750," *JEH* 25 (1965): 1–18; and Eric Kerridge, *The Agricultural Revolution* (New York, 1968). Valuable treatments of the development of a commercial economy include Barry Emmanuel Supple, *Commercial Crisis and Change in England, 1600–1642* (Cambridge, 1959), and Ralph Davis, *The Rise of the Atlantic Economies* (New York, 1973).

hectic boom years of the 1660s and 1670s, the first Eastern Shore settlers plunged into a thoroughly commercialized economy. Only with time would a balance be struck between the new world of the market and the old of stable rural farming villages.[2]

THE EARLY MARKET ECONOMY IN GEOGRAPHICAL PERSPECTIVE

Eastern Shore colonists first had to deal with the land. The English farmers among them well knew that an agricultural economy was shaped by the soil, the waterways, and the climate of a region. They had to learn to accept the inevitable limitations that nature placed on them while in their very understanding of the environment they gained freedom to respond to new opportunities created by the spread of market agriculture. Despite the awe that surely overcame the first of these English farmers when they confronted the vast, virtually uninhabited woodlands that stretched along the Eastern Shore of Maryland, those colonists who had been born in rural England must quickly have realized the potential of the region. The weather was mild compared to what most had known in England, and although the region lay well north of the region where tobacco growing had begun in Virginia, temperatures remained above freezing long enough each year to allow completion of the delicately timed process of planting and picking tobacco. Equally obvious to the first English settlers were the region's two central physical features: the large number of navigable creeks and rivers that connected the interior to the Chesapeake Bay and thus to the Atlantic; and the miles of level or gently sloping, heavily forested farmland awaiting ax and harrow. In short, the Eastern Shore, with its ample waterways and virgin forest land, bore a marked resem-

---

2. My understanding of the settlement of the Eastern Shore has been helped immeasurably by discussions with Lois Green Carr, Lorena S. Walsh, and Russell R. Menard. See Lois Green Carr, "County Government in Maryland, 1689–1709," Ph.D. dissertation, Harvard University, 1968; Russell R. Menard, "Economy and Society in Early Colonial Maryland," Ph.D. dissertation, University of Iowa, 1975; and Lorena S. Walsh, "Charles County, Maryland, 1658–1705: A Study of Chesapeake Social and Political Structure," Ph.D. dissertation, Michigan State University, 1977.

blance to those regions of England to which commercialized agriculture had recently come.[3]

The development of market agriculture on the Eastern Shore paralleled the spread of settlement up the region's two major rivers: the Great Choptank and the Chester. The Great Choptank wound around what would become the southern and eastern boundaries of Talbot County, and the Chester, some twenty miles to the north, cut through what would be Kent County. The Great Choptank, because it was closer than the Chester to the mouth of the Chesapeake, could be reached more readily by both colonists and English traders. Settlement thus initially concentrated in the Great Choptank area, that is, in Talbot County, and as long as the Atlantic tobacco trade remained the chief outlet for the region's produce, Talbot farmers had readier access to the market. Only with time, as trading patterns and farming practices changed, would the center of economic life shift north to the Chester area.

Neither the Great Choptank nor the Chester was a large waterway. Both were dwarfed by the earlier settled James and Potomac rivers and both were deep enough to allow English merchant ships to navigate only fifteen miles or so upstream. Colonists therefore stayed near the coast, where the many tributaries of the two rivers and the numerous creeks that emptied directly into the bay provided a convenient means of getting goods to market. Few moved far inland, for few could or wished to live independent of Atlantic trade. Accordingly, the bay and its rivers, by providing the link to English commerce, molded the pattern of settlement: the Eastern Shore became a coastal society and Talbot County planters dominated the region's early economic development.[4]

While the spread of tobacco planting followed the river sys-

---

3. On geographical influences on history, see Edward Whiting Fox, *History in Geographic Perspective: The Other France* (New York, 1971), pp. 19–32; Allan Kulikoff, "Historical Geographers and Social History: A Review Essay," *Historical Methods Newsletter* 6 (1973): 122–128; Carville V. Earle, *Evolution of a Tidewater Settlement System: All Hallow's Parish, Maryland, 1650–1783,* University of Chicago Department of Geography Research Paper no. 170 (Chicago, 1975), pp. 5–37.

4. Settlement information comes from the Talbot County Rent Roll of 1706–1707, Lloyd Collection, MS 2001, MHS (hereafter cited as Lloyd Rent Roll of 1706). See also the Kent-Cecil Rent Roll, no. 1 vol. 5 of Rent Rolls, MHS.

tem, the condition of the soil also shaped the economy. The Eastern Shore had originally been formed from sediment washed by melted glacial ice from watersheds of the Susquehanna and Delaware rivers. This sediment created two terraces, the Wicomico and the Talbot, of different ages and characteristics. The Wicomico was the older terrace. It ran from north to south through the heart of the Eastern Shore to the Great Choptank River and contained sandy soils; the Talbot terrace ran along the Chesapeake Bay, was longer and younger than the Wicomico, and was composed of finely textured silts and clays. The older, inland formations of the Wicomico terrace were generally more fertile than those of the Talbot terrace.[5]

One result of the process of soil formation was that the quality of farming land generally improved as one moved from west (the bayside) to east (inland). Most of the bayside areas, where seventeenth-century settlement concentrated, provided merely adequate farming acreage that produced, in comparison with other regions of the Chesapeake, only average yields and low-quality tobacco. This was especially true of the area around the mouth of the Chester River and on Kent Island (see Map 3). To the south, in Talbot, extremely rich soil deposits on many bayside necks compensated colonists somewhat for the generally poor quality of the land.[6]

Soil conditions also improved, on the whole as people moved from south (Talbot) to north (Kent). The Wicomico terrace—the older, richer of the two—was much wider in the north. Its soil groups typically yielded high-quality tobacco crops of average size. Settlers found such soil in Kent upstream from Chester-

5. USDA, *Soil Survey of Talbot County, Maryland* (Washington, D. C., 1963), pp. 73–78.

6. Ibid., pp. 2–4, 33–43, 82, map following p. 84; USDA, *Soil Survey of Queen Anne's County, Maryland* (Washington, D. C., 1966), pp. 4–5, 29–43, map following p. 117; USDA, *Soil Survey of Dorchester County, Maryland* (Washington, D.C., 1963), pp. 4, 24–34, map following p. 66; USDA, *Soil Survey of Kent County, Maryland* (Washington, D.C., 1933), endpaper map. See also "Geological Map of Kent County, 1837," Map Collection, Box 29, Folder 13, MHR. In USDA, *Soil Survey of Prince George's County, Maryland* (Washington, D.C., 1967), p. 141, estimates are given of current tobacco yields per acre on soil types that were common on the colonial Eastern Shore. Detailed but technically imprecise data on soil conditions in 1783 are provided in the Maryland Assessment of 1783, Talbot, Queen Anne's, and Kent County Return of Land Reports, MHR.

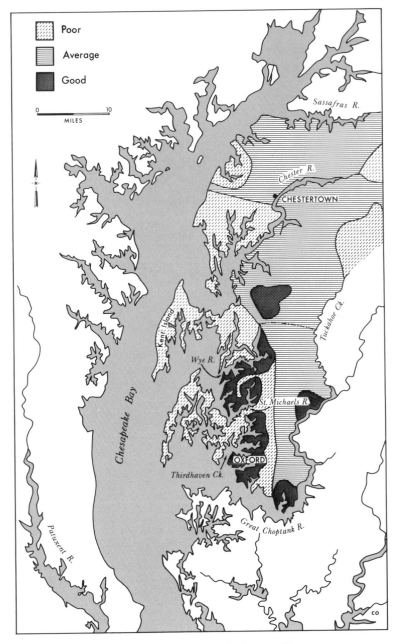

Map 3. Soil conditions on the Eastern Shore

town, the eighteenth-century port, and in most of Queen Anne's County (except on Kent Island and Wye Neck), but only well inland in Talbot. If farmers ventured farther south than Talbot, they confronted the level, poorly drained and marshy lands of Dorchester County.[7]

Soil patterns help to explain two stages in the spread of a commercial economy on the Eastern Shore. During the first, which lasted from the 1660s into the early eighteenth century, settlement remained along the bayside and trade occurred with most English ports. The south (Talbot), because of its location rather than its soil, had the advantage over the north. During the eighteenth century, traders began to differentiate between north and south, between Talbot on the one hand and Kent (and Queen Anne's) on the other. The south, with its low-quality tobacco, attracted chiefly Liverpool, Whitehaven, and Glasgow merchants who wanted a cheap product for reexport to France. The north, as settlement moved inland, began to draw London shippers, who preferred to market the high-quality crop that could be grown in the interior. In short, the opening of the interior of the Eastern Shore, together with the growing sophistication and specialization of the marketing practices of English merchants, drew Talbot and Kent–Queen Anne's into separate economic worlds. Later in the eighteenth century, the advent of cash grain farming would accelerate this process.[8]

LABOR: IMMIGRATION AND POPULATION GROWTH

In 1660 the agricultural resources of the Eastern Shore awaited exploitation. Nothing could be done—trees could not be felled, crops planted, or tobacco dispatched to Europe—without settlers, but happily settlers were plentiful. All initially set themselves to the hard physical task of bringing land into production. They began raising corn and beef for sustenance and producing

7. See sources cited in note 6.

8. The activities of English merchants in specific areas of the Eastern Shore can be traced in probate and county court records. See, in particular, Talbot County Court Records, Kent County Court Records, and Maryland Inventories and Accounts, MHR.

tobacco to exchange for English trade goods. They could have spent their lives this way, working their own farms and dividing their time between subsistence and commercialized agriculture, but they chose not to. The lure of the market—of increasing tobacco production so that they could purchase more of the merchandise shipped from Europe to the Chesapeake—was strong, and, given the ample supply of virgin farmland on the Eastern Shore, the only real limit on the quantity of tobacco they could produce was the number of laborers they had at their command. London and Bristol merchants solved this problem for Eastern Shore landowners by inducing the English and Irish poor to come to the Chesapeake as servants and by forcing African and West Indian blacks to comes as slaves. With this immigrant labor, free settlers gradually transformed their small, family-worked farms into commercialized plantations. Only as the land was cleared and occupied and as declining tobacco prices restricted economic opportunity would immigration slacken.[9]

From 1660 to the early 1670s, most of the immigration to Talbot and Kent was free. Some settlers came to escape religious persecution in Virginia or disease in the West Indies, others to convert an English inheritance into a New World fortune. Most, however, were men of modest means who left the great English ports of London and Bristol and ventured to the Eastern Shore in search of a better future. To a considerable degree, their decisions to come to the Chesapeake reflected economic conditions in England.[10]

9. Table 2 gives data on population growth and lists source material. For recent analyses of Maryland population growth, see Lorena S. Walsh and Russell R. Menard, "Death in the Chesapeake: Two Life Tables for Men in Early Colonial Maryland," *MHM* 69 (1974): 211–227; and Russell R. Menard, "Immigrants and Their Increase: The Process of Population Growth in Early Colonial Maryland," in *Law, Society, and Politics in Early Maryland,* ed. Aubrey C. Land, Lois Green Carr, and Edward C. Papenfuse (Baltimore, 1977), pp. 88–110. Seventeenth-century Virginia population growth is discussed in Edmund S. Morgan, *American Slavery, American Freedom: The Ordeal of Colonial Virginia* (New York, 1975), pp. 395–432; and Kevin P. Kelly, "Economic and Social Development of Seventeenth-Century Surry County, Virginia," Ph.D. dissertation, University of Washington, 1972.

10. A general introduction to the questions raised in this paragraph is given by Mildred Campbell, "Social Origins of Some Early Americans," in *Seventeenth-*

At first free immigration was heavy; after 1666, the pace slowed substantially. Not only did the rebuilding of London after the disastrous fire of 1666 provide employment at home for countless artisans and laborers, but through the end of the decade, unusually good wheat harvests kept the cost of living low and made migration to the Chesapeake less attractive. Then, just as the English prosperity of the late 1660s passed, conditions took a turn for the worse in Maryland and Virginia. A hurricane destroyed part of the 1670–71 tobacco crop and briefly disrupted trade with Europe, and the next year, with the outbreak of a new naval war between England and the Dutch, immigration virtually came to a standstill. Talbot County's taxable population, which between the first settlement around 1660 and 1667 had grown to 620 people, had reached only 712 by 1672 (see Table 2 for complete figures and the definition of "taxables"). During the next year, the taxable population actually decreased. Nonetheless, by 1672, if the small number of colonists living in Kent were added in, well over 1,000 colonists, most of them white, male adults, lived on the Eastern Shore and had begun to plant tobacco.[11]

Free immigration would, of course, continue. Many people

Century America: Essays in Colonial History, ed. James Morton Smith (Chapel Hill, N.C., 1959), pp. 63–89. David W. Galenson has written an important response to Campbell's article in "'Middling People' or 'Common Sort'?: The Social Origins of Some Early Americans Reexamined," *WMQ* 35 (1978): 499–524. See also Russell R. Menard, "From Servant to Freeholder: Status Mobility and Property Accumulation in Seventeenth-Century Maryland," *WMQ* 30 (1973): 37–64. Studies of nineteenth-century American immigration that stress family linkages between successive waves of immigrants as much as the push-pull mechanisms of the market do not appear to apply to the servant trade in the early colonial Chesapeake.

11. See Table 2 and Graph 3. Statements about English economic conditions draw on W. G. Hoskins, "Harvest Fluctuations and English Economic History, 1620–1759," *Agricultural History Review* 16 (1968): 19, 29–30; Elizabeth Boody Schumpeter, "English Prices and Public Finance, 1660–1882," *Review of Economic Statistics* 20 (1938): 21–37; E. H. Phelps Brown and Sheila Hopkins, "Seven Centuries of the Prices of Consumables Compared with Builders' Wage Rates," *Economica* 23 (1956): 296–313. For a more general discussion of economic conditions during the Restoration, see Christopher Hill, *The Century of Revolution, 1603–1714* (New York, 1966), pp. 220–221, 317–321; and Charles Wilson, *Profit and Power: A Study of England and the Dutch Wars* (London, 1957), pp. 148–151. Information on conditions in the Chesapeake is found in *CSPCS, 1661–1668,* pp. 381, 509, 515–516; *1669–1674,* p. 135.

Table 2. The taxable population of Kent, Talbot, and Queen Anne's counties, 1660–1713

Year	Kent	Talbot	Queen Anne's	Total
1660	152	–		–
1664	140	225		365
1665	–	446		–
1667	–	620		–
1668	155	630		785
1669	158	–		–
1670	163	776		939
1671	257	785		1,042
1672	–	712		–
1673	–	856		–
1675	300	1,018		1,318
1677	298	1,130		1,428
1678	303	–		–
1679	–	1,153		–
1680	–	1,304		–
1681	–	1,297		–
1683	–	1,348		–
1684	–	1,365		–
1685	–	1,299		–
1686	401	–		–
1687	–	1,542		–
1688	–	1,540		–
1694	447	1,504		1,951
1695	467	1,509		1,976
1696	515	1,379 (?)		–
1697	537	1,517		2,054
1698	581	1,517		2,098
1699	597	1,644		2,241
1700	691	1,854		2,545
1701	813	1,976		2,789
1702	840	–		–
1704	834	1,970		2,804
1706	850	2,050		2,900
1706	505	1,406	989	2,900
1707	–	1,406	–	–
1708	–	1,372	–	–
1709	–	–	1,054	–
1710	1,047	1,407	1,050	3,504
1711	–	–	1,071	–
1712	1,106	1,432	1,069	3,607
1713	–	–	1,067	–

NOTE: Through 1676, the courts levied a head tax for freemen aged 16 and over, male servants aged 10 and over, and slaves, male and female, aged 10 and over. In 1676 the definition of "taxable" became white males, free and

would come to join relatives; others would be merchants and craftsmen whose capital and entreprenurial skills would be vital to the developing tobacco economy. After the early 1670s, however, the pattern of immigration would be shaped less by the desire of free men to take up land than by the desire of those who already owned farms to acquire laborers, clear new acreage, and increase tobacco production.

Rural England provided the initial source of dependent labor. English villagers, to be sure, hesitated before contracting to work in the Chesapeake. However poor, they had traditionally been shielded from complete destitution by their neighbors. Land, kin, and occupation had tied them to a community, and such ties provided what safety they had in a world where poverty, famine, and plague were all too common. The commercialization of seventeenth-century English agriculture, however, cut many of these bonds. Community land, long held in common, was parceled out to individual proprietors, enclosed, and devoted to cash crops rather than to food for the local population. Small holders were bought out by wealthier villagers and children found themselves left with no land to inherit. Those who lost out became day laborers, artisans, or tenants with short-term leases, and their meager incomes left them desperately vulnerable to a sudden rise in food prices or contraction of employment opportunities. As the English population continued to grow through the mid-seventeenth century, so did the number of people forced off the land and into the ranks of the poor. In order to escape their predicament, many of England's poor

---

servant, aged 16 and over, and all slaves aged 16 and over. At least two boundary changes affect the figures in the table. In 1706 Queen Anne's County was formed out of sections of Talbot and Kent. Between 1706 and 1710, people who had previously been counted in the records of Cecil County were put on the tax list in Kent.

SOURCES: Taxable figures are found in the county court records (generally the November session), and beginning in the 1690s, in parish records, MHR. Additional taxable totals are found in *AM,* vol. 2, p. 341; vol. 15, p. 51; vol. 25, pp. 256–258 (occasionally listed incorrectly); vol. 28, pp. 51–52. In Queen Anne's, a separate levy book, now at MHR, was kept. See also Arthur Karinen, "Numerical and Distributional Aspects of Maryland Population, 1631–1840," Ph.D. dissertation, University of Maryland, 1958.

moved to London and Bristol, where they were offered the chance to become servants of Chesapeake landowners.[12]

The terms of servitude seemed attractive. Merchants gave the poor free passage to Maryland in return for the right to sell their labor for a specified period of time to a Chesapeake planter; the proprietary government of the colony guaranteed the servant, when free, a small stake of food, clothing, and tools and the right to patent a tract of land. Merchants profited directly from the trade in servants, planters because they were provided with cheap labor, and the government because the system encouraged settlement and made the colony more viable. Servants had the promise that they could become independent proprietors. If the promise were kept and if better economic opportunities did not develop elsewhere, English laborers would continue to come to the Eastern Shore.[13]

The course of the tobacco trade and conditions in England regulated the commerce in servants (see Graph 3). As the struggle between the English and Dutch for control of the North Atlantic subsided in the mid-1670s, Eastern Shore planters began getting their first major shipments. Relatively high tobacco prices maintained the demand for servants, while a slump in the real wages of London workers provided the impetus that drove many to the New World. The trade in servants peaked in 1680, when English merchants delivered at least 100 men, women, and children. Immigration then virtually stopped as a result of the collapse of the tobacco market and the improvement of employment opportunities in the port cities of southern England.[14]

In 1684 the recession temporarily ceased. In England, new, higher tobacco duties were soon to go into effect; consumers

12. In addition to the sources listed in note 1 above, see David Hey, *An English Rural Community: Myddle under the Tudors and Stuarts* (Leicester, 1974); J. D. Chambers, *Population, Economy, and Society in Pre-Industrial England* (Oxford, 1972); and W. G. Hoskins, *The Midland Peasant: The Economic and Social History of a Leicestershire Village* (London, 1957).

13. For a fuller discussion, see "The Land System," below, and Abbot Emerson Smith, *Colonists in Bondage: White Servitude and Convict Labor in America, 1607–1776* (Chapel Hill, N.C., 1947).

14. Phelps Brown and Hopkins, "Seven Centuries of the Prices of Consumables," p. 313; Hoskins, "Harvest Fluctuations," p. 29.

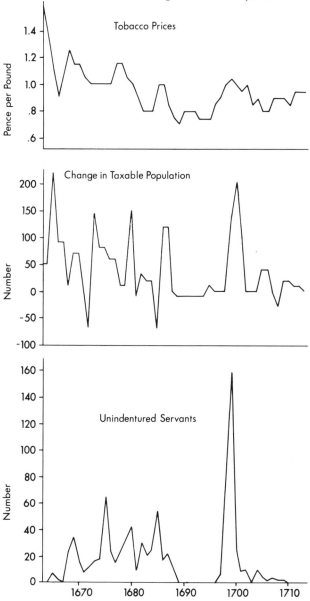

Graph 3. Tobacco prices, changes in taxable population, and number of unindentured servants arriving in Talbot County, 1665–1713.

Sources: Russell R. Menard. "Farm Price of Maryland Tobacco, 1659–1710," *MHM* 68 (1973): 80–85; Inventories, MHR; Talbot County Records, MHR. See also Table 2.

anticipated that the duties would force up tobacco prices, and the demand for the product improved. In the Chesapeake, increased demand for tobacco put planters in a better position to buy laborers and set them to work profitably. After shiploads of immigrants began arriving, Kent County's taxable population grew by some 200 people, while in Talbot between 1685 and 1687, the taxable population climbed from 1,299 to 1,542. Many of the people added to the county tax lists during this period were servants; at least half, however, were not. Around 1685, it seems certain, Eastern Shore whites witnessed the first substantial importation of slaves. Just as significant, in the wake of the boom of the mid-1680s numerous former servants who had arrived half a decade before and had now served out their time collected their freedom dues and left the Eastern Shore. From the 1680s on, this pattern would continue: poorer colonists, after getting their start in Talbot or Kent, would head for less settled areas in Delaware and Pennsylvania.[15]

After the boom of the mid-1680s, the recession returned. Tobacco prices continued their downward course, and neither merchants nor planters registered much enthusiasm for the servant trade. When King William's War began in 1689, two new problems beset those who depended on the tobacco economy. The first was created by the English government, which, in order to defend its commercial interests, placed restrictions on the number of ships that could be sent to the colonies. At the same time, the presence of hostile French men-of-war in the North Atlantic made shipping more risky and insurance more costly. These conditions increased the expense of freighting goods between England and America, and, as a result, Chesapeake planters got less for their tobacco and had to pay more for English merchandise. Not surprisingly, few servants found their way to the Chesapeake.[16]

15. Note the totals for taxable population and the importation of unindentured servants given in Table 2 and Graph 3. Because no records exist of slave importations or the out-migration of poor whites, this paragraph is speculative. Data from the inventories about the prevalence of servants and slaves as well as evidence on population changes in Table 2 serve as the basis for my conjectures.

16. Detailed information on the wartime disruption of commerce is available in William A. Shaw, ed., *Calendar of Treasury Books*, 32 vols. (London, 1904–1957), vol. 9, pt. 2, pp. 478–479; pt. 4, pp. 1364–65; pt. 5, pp. 1932–39; vol. 10,

Meanwhile, in England, pressure built that would send the last major surge of white immigrants to the Eastern Shore. Through the late 1690s, bad harvests adversely affected the cost of living, while the war disrupted normal patterns of employment. When peace broke in 1697, not only were a great number of poorer English people ready to come to the Chesapeake, but tobacco planters, once again able to get their crop safely and cheaply to market, were eager to contract for laborers. In the five years from 1697 through 1701, more servants came to the Eastern Shore and to the Chesapeake in general than during any similar period in the seventeenth century. This boom, however, was to be the final one. The resumption of hostilities betwen England and France in 1702 plunged the Chesapeake economy into another decade-long depression, and when in 1713 the Treaty of Utrecht finally concluded Queen Anne's War, peace did not bring with it a resumption of the servant trade. Unfree white laborers would still come to the Eastern Shore, but their numbers would be few and most would be convicts whom the English government allowed to exchange prison terms for sentences of servitude in the colonies.[17]

During only two relatively short periods—one from the mid-1670s to the mid-1680s, the other between 1697 and 1701—had the shipment of servants to the Eastern Shore played a critical role in population growth and economic development. Seen in the perspective of the entire Chesapeake, the pattern was common enough: throughout Maryland and Virginia over the last quarter of the seventeenth century, servants had gradually be-

---

pt. 1, p. 430; and in *CSPCS, 1689-1692*, pp. 183, 381-382; *1693-1696*, pp. 518-519; *1702-1703*, pp. 45-46, 259-260. Little is available on credit resources of English merchants; my statement is speculative, based on study of Talbot and Kent county inventories and accounts. The credit crisis of the 1690s, however, has been documented by D. W. Jones, "London Merchants and the Crisis of the 1690s," in *Crisis and Order in English Towns: Essays in Urban History*, ed. Peter Clark and Paul Slack (Toronto, 1972), pp. 311-355.

17. For conditions in England, see Hoskins, "Harvest Fluctuations," pp. 29-30; for the state of the tobacco market, see Appendix. The magnitude of the 1697-1701 immigration boom in other parts of the Chesapeake was determined by a survey of Virginia Court Order Books, Virginia State Library, Richmond, and Maryland County Court Records, MHR. Additional information on population growth can be found in *AM*, vol. 25, pp. 256-258.

come a less and less important form of labor. In many regions, the 1697 boom had reversed this trend, but as on the Eastern Shore, the return to servant labor during this brief period of peace and high crop prices had not had lasting effects.

One explanation for the fact that relatively few servants came to the Chesapeake in the late seventeenth century was the state of the tobacco economy. By the 1680s, planters were lucky to get a penny per pound for their crop—a price at which they could just about break even—and with the onset of two decades of war in 1689 and the resulting rise in shipping costs, many abandoned efforts to expand tobacco production. Except during the 1697–1701 boom, most settlers remained content with the labor they already had and some devoted more time to the cultivation of food crops and the fashioning of simple household items. The tobacco trade, of course, did not collapse, but Chesapeake exports remained at about the same level throughout the war years. The risks of war, the price of tobacco, and the cost of freight consequently played a part in the demand for labor, and these conditions help to explain the pace of the servant trade to Maryland and Virginia. Even so, the failure of the trade to revive after 1713, when peace returned and tobacco prices rose, suggests that other factors affected the movement of people from England to the Chesapeake.[18]

Immigration also slowed because of problems on the supply side of the servant trade. The number of servants sent to the Chesapeake had to grow constantly and rapidly simply to maintain the ratio of free landowners to servile laborers in Maryland and Virginia. The trade could grow at this rate as long as the expansion of the lower and middle strata of rural English society, from which most servants were drawn, continued. Roughly midway through the seventeenth century, however, deaths began to outnumber births in rural England, and within a generation, a supply problem arose. Moreover, as the rate of English population growth declined, opportunities for upward mobility opened up and tempted English men and women to take their chances at home. If the English economy suffered because limited population growth reduced the rate of demand,

18. Tobacco prices are shown in the Appendix.

the same demand conditions affected the market for tobacco and made the Chesapeake a less inviting place.[19]

Still, merchants could have turned elsewhere for servants: to the destitute in England's increasingly crowded commercial centers, to convict laborers, to impoverished Catholic tenants in Ireland, or even to those escaping religious troubles and economic misfortune on the European continent. In fact, all of these sources were tapped, but not necessarily to supply Maryland and Virginia with settlers. Newer areas offered immigrants more. As early as 1681, William Penn's colonization of the territory north of Maryland diverted ships from the Chesapeake to the Delaware; while the initial surge into the region lasted only until 1685, Pennsylvania and Delaware remained competitors for the labor of English people who came to the New World. Similarly, the settlement of South Carolina during the 1680s drew potential colonists from the Chesapeake, and thereafter the Carolina government attempted to attract immigrants with lucrative land grants.[20]

In sum, even if in the late seventeenth century falling tobacco prices and rising wartime costs had not made the purchase of servants more difficult for Chesapeake landowners, conditions in England and competition with other colonies for settlers would have created a shortage of white laborers in Maryland and Virginia. To the shortage of white laborers, however, there was a solution.

---

19. Only the outlines of seventeenth-century English population growth are known. The most important works on this subject include Chambers, *Population, Economy, and Society;* E. A. Wrigley, "Mortality in Pre-Industrial England: The Example of Colyton, Devon, over Three Centuries," in *Population and Social Change,* ed. D. V. Glass and Roger Revelle (London, 1972), pp. 243–273; G. S. L. Tucker, "English Pre-Industrial Population Trends," *EHR* 16 (1963): 205–218; Ronald Lee, "Population in Preindustrial England: An Econometric Analysis," *Quarterly Journal of Economics* 87 (1973): 581–607; E. A. Wrigley, "Family Limitation in Pre-Industrial England," *EHR* 19 (1966): 82–109; and W. G. Howson, "Plague, Poverty, and Population in Parts of Northwest England, 1580–1720," *Transactions of the Historic Society of Lancashire and Cheshire* 112 (1960): 29–55.

20. Gary B. Nash, *Quakers and Politics, Pennsylvania, 1681–1726* (Princeton, 1968), pp. 48–67; Converse D. Clowse, *Economic Beginnings of Colonial South Carolina, 1670–1730* (Columbia, S.C., 1971), pp. 50–54, 73–76, 104–106; Richard Waterhouse, "South Carolina's Colonial Elite: A Study in the Social Structure and Political Culture of a Southern Colony, 1670–1760," Ph.D. dissertation, Johns Hopkins University, 1973, pp. 8–50.

Talbot and Kent county farmers could also buy slaves. By the time white settlers arrived on the Eastern Shore, European nations had been involved in the African slave trade for over a century and a half. Around 1500, the Portuguese had begun buying slaves from African tribes that were willing to sell war captives. At first the Portuguese put these captives to work on sugar plantations on the island of São Thomé, near the African mainland. By mid-century they had moved across the South Atlantic and introduced sugar culture and slave labor to Brazil. With this move they had taken a decisive step toward creation of a commercial system that would eventually make African laborers available to Chesapeake tobacco producers.[21]

Encouraged by Portugal's success, other nations soon entered the trade. First the Dutch, then the English and French sent ships to Africa, and the struggle to maintain a foothold for trade on the coast repeatedly drove these European powers to war with each other. Slavery spread from Portuguese Brazil to the Spanish possessions in South and Central America, to the Caribbean, and then gradually to the North American colonies. Where sugar proved difficult to grow, Europeans put Africans to work digging for minerals, producing pitch and tar, cultivating grain, and tending rice. To procure slaves, merchants brought to Africa textiles from the East Indies, iron and copper from the Baltic, and woolens and gunpowder from their own countries. Incessant demand for more slaves was translated into pressure on the tribes supplying captives to expand the range and increase the frequency of their raids on other Africans. In all, before the end of the seventeenth century some million and a half people were torn from their native Africa and, if they did not die on the gruesome passage to the New World, became the permanent chattel of European colonists.[22]

At first, all this—the greed, warfare, and international commerce that fueled the slave economies—mattered little to the English settlers of the Chesapeake. They lived far from the

21. The best summary of the origins of the slave trade is to be found in Philip Curtin, Steven Feierman, Leonard Thompson, and Jan Vansina, *African History* (Boston, 1978), pp. 213–248.

22. Ibid. On the volume of the slave trade, see Philip D. Curtin, *The Atlantic Slave Trade: A Census* (Madison, Wis., 1969).

South Atlantic sugar colonies, and in any case had servants who could plant tobacco. They dealt with tobacco merchants who seldom had the capital to finance slaving voyages from Africa all the way to the Chesapeake. These same merchants knew that the Maryland and Virginia governments would grant shippers negotiable land rights (headrights) for anyone, black or white, they brought to the tobacco colonies, and for this reason, they could profit as readily from servants, who cost very little, as from slaves, who could not be obtained without a substantial outlay of funds.

In the 1670s this situation began to change. By that time there were men in London and Bristol who had accumulated enough money from tobacco to venture some in the slave trade. Few of them participated personally in the Royal African Company, which the English government chartered in 1672 and granted a monopoly over trade on the African coast, but they were able to obtain from the company consignments of slaves for the Chesapeake. Not until the 1690s, however, after the headright system had ended and white immigration to Pennsylvania and Carolina had begun, did merchants regularly bring large shipments of slaves directly from Africa to Maryland and Virginia.[23]

Until that time, most Africans brought to the Chesapeake had already endured enslavement in the West Indies. After the mid-seventeenth century, the concentration of landholding and the fall of sugar prices in Barbados drove small planters from the island, and some resettled with their slaves in the tobacco colonies. Other slaves were bought in the Caribbean and sold in the Chesapeake by New England merchants. If, however, the initial brutalization of Africans by English people in the Caribbean and the steady flow of commerce between the islands and the mainland provinces made it easy for Chesapeake farmers to drift into slave owning, it is equally clear that there was no rush to replace English laborers with black African field hands. Slavery came slowly to the Chesapeake.[24]

23. Details about merchants involved in the tobacco and slave trades may be found in the London Port Books, E. 190, PRO; K. G. Davies, *The Royal African Company* (London, 1957), pp. 377–390; *CSPCS, 1669–1674*, p. 552; and Elizabeth Donnan, ed., *Documents Illustrative of the History of the Slave Trade to America*, 4 vols. (Washington, D.C., 1931–35), vol. 4, p. 55.
24. The literature on the origins of slavery in the Chesapeake is extensive, but

On the Eastern Shore the spread of slavery followed the pattern that existed throughout the tidewater regions of Maryland and Virginia. The black population grew steadily but gradually. From some 300 men, women, and children in 1680, the number of blacks in Talbot, Kent, and Cecil increased to perhaps 1,390 by 1704 and then to around 1,640 by 1710. Only once or twice—in 1685 and perhaps during Queen Anne's War—did English slave ships come directly to the Eastern Shore from Africa; at other times, planters bought from their neighbors across the bay or from merchants in the Caribbean trade. The position of the Eastern Shore in the slave trade was not, however, the only explanation of the gradual development of slavery in the region.[25]

In the seventeenth century, Eastern Shore planters showed no distinct preference for slaves over servants. To establish this point, it is necessary to recall briefly the supply situation. Through 1689, planters had a fairly easy time buying servants and a good deal more difficulty getting slaves. To acquire more slaves, they would have had to increase the amount they were willing to pay for them enough to make it worthwhile for merchants to reroute their slaving vessels from the South Atlantic to the Chesapeake. If planters had done this, not only would local slave prices have increased, but so would the slave–servant price ratio. Until the end of the seventeenth century, no such changes

---

the most significant statements for the purposes of my work are Russell R. Menard, "From Servants to Slaves: The Transformation of the Chesapeake Labor System," *Southern Studies* 16 (1977): 355–390; Allan Kulikoff, "The Origins of Afro-American Society in Tidewater Maryland and Virginia, 1700–1790," *WMQ* 35 (1978): 226–259; and Morgan, *American Slavery, American Freedom,* pp. 295–315. Morgan explores the relationship of English treatment of the English poor and of the Indians to the willingness of planters to enslave Africans. He also conjectures that over the seventeenth century the life expectancy of slaves improved and they became better investments.

25. The 1680 figure is an estimate based on the prevalence of slaves in the Inventories, MHR. The 1704 census, printed in *AM*, vol. 25, p. 257, lists 820 adult slaves for the three-county area. Between 450 and 570 children must be added to the number of adult slaves. These estimates reflect the ratio of adults to children in the inventories and in the 1710 census. The 1710 figure comes from the 1710 and 1712 census data in *AM*, vol. 25, p. 258. But the Kent total for 1710 is clearly wrong, either the 1710 or 1712 total for Cecil is wrong, and the Queen Anne's figure for 1712 is also incorrect. In 1710 the slave population probably reached 1,640 but may have been no more than 1,530.

in price levels occurred (see Table 3). Slave prices did go up during the boom of 1697–1701, but the failure of servant prices to rise correspondingly can be attributed to the unusual availability of English laborers during this period. Put another way, through the seventeenth century, planters willingly bought both servants and slaves, but they would not pay the extra amount required to shift from servant labor to a slave labor system.[26]

During Queen Anne's War, in contrast, landowners began investing more systematically in slaves. This changing attitude was reflected in the movement of prices for labor. Despite the fact that servants were in short supply and slaves more available than before, the slave-servant price ratio rose to a level significantly higher than it had been during the late seventeenth century. With the difficulty of obtaining adequate returns from a short-term investment in a servant during the years of low wartime tobacco prices, the planters who could acquire black laborers did so. Though whites had finally come to prefer black laborers, their initial satisfaction with servants had delayed the spread of slavery.[27]

Equally important in accounting for the gradual development of a slave labor system was the fact that most Africans carried to the Eastern Shore were men. In the 1680s, the ratio of men to women among blacks listed in Talbot inventories was 2.5:1.0. By 1700 the inventory ratio had fallen to about 1.5:1.0 in Talbot but remained over 2:1 in Kent. This imbalance in the sex ratio made natural population growth unlikely. In the 1680 inventories, only two children were recorded for every ten adults, a ratio that rose to six children per ten adults by 1700. There is no indication that the large planters, those with some control over the labor supply, wished to buy female slaves, for the sex ratio on plantations with ten or more slaves was always higher than on small farms. Considering the short life expectancy in the

26. See Table 3. The assumption in this paragraph is that in the absence of change in the relative supply of slaves and servants, any change in preference would have changed the slave–servant price ratio.

27. See Table 3. The assumption here is that with servants becoming less available, the rise in the slave-servant price ratio indicates a change in preference.

Table 3. Inventory values of male servants with three or more years to serve and male slaves, 1670–1713 (in pounds)

| | Slaves | | | Servants | | | | | |
| | | | | With three years to serve | | | With four or more years to serve | | |
Period	Number	Range	Average	Number	Range	Average	Number	Range	Average
1670–79	4	£20–30	£23	8	£7–10	£8	6	£5–12	£ 9
1680–87	4	20–25	23	6	8–10	9	10	6–12	10
1688–96	5	22–25	24	0	–	–	1	10	10
1697–1701	10	24–33	27	4	6–9	8	19	6–12	10
1702–1713	17	20–30	27	5	6–10	8	9	7–11	9

NOTE: One £13 slave evaluation and one £18 servant evaluation from 1670–79 excluded.
SOURCE: Talbot inventories, Inventories and Accounts, MHR.

Chesapeake, planters wanted the immediate rewards offered by the exploitation of a male field hand. Only slowly did they undertake a different organization of the labor system. By and large, the imbalance between men and women, high mortality, the physical separation of black men and women on distant farms, and the lack of initiative on the part of planters to encourage family life among their captives limited the growth of the slave population. Throughout the early colonial period, slaves accordingly remained a small part of the Eastern Shore's labor force, smaller, in fact, than in most other regions of the Chesapeake. Still, their numbers had increased fivefold between 1680 and 1710, making a small but growing class of whites increasingly dependent on their labor.[28]

Servant labor had supplemented free, and, in turn, slaves had gradually replaced servants. At the same time, the pace of immigration itself had slowed, and the development of the Eastern Shore had increasingly come to depend on natural population growth—on the efforts of each generation of white settlers to leave enough children to balance the death rate.

The story of natural growth of the white population can be rather simply outlined. From the 1680s on, more births than deaths occurred among the landed settlers, while among nonlanded inhabitants, deaths far exceeded births because few men married and fathered children. Of course, many nonlanded freemen became landowners and married, but the number of landed and nonlanded free males remained relatively equal because of the periodic arrival of poor immigrants. As long as the excess of births over deaths among landed families was less than the excess of deaths over births among nonlanded residents, no natural population growth occurred.[29]

The free population was predominantly male. Consequently,

28. Inventories and Accounts, MHR. On life expectancy, see Russell R. Menard, "A Profile of the Maryland Slave Population, 1658–1730: A Demographic Study of Blacks in Four Counties," *WMQ* 32 (1975): 29–54; and Allan Kulikoff, "A 'Prolifick' People: Black Population Growth in the Chesapeake Colonies, 1700–1790," *Southern Studies* 16 (1977); 391–428.

29. This analysis, as will be shown below, draws basically on the Maryland Wills, MHR.

marriage opportunities were limited. Before 1683, roughly two out of every three immigrants were male. Among servants who came to Kent and Talbot during the 1670s and 1680s, males outnumbered females three to one, a circumstance that perpetuated the imbalance in the sex ratio of the free population. Even if remarriage by widows allowed more than half the planters to find wives, women had the upper hand in selecting mates and, not surprisingly, they chose men of property and accomplishment. Wills indicate that most landowners married and that most other men did not. The scarcity of women separated male society into two classes: those with land and wives and those with neither. If some men in the latter class married and entered the former, new, predominantly male immigration replenished the ranks of the unmarried and kept the sex ratio hovering below two.[30]

The imbalance between males and females adversely affected the growth of the population. An initial indication of the course of population growth may be obtained by a construction of replacement rates from Talbot, Kent, and Queen Anne's county wills. These rates measure the number of male heirs left by a deceased male planter. The native-born population will increase only if the replacement rate is above one. Because the rate depends on the number of male births over the life span of a deceased male planter, it may be taken as an indicator of population growth before the period for which it is constructed. The higher rates that prevailed on the Eastern Shore from 1694 on (see Table 4) suggest that the birth rate rose in the 1680s among the free, English-born population.[31]

The increase in the replacement rates in 1694 does not indicate that natural population growth had begun. While rates above one generally reflected natural increase in the population, Eastern Shore rates come increasingly from the wills of landed

30. Talbot County Court Records, MHR, contain information on servants. A general treatment can be found in Menard, "Immigrants and Their Increase," pp. 88–110, but especially p. 96, Table 4.1. Also of importance is Lois Green Carr and Lorena S. Walsh, "The Planter's Wife: The Experience of White Women in Seventeenth-Century Maryland," *WMQ* 34 (1977): 542–571.

31. See Table 4 and the discussion in T. S. Hollingsworth, *Historical Demography* (Ithaca, N.Y., 1969), pp. 377–379.

Table 4. Male replacement rates derived from Talbot, Kent, and Queen Anne's county wills, 1669–1713

Period	A Number of wills	B Number of sons	C Replacement rate (B/A)
1669–73	15	4	0.3
1674–78	54	36	0.7
1679–83	30	26	0.9
1684–88	63	62	1.0
1689–93	17	8	0.5
1694–98	60	82	1.4
1699–1703	97	136	1.4
1704–1708	95	142	1.5
1709–13	121	185	1.5

SOURCE: Wills, MHR.

planters, those most likely to have married and left heirs. During the period 1669–73, 50 percent of those leaving wills in Talbot had land; between 1674 and 1678, 75 percent were landed; by the period 1684–88, 85 percent of those in the records were landowners. Not until the eighteenth century did a nonlandowner mention a son in his will. The increasing exclusion of the nonlanded consequently greatly inflates replacement rates given in Table 5.[32]

The second column in Table 5 gives male replacement rates (per 100 males) for Talbot County landowners. The increase again occurs in 1694, suggesting that for this segment of the population conditions continued to improve in and after the 1680s. Not only did large families—by Eastern Shore standards—become more commonplace, but fewer and fewer landowners remained childless. Surprisingly (for one would expect wills to underrepresent female heirs), the number of girls exceeded the number of boys in the 1684–88 group of Talbot wills. If most of these girls lived to become adults, their survival helped adjust the sex ratio in the late 1690s and early eighteenth century and provided a foundation for natural population growth.[33]

32. Maryland Wills, MHR.
33. Ibid.

Table 5. Number of children and family size of Talbot County landowners who left wills, 1674-1713

Period	Children per 100 male landowners		Percent of male landowners with given number of children			Number of wills
	Male	Female	5+	4-1	0	
1674-78	133	104	11	63	26	27
1684-88	117	139	22	53	25	36
1694-98	164	146	30	52	18	44
1709-1713	182	140	30	59	12	65

SOURCES: Wills, MHR; Lloyd Rent Roll of 1706, MHS. Periods selected to illustrate general trends.

While the predominance of males on the Eastern Shore kept replacement rates low, marriage patterns and life expectancy among Talbot and Kent whites may also have played a part. Unfortunately, the family reconstitution studies on which knowledge about marriage and deaths in seventeenth-century England and New England are based cannot be duplicated for most early colonial Chesapeake counties. The best that can be offered at this point is a series of conjectures based on the life histories of a dozen prominent families and the incomplete registers of the Quakers of Talbot and Dorchester counties. Men in prominent Eastern Shore families married at the average age of 26.9 years; men in Quaker families at the age of 25.2 years. Women married earlier, on the average at age 21.8 (Eastern Shore families) or 20.4 (Quaker). The figures are not too reliable and include marriages over the period 1658-1750, but they suggest that on the Eastern Shore a significant portion of the women were married under the age of 20 to men six or seven years older than they. Marriage in these circumstances did not preclude large families and high replacement rates.[34]

34. Family genealogies are to be found in the early volumes of *MHM* and in typescript at MHS. For example, see Oswald Tilghman, "Tilghman Family," *MHM* 1 (1906): 181, 280, 290, 369. For an early study look at Michael James Kelly, "Family Reconstitution of Stepney Parish, Somerset County, Maryland," master's thesis, University of Maryland, 1971, pp. 21-22, 43-44.

The age of death may be more critical in explaining the low replacement rates. The age of death is known for 52 planters born in seventeenth-century Talbot and Kent counties and 20 women (all of whom lived at least to the age of 20). The average age of death for the men was 52.1 years and for the women 48.6 years. Again, the figures are only of limited value, and the difference in male and female mortality is insignificant, but the impression is that life expectancy was short relative to that of settlers in New England. In fact, a more comprehensive study of the early colonial Chesapeake suggested that male immigrants who reached the age of 20 died at the average age of 43. The early age of death may be explained by the increased possibility of mortality during the first years immigrants spent (the "seasoning" period) in the hot, damp environment of Maryland. Life may also have been cut short by epidemic disease, for aggregate figures taken from the wills show sharp peaks in the number of deaths in 1685, 1699, and 1709, and references can be found in the inventories to smallpox in 1709.[35]

In any case, replacement rates improved in the 1690s. Many native-born children became socially, economically, and psychologically free of their parents, and the economic boom of 1697 provided the impetus they needed to marry and have children of their own. The boom of 1697, however, also brought shiploads of male servants to the Eastern Shore. The addition of these immigrants to the population reversed the falling trend in the sex ratio and brought society back to a point where deaths among the nonlanded population exceeded population growth among the landed. This reversal makes the population boom after 1704 all the more impressive.[36]

Between 1704 and 1710, the population of the Eastern Shore grew enormously: from 8,940 people in Kent, Talbot, and Cecil

35. Data come from genealogical sources discussed in note 34 above. On life expectancy, see Walsh and Menard, "Death in the Chesapeake," pp. 211–227; Daniel Blake Smith, "Mortality and Family in the Colonial Chesapeake," *Journal of Interdisciplinary History* 8 (1978): 403–427; and the exceptionally fine article by Darrett B. Rutman and Anita H. Rutman, "Of Agues and Fevers: Malaria in the Early Chesapeake," *WMQ* 33 (1976): 31–60.

36. Analysis based on Tables 4, 5, and 6.

in 1704 to 12,150 people in the four counties that made up the same region in 1710 (see Table 6). This increase occurred despite the wartime recession in the tobacco trade, which virtually cut off immigration to the Eastern Shore and forced several hundred newly freed servants to abandon the region forever. The new families formed during the earlier boom years, however, continued to have children, and an exceedingly high birth rate more than made up for the losses from the population. From this time on, native-born planters, not immigrants, would predominate in Talbot and Kent, and the peopling of the Eastern Shore would be less directly affected by the Atlantic economy.[37]

Marriage patterns indicate the demographic transition that had taken place. Between 1700 and 1704, parish registrars recorded two or three times as many marriages as during similar periods a decade earlier. In St. Peter's, a parish with 1,200 white inhabitants in central Talbot County, the Anglican minister performed 100 marriages. Over the same period in St. Paul's, a slightly larger parish located in part of Kent and Talbot counties, the church married 103 couples. Even by the standards of rural England, this number of marriages corresponded to a relatively high rate.[38]

If a fundamental change had occurred in the population composition of the region, then the wills of planters who died after 1704–1710 should further confirm the transition. In particular, when the planters who had children between 1704 and 1710 died, the number of heirs in the wills should have increased. This is exactly what the wills show. In the late 1720s, replacement rates rose to an exceptionally high level. They remained high through the 1730s. Planters who had married in the 1704–1710 period now left large families when they died.[39]

37. Population figures are given in Table 6. Note that as servants arrived on the Eastern Shore, the ratio of the total population to the number of taxables fell. As freed servants left and children were born, the ratio rose. Manipulating the 1704 and 1710 census data, I have estimated that during this period no fewer than 450 adult males left the Eastern shore.

38. Eastern Shore Anglican Parish Records, MHR.

39. Maryland Wills, MHR.

Table 6. Composition of white population in Talbot, Kent,
Cecil, and Queen Anne's counties, 1697–1710 (in thousands)

	1697	1700	1704	1710
Men			3.0	3.3
Women			1.8	2.5
Children			2.8	4.8
Total whites			7.6	10.6
Slaves			1.3	1.6
Total population	8.4	8.8	8.9	12.2
Taxable population	3.0	3.4	3.8	4.2
Ratio of total to taxable population	2.8	2.6	2.3	2.9

SOURCES: MA, XXV, 255–258 (adjusted). See also the sources and figures listed in Table 2.

In short, in the 1680s a gradual improvement had begun in the ability of the settler population to replace itself. Enough planters married, lived, and had children during that decade so that by the 1690s replacement rates rose above one. Simultaneously, with the contraction of economic opportunity in the local economy, immigration decreased and the number of men leaving the region increased. Both factors helped balance the sex ratio and further improved the chances of white Eastern Shore residents to replace themselves. The renewed prosperity during the 1697 boom added another stimulus to population growth by encouraging those who remained in the region to marry earlier. As native-born inhabitants more and more replaced English settlers in the white population, life expectancy may also have lengthened. Put in a broader context, the impact of the Anglo-Chesapeake tobacco economy on the growth of the Eastern Shore population had clearly changed with time. Through the 1680s, the market encouraged rapid development of a male immigrant society. Increasingly after the 1680s, conditions in the Atlantic economy helped perpetuate a stable, family-oriented society by discouraging immigration and by forcing many of those whites who came to leave after their period of servitude ended.

The Land System

Most Eastern Shore settlers came from a nation where the agrarian structure separated the ownership of land from its actual farming. In seventeenth-century England, perhaps three-fourths of the arable and pasture land rested in the hands of landlords—the government, nobility, gentry, and church—who did not farm it themselves. Tenants, generally with leases for several years or of one or two lives' duration, managed this portion of England's agriculture. Owner-operators, freeholders, and those with inheritable copyhold tenures controlled no more than one-fourth of the nation's farming acreage. In the case of neither owner-operators nor tenants were individual holdings large. In both cases, middling farmers, those with more than two but less than thirty acres, were being forced out as larger owners aggrandized their holdings.[40]

The promise of land attracted many to the Eastern Shore. There they found, just as in England, that market agriculture shaped the land system. The movement of tobacco prices, population increases, alternative investment possibilities, and costs affected choices and opportunities to patent and buy land. Over the period from 1658 to 1713, however, the land system changed. Families played an increasingly important role in the control and distribution of real property. Purchases became less speculative and planters exercised more caution in investing. The land market changed from one in which immigrants bought land during recessions when the supply of and demand for servants was down to a market in which families acquired land when rising crop prices and expanding credit provided them with the opportunity.

The partition of land among the original settlers occurred through the headright system. Since 1633 the proprietary gov-

40. Particularly useful on the English land system have been Margaret Spufford, *Contrasting Communities: English Villagers in the Sixteenth and Seventeenth Centuries* (Cambridge, 1974), pp. 46–167; L. A. Clarkson, *The Pre-Industrial Economy of England, 1500–1750* (London, 1971), pp. 61–68; Jan de Vries, *The Economy of Europe in the Age of Crisis, 1600–1750* (Cambridge, 1976), pp. 75–82; F. M. L. Thompson, "The Social Distribution of Landed Property in England since the Sixteenth Century," *EHR* 19 (1966): 505–507; and H. J. Habbakuk, "English Landownership, 1660–1740," *EHR* 10 (1940): 2–17.

ernment had granted immigrants, freed servants, and people who transported others to the colony the right—known as a headright—to have land surveyed and patented. Since mid-century, this right had been fifty acres per person. The system, as has been noted, provided incentives to merchants to supply the colony with indentured servants. For each laborer the merchant received a headright that he could market or convert to a patent and sell. At the same time, the headright system provided middling English yeomen an opportunity to acquire land in the Chesapeake.[41]

Although land so granted was not free, it was at least inexpensive. The chief expense was that of coming or bringing someone to the Chesapeake. In the 1670s, transporting a servant from Ireland to Maryland cost in the neighborhood of £4 to £5. Contracts for shipping people from Hull, England, stated the going rate as £6 per servant and £12 per freeman. Converting the headright into a salable tract also cost something. A merchant or planter first obtained a warrant from the land office, for roughly 30 pounds of tobacco. He then took the warrant to a surveyor, who would ride to the tract site, survey the property, and enter a description of the plot on the warrant, charging 110 pounds of tobacco for laying out fifty acres. The owner returned the warrant to the land office, where the chancellor charged 240 pounds of tobacco for drawing up and sealing the patent. Before the procedure was completed, clerks, secretaries, and surveyors had collected at least 400 pounds of tobacco.[42]

41. The headright system is discussed in Russell R. Menard, "Immigration to the Chesapeake Colonies in the Seventeenth Century: A Review Essay," *MHM* 68 (1973): 323–329. Documents describing its workings can be found in *AM*, vol. 3, pp. 47–48, 99–100, 221–228, 231–237; vol. 5, pp. 54–55, 63–64. See also Clarence Pembroke Gould, *The Land System in Maryland, 1720–1765*, Johns Hopkins University Studies in Historical and Political Science, Series 31, no. 1 (Baltimore, 1913).

42. Passage costs are discussed in Smith, *Colonists in Bondage*, pp. 36–38; and examples can be found in *AM*, vol. 57, p. 416; vol. 68, p. 157; vol. 69, pp. 107–109, 127; *CSPCS, 1577–1660*, pp. 56, 311; and the Bristol Deposition Books, Bristol Record Office, England (microfilm at Colonial Williamsburg Library, Virginia). On survey costs, consult *AM*, vol. 2, pp. 392–394; vol. 13, pp. 507–511; and Gould, *Land System*, pp. 9–10, 15–16. An excellent study of the land system in Virginia is included in Michael Lee Nicholls, "Origins of the Virginia Southside, 1703–1753: A Social and Economic Study," Ph.D. dissertation, College of William and Mary, 1972), pp. 17–78.

Accordingly, if an immigrant had £4–£6 (1,000 to 1,400 pounds of tobacco) for passage and 400 pounds of tobacco for land, he could acquire for farming 50 acres on Maryland's Eastern Shore. Most people who came to the region after the 1670s did not have this type of capital. Instead, they accepted passage on a merchant ship in return for selling their services once they reached Maryland. Headrights became the property of ship captains who sold them rather than convert them to patents. This procedure allowed the captain to return quickly to England with a cargo of tobacco and left to local speculators the chance of reselling the headright.[43]

In the mid-1660s, settlers and speculators patented as many as eighty tracts a year in Talbot County. Again in the mid-1680s, an unusually large number of people took out patents in Talbot County. In both cases, the flurry of patenting activity soon led to extensive buying and selling of land. The time lag between patenting and sales, however, involved something more than speculators putting recently obtained land on the market. Chesapeake settlers had three principal options when they invested in the agricultural economy: patenting land, buying land, and purchasing labor. Because tobacco cultivation required little land in a given year, planters benefited when they responded to higher staple prices by purchasing a servant's contract rather than more farming acreage. On the other hand, patenting land, once a person had been transported to the Chesapeake, cost little additional tobacco, and because nonresidents—speculators, merchants, and provincial officeholders—obtained many of the headrights for patents, little money was drawn out of the local agricultural economy. People consequently patented land when tobacco prices were high and servants were being brought to the Chesapeake. They generally bought and sold land when tobacco prices dropped and few servants were available.[44]

In 1658 the initial land boom on the Eastern Shore began.

43. See Abbot Emerson Smith, "The Indentured Servant and Land Speculation in Seventeenth-Century Maryland," *American Historical Review* 60 (1934–35): 467–472.

44. This analysis is based on patents in the Lloyd Rent Roll of 1706, MS 2001, MHS, and on deeds of sale in the Talbot County Land Conveyances, MHR. See Graph 4.

Through 1663, proprietary agents parceled out large, essentially speculative patents to wealthy immigrants and western shore adventurers. While patenting continued after the early 1660s, the focus of activity turned to land sales. Speculators sold land readily and cheaply to numerous settlers arriving in the Great Choptank and Chester river regions. With tobacco prices low and servants few, immigrants put their savings in land rather than labor. In Talbot and Dorchester counties, the boom lasted through 1672; in Kent, the slower initial settlement of the county prolonged the boom through 1677. Rising land prices probably deterred some potential buyers, while more stable tobacco prices and an increased supply of servants affected the choices of others (see Graph 4).[45]

Between 1682 and 1693, land sales again soared as recently patented land came on the market. Low tobacco prices and the limited availabililty of labor—except in 1685—helped to sustain the boom, but spiraling land prices kept sales from reaching the level they had attained earlier. The end of the headright system in 1683 probably mattered little. Under the new land policy that took effect the following year, the land office continued to issue warrants for as little as 240 pounds of tobacco, and a planter could patent a 50-acre tract for not much more than 600 pounds of tobacco, much less than the purchase price (about 1,500 pounds for 50 acres). Most settlers, however, preferred to purchase improved bayside farms rather than patent virgin inland tracts, and the heavy demand for the limited amount of land near the bay pushed up prices.[46]

In summary, through the early 1690s, speculation and investment dominated the land market. Planters and merchants generally obtained patents for future sale. Residents purchased land only when servants were not available, tobacco prices were low, and buyers had little chance of using acreage immediately.

During King William's War, however, the character of the land market changed. The wartime depression dampened plant-

---

45. See sources cited in note 44. Land prices are also given in Paul G. E. Clemens, "From Tobacco to Grain: Economic Development of Maryland's Eastern Shore, 1660–1750," Ph.D. dissertation, University of Wisconsin, 1974, p. 169. Tobacco prices are given in the Appendix.
46. See Graph 4.

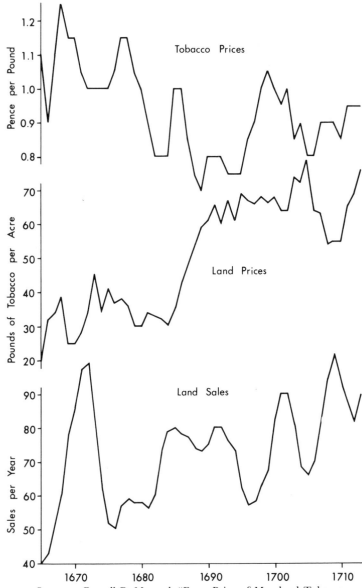

Graph 4. Tobacco prices, land prices, and land sales on the Eastern Shore, 1665–1713.

Tobacco Prices

Land Prices

Land Sales

SOURCES: Russell R. Menard, "Farm Price of Maryland Tobacco, 1659–1710," *MHM* 68 (1973): 80–85; Inventories, MHR; Eastern Shore Land Records, MHR.

ers' economic outlook, and despite the absence of alternative investment opportunities, they did not buy land. In 1694 the reopening of the land office, closed since 1690 in the wake of the Glorious Revolution, further restricted land sales by again making patents available for those with the capital to speculate. Only in 1697, with peace and higher tobacco prices, did land sales pick up. Planters now put money into both servants and land, and when depression struck in 1702, they curtailed investments in both. With the boom economy a thing of the past, few settlers would risk their savings, unless rising tobacco prices promised good returns.[47]

The decline in speculation reflected the changing nature of the land market. Speculators had seldom withheld land from sale. Most acquired land in large blocks and sold it quickly; they profited not from artificially high prices but from the volume of their transactions. In the 1660s, Eastern Shore landowners had sold nine tracts of over 1,000 acres. In the 1670s, they sold eight such tracts; in the 1680s, seven; during the next two decades, eleven; and during the second decade of the eighteenth century, none. Nor did the patent system provide a means for much large-scale speculation. Before 1680, only thirty-one tracts of over 1,000 acres were patented in Talbot County and only one of over 3,000 acres. Most went to London and Bristol merchants or to prominent planters residing on the western shore, all of whom quickly transferred their grants to settlers. These large patents accounted for less than one-fifth of the land distributed under the headright system. After 1680 hardly any 1,000-acre patents were made on the Eastern Shore.[48]

This decline in the sale and patenting of large tracts paralleled a gradual curtailment of trading activity by individual planters. In the 1660s, when Talbot and Dorchester counties were still on the frontier of the Chesapeake economy, those who sold land

47. See Graph 4.
48. Talbot County Land Conveyances, MHR, and Lloyd Rent Roll of 1706, MHS, provide data on the size of patents and land tracts. The only study of an Eastern Shore speculator is Frank B. Edmondson and Emerson B. Roberts, "John Edmondson—Large Merchant of Tred Haven Creek," *MHM* 50 (1955): 219–233. Between 1663 and 1696, Edmondson bought or patented 16,680 acres in Talbot County and sold 12,560. He also owned extensive acreage in Dorchester County and western Delaware. He died heavily in debt.

averaged two conveyances during the decade. By the early eighteenth century, only one seller in two from Talbot and one in three from Dorchester handled more than one property transaction per decade. Men were selling land less frequently and in smaller amounts. The frontier had disappeared, land had been cleared, and families were settling into the rugged task of making money from tobacco and passing what they could save on to their children.[49]

During the seventeenth century, the land system operated to dispense generous allotments of arable and wooded land to a great number of immigrants. Throughout the period, about half the free males in Talbot and Kent owned land, and the land remained rather evenly distributed. In 1680, for example, only 15 percent of the planters in Talbot had fewer than 100 acres, 35 percent had between 100 and 299 acres, 39 percent had between 300 and 999 acres, and but 11 percent could be classified as large landowners, or men with over 1,000 acres. By the eighteenth century, numerous estate divisions among second-generation sons and purchases by new arrivals had augmented slightly the importance of small family farms of under 300 acres, but the basic agrarian structure of the region remained unchanged. There had also been some growth, from around 4 percent in the 1680s to about 11 percent two decades later, in the prevalence of women in the ranks of the landowners. During the earlier period, with few women present and with numerous opportunities for widows to remarry, women seldom acquired or long maintained title. As immigration subsided and the sex ratio approached unity, women played a larger role in the control of land. For these women and men, the promise that had first brought them to the Eastern Shore had been fulfilled.[50]

By the early eighteenth century, the Eastern Shore's economy no longer operated as it had when settlement began. Free colonists first worked their fields themselves, then imported ser-

49. The information in this paragraph comes from Dorchester County Land Records, MHR, and the Talbot County Land Conveyances, MHR.
50. Lloyd Rent Roll of 1706, MS 2001, MHS. In the early eighteenth century, 13 percent owned fewer than 100 acres, 47 percent owned 100–299 acres, 30 percent owned 300–999 acres, and 10 percent owned 1,000 acres or more.

vants to tend the tobacco crop, and finally shifted, if they had the capital to do so, to slave labor, as the supply of servants ran out. Just as important, after the 1680s, immigrants—free, servant, and slave—had come in ever smaller numbers to the region, and the development of the Eastern Shore fell more and more into the hands of native-born whites and blacks. Planters who had originally thought of land as a speculative commodity quickly converted their acreage into a productive asset, which thereafter became the basis of family farms. While through the 1680s economic life had revolved around immigrant male planters who had a penchant for buying and selling labor and land as the market dictated, by the first decade of the new century the economy centered on native-born families who had settled into the routine of making a living from plantations inherited from an earlier generation of colonists. Planters still watched the movement of tobacco prices and still adjusted their behavior to changes in the cost and profit of agricultural production, but farm and family now stood between them and the market and gave to rural life a stability much like that their parents had known in England.

Several explanations may be given for this transformation. In part, the growing stability of economic life simply reflected the passage of time. As land filled up, opportunity contracted, immigration shifted elsewhere, the poor left, and second- and third-generation landowners took over. Such a process—settlement, crowding, and out-migration—occurred in virtually every English colony. The rate of the process depended primarily on the population the land could support, which in turn reflected the relationship (or lack of it) of local agriculture to the market. In the areas where the Atlantic economy had little impact, the process generally occurred very slowly, and stopped only after family lands had been divided among heirs over the course of several generations and the size of individual holdings had become too small to raise the corn and livestock needed to provide an acceptable standard of living. In areas such as the Eastern Shore, where farmers constantly tried to increase their holdings of land and labor to take advantage of the market, the disappearance of opportunity for new immigrants and the emergence of a native-born elite generally proceeded more quickly.

In such a situation, however, the possibility remained that a change in market conditions could create new opportunities, make land more productive, and again transform the local economy.[51]

The market thus affected the pace of development on the Eastern Shore. Just as certainly, market relationships shaped the character of that development. English labor conditions, the demand for tobacco in Europe, slaving voyages in the South Atlantic, and the competition for immigrants with other colonies all helped mold the life an Eastern Shore settler lived. The growth of population and the intensification of cash farming in seventeenth-century England created the conditions that freed and forced people to come to the New World. They were drawn to the Eastern Shore more rapidly and in greater numbers than they otherwise would have been by the prosperity that prevailed during the boom years in Anglo-Chesapeake trade. When the boom ended, many fewer came. Immigration slowed in part because of the wartime depression in the tobacco trade, but also because the supply of English people available for the colonies had decreased and because newer settlements, especially in Pennsylvania and the Carolinas, began to attract immigrants away from the Eastern Shore. In response, rich Talbot and Kent

51. The New England experience has been described, but without reference to the market, in Kenneth A. Lockridge, "Land, Population, and the Evolution of New England Society, 1630–1790," *Past & Present*, no. 39 (1968), pp. 62–80; Philip J. Greven, Jr., *Four Generations: Population, Land, and Family in Colonial Andover, Massachusetts* (Ithaca, N.Y., 1970); and Susan L. Norton, "Population Growth in Colonial America: A Study of Ipswich, Massachusetts," *Population Studies* 25 (1971): 433–452. In the New England case, it must be emphasized that once a certain population density threshold was reached, people left and new towns were begun. For a different picture of New England, emphasizing the relationship between commerce and agriculture, see Carl Bridenbaugh, *Fat Mutton and Liberty of Conscience: Society in Rhode Island, 1636–1690* (Providence, 1974); and Darrett B. Rutman, *Husbandmen of Plymouth: Farms and Villages in the Old Colony, 1620–1692* (Boston, 1967). The Lockridge analysis, noted above, should be compared with Duane E. Ball's "Dynamics of Population and Wealth in Eighteenth-Century Chester County, Pennsylvania," *Journal of Interdisciplinary History* 6 (1976): 621–644. For a sophisticated attempt to apply these ideas to the Chesapeake, see P. M. G. Harris, "Integrating Interpretations of Local and Regionwide Change in the Study of Economic Development and Demographic Growth in the Colonial Chesapeake, 1630–1775," *Working Papers from the Regional Economic History Research Center* 1, no. 3 (1978): 35–72.

planters turned to black slaves. The blacks whom planters put to work on the Eastern Shore had been bought in Africa, first enslaved and broken to fieldwork in the Caribbean, and then sold north to the Chesapeake. At each step, the evolution of the Eastern Shore's economy had been shaped by relationships to distant lands and international commerce.

Chapter 3

Settlement: Economy
and Society

The white settlers of the Eastern Shore shared with their fellow English immigrants to the American colonies the economic aspirations and practices of rural English people: they came to obtain land, establish families, and raise crops and livestock. Land gave them not only a means of making a living but also an assurance that they could bequeath something of value to the next generation. Marriage, the rearing of children, and the obtaining of servants allowed them to care for their households and cultivate their land. Farming, in turn, promised them not only food for subsistence but also produce for the market. As was generally true in agricultural economies, some inhabitants of the Eastern Shore found fruitful ways to combine the managing of their cattle and crops with work as artisans and merchants. Not surprisingly, the social structure that gradually emerged on the Eastern Shore, much like the ordering of people in rural England, reflected the slow acquisition of property through farming and trade and the choices fathers and mothers made in transferring their holdings to sons and daughters.

What, then, was distinctive about economic life on the Eastern Shore? What set off the Eastern Shore from other New World settlements and from rural England? Answering these questions entails the investigation of three related problems: (1) the extent to which production of tobacco as an export crop dominated the economy; (2) the way this basic commitment to market agriculture shaped the social and occupational structure of the region; and (3) the opportunities this society held out, both to planters and to those who lived indirectly off the tobacco economy as merchants and artisans, to accumulate wealth. Such inquiry will, however, demonstrate that by entering a market economy Eastern Shore settlers did not abandon completely the world they had known in England. For not only did they turn to tobacco planting without giving up their traditional reliance on land, family, and farming, but, in adopting market agriculture, they did nothing that had not already occurred in many of the English communities they had left. What in fact stands out most sharply about the seventeenth-century Eastern Shore is not how different it was from rural England but how different it became from settlements in New England and the Caribbean.

ECONOMIC ORGANIZATION

The English settlers of the seventeenth-century Chesapeake came from a remarkably diversified agrarian economy. In the grass-growing north of England, sheep and cattle raising predominated. To the south, mixed farming prevailed; farmers combined attention to dairying, sheep tending, and cattle grazing with corn growing. As the English economy became more specialized, northern farmers sold livestock south in return for grains. The evolution of English inheritance laws and farming practices imposed on this rural world two forms of social organization. Some farming was largely a communal venture. Villagers decided together about the use of arable land and pastured their livestock in common fields. All lived in close proximity as a tightly knit community. In other parts of England, each farmer managed individually his own arable, pasture, and woodland. Farm houses tended to be more dispersed, and manorial control, which often helped to provide social cohesion in the common-field villages, was lacking. In virtually every region, the nuclear household of parents, children, and possibly servants formed the basic unit of production. Farms were small—unless extended by common-field rights they generally came to less than thirty acres—and a small but growing part of their output went to the market.[1]

1. The best summaries of English agriculture are in Joan Thirsk, "The Farming Regions of England," in *The Agrarian History of England and Wales,*

English people on the Eastern Shore preserved much of this economic heritage. The nuclear household, if initially weakly rooted in a society of male immigrants, eventually prevailed, although in a fashion adapted to the tobacco economy. Land was plentiful and many inhabitants acquired large tracts of un-cleared woodlands, but they actually cultivated no more than they would have on a twenty-acre farm in England. Farmers practiced a form of mixed agriculture, balancing market and subsistence production. While the importance of tobacco as a market crop distinguished the Eastern Shore's economy, corn production and livestock raising also played important roles.[2]

The involvement of Eastern Shore residents in the Atlantic tobacco trade nonetheless gave to their lives a new economic texture. When staple prices peaked and households channeled most of their energy into tobacco production, the Eastern Shore became part of a highly specialized economy. London and the outports supplied the goods, labor, and services planters de-manded, and a numerous class of local merchants and merchant planters acted as middlemen in the Atlantic trade. The prof-itability of tobacco production thus led to an international divi-sion of labor, and efforts of the planter class during the late seventeenth century to maintain its income in the face of low crop prices and a contracting supply of servants pushed the society inexorably toward a labor system based on slavery.[3]

The typical Eastern Shore landowner farmed 250 acres and raised tobacco, livestock, and corn. Because corn was a hardy, nutritious, high-yield crop that required little cultivation beyond weekly weeding, it replaced traditional English grains (wheat and rye) as the staple of the settlers' diet. To the extent that the introduction of corn freed land and labor for tobacco produc-

---

1500–1640, ed. Joan Thirsk (Cambridge, 1967), pp. 1–112, especially pp. 2–15; E. L. Jones, "Agriculture and Economic Growth in England, 1660–1750: Ag-ricultural Change," *JEH* 25 (1965): 1–18; and Eric Kerridge, *The Agricultural Revolution* (London, 1967).

2. Statements on Eastern Shore farming are based on information in the Wills, MHR, and the Inventories and Accounts, MHR.

3. Ibid. See below and the stimulating discussion in Immanuel Wallerstein, *The Modern World-System: Capitalist Agriculture and the Origins of the European World Economy in the Sixteenth Century* (London, 1974), pp. 66–131.

tion, the Indian crop made a significant contribution to the development of market agriculture on the Eastern Shore. In the unfenced and overgrown timberland adjacent to the cornfield, a planter could let his livestock graze at will and be confident that the animals would thrive. Herds grew quickly, undoubtedly supplemented by imported animals, so that by the 1680s most farmers were at least as well off as their rural English contemporaries. Householders in the late seventeenth century generally owned well over a dozen cattle and an equal number of swine.[4]

Raising cows, steers, and hogs not only made the farm more self-sufficient but also gave many planters a way of eking out a slightly larger income. As the landless population on the Eastern Shore grew, the local market for beef and pork expanded, and the steady drop in livestock prices over the course of the century testified to the ability of farmers to meet the new demand for food. At the same time, sheep herds became increasingly common. Settlers from the agrarian counties around London and Bristol came from communities long attached to sheep farming, and once sufficient land on the Eastern Shore had been cleared of timber and heavy underbrush, and predatory animals, especially wolves, had been brought under control, planters began to build up sheep herds to supplement the food they already obtained from cows and hogs. Traditional concern for sheep raising, moreover, was reinforced by market conditions, for with the downturn in tobacco prices, local production of wool became an important alternative to imported European cloth.[5]

4. The importance of corn to the farmers on the Eastern Shore can be readily determined from the Inventories and Accounts, MHR; but see also "Peter Kalm's Description of Maize, How It Is Planted and Cultivated in North America, Together with the Many Uses of This Crop Plant, 1751–1752," *Agricultural History* 9 (1935): 98–117, especially pp. 109–110; and Edmund S. Morgan, *American Slavery, American Freedom: The Ordeal of Colonial Virginia* (New York, 1975), pp. 71–91. On English livestock farming, see the sources listed in note 1 above and David Hey, *An English Rural Community: Myddle under the Tudors and Stuarts* (Leicester, 1974), pp. 61–64. In Talbot County inventories from the 1680s, the average number of cattle per household was 21, sheep 4, and swine 18; for the first decade of the eighteenth century, the comparable figures were 17, 10, and 16. The Appendix discusses problems in the use of inventories.

5. The price of a cow and calf fell from over 50 shillings in the 1660s to about 40 shillings by the first decade of the eighteenth century. Sheep prices fell from 10 or 11 shillings in the 1680s to 7 or 8 shillings two decades later; see Paul G. E. Clemens, "From Tobacco to Grain: Economic Development on Maryland's East-

Once farmers were assured of food, their most vital concern was the tobacco crop. The larger the crop, the better their position in the market economy. While soil conditions affected crop size somewhat, the most important measure of the productive capacity of a household was the labor force at a planter's command. On the largest estates, male workers substantially outnumbered female, and despite the ease with which rich planters could acquire servants, far more blacks than whites labored in the fields. Henrietta Maria Lloyd's plantations, inventoried in 1697, typified the organization of production by the wealthy. At the death of her husband, Lloyd acquired six plantations, four in the tidewater region around the Wye River and two inland near Tuckahoe Creek. She managed them carefully and avoided remarriage and loss of control. Lloyd commanded thirty-two slaves, two women servants, and five overseers, the equivalent (if women and older children helped with the cultivation) of a work force of twenty-three male field hands. On no farm did she employ more than ten workers. Only on one farm, the home plantation, did she grow more than 10,000 pounds of tobacco. On the others, yearly production ran between 4,000 and 7,000 pounds. Considered together, her laborers in 1697 raised a crop of 37,000 pounds of tobacco, about 1,610 pounds per male field hand or 1,300 pounds per worker (see also Table 7). Lloyd and the other large slave owners of the Eastern Shore, unlike the great planters in the Caribbean, built their estates by establishing numerous small farms, each with its own overseer and complement of laborers.[6]

---

ern Shore, 1660–1750," Ph.D. dissertation, University of Wisconsin, 1974, pp. 163–166. On the increase in the number of sheep in the seventeenth-century Chesapeake, see the figures in note 4 above and Lorena S. Walsh, "Charles County, Maryland, 1658–1705: A Study of Chesapeake Social and Political Structure," Ph.D. dissertation, Michigan State University, 1977, pp. 267–269, 280–281. An excellent discussion of colonial sheep husbandry is in Carl Bridenbaugh, *Fat Mutton and Liberty of Conscience: Society in Rhode Island, 1636–1690* (Providence, 1974), pp. 49–56.

6. Inventories and Accounts, vol. 21, p. 213 (Henrietta Maria Lloyd, 1697), MHR. For other large slave owners, see Inventories and Accounts, vol. 8, p. 353 (Bryant Omaly, 1685); vol. 15, p. 189 (Henry Coursey, 1697); vol. 17, p. 78 (Peter Sayer, 1697), MHR. There were fewer slaves on the Eastern Shore than in other settled parts of colonial Maryland. In 1704, for example, the ratio of white to black taxables in Talbot County was 3.33:1 but only 1.89:1 in Charles County.

Table 7. Tobacco production per field hand and per worker on Talbot County farms, 1671–1713

Type of farm	Number of inventories	Output per male field hand (pounds)	Output per worker (pounds)
Large slave estate	4	1,800	1,650
Smaller slave-servant estate	10	1,230	1,050
Servant estate	32	1,740	1,410
Small landowner or tenant	37	1,310	1,100
Total (or average)	83	1,570	1,360

NOTE: Output per male field hand was determined by dividing each crop by the sum of the number of adult male workers, two-thirds the number of adult female workers, and one-half the number of children aged 10 to 15. Output per worker was calculated by dividing the crop total by the number of male and female servants and slaves over age 14. In both calculations, the white family was assumed to have contributed one adult male worker (master or overseer). In the case of small landowners and tenants, both estimates counted the wife as a worker (but in the field-hand estimate the divisor was 1.66 rather than 2.0).

SOURCE: Inventories and Accounts, MHR. Only inventories with specifically designated crop tobacco totals were used.

Smaller planters were more dependent on their own labor and that of servants than on the use of slaves. At his death in 1705, Nicholas Goldsborough, for example, had working for him a servant man, a servant woman, two older servant boys, two orphan girls, a black woman, and an older black youth. Typically, smaller planters were married, had three of four young children, and lived apart from grandparents and grandchildren. Sons and daughters in these families often left home soon after they had reached maturity and hence did not contribute directly to the tobacco production of the household. While their own children did little work, most small planters had two or three servants, more often women and children than men, and occa-

---

For comparative figures see *AM*, vol. 25, p. 257; and Walsh, "Charles County, Maryland," pp. 450–455. On the West Indies, consult Richard S. Dunn, *Sugar and Slaves: The Rise of the Planter Class in the English West Indies, 1624–1713* (Chapel Hill, N.C., 1972), pp. 46–83, 188–223.

sionally a slave to help in the fields. Planters, of course, bought servants, especially adolescents, directly from English ship captains, but they also hired laborers from neighboring landowners and contracted with indigent immigrants for their services. In addition, orphans from nearby plantations frequently stayed in the home. Output on the farms of these middling planters averaged between 3,500 and 5,500 pounds of tobacco (£14 and £23) annually. Goldsborough produced somewhat more, 6,370 pounds in 1705—by no means an enormous crop, considering the household he supported. As in rural England, small farmers, living with only their immediate family, servants, and orphans, constituted the most numerous class in society and accounted for by far the largest share of agricultural production (see Table 8).[7]

Planters without servants and slaves made up no more than one-fifth of the landed population. Most were young, without older children, and upwardly mobile. In these households the wife probably assisted in the fields during April and May, when planting began. Such partnerships at times produced large crops, occasionally as much as 4,000 pounds of tobacco, although on most such farms returns of 1,500 to 2,000 pounds of tobacco were clearly more common. If the farmer was a tenant, he suffered from two handicaps that did not affect the small landowner. The first was that he had more difficulty marrying because he had less to offer. Second, a portion of his income went to his landlord. Out of a 1,500-pound crop, the tenant often lost 600 pounds of tobacco or more in rent. For those of the free, nonlanded population who were unsuccessful in leasing land and establishing a household, sharecropping agreements and part-time labor sufficed to get them lodging and victuals with a small planter. Because of the problems planters had purchasing servants and slaves, landless residents could often negotiate attractive terms for the use of their labor. In some cases, both a husband and his wife would be hired, the husband to assist with planting the crop, fencing the farm, and watching the livestock, the wife to care for the household. At the same time, the growing prevalence of tenancy and sharecrop-

7. See Tables 7, 8, and 11; Inventories and Accounts, vol. 25, p. 194; vol. 26, p. 66 (Nicholas Goldsborough, 1705–1706), MHR; and *AM*, vol. 54, pp. 380, 450.

Table 8. Household income from tobacco and share of market, Talbot County, c. 1704

Type of household	Average work force	Average income, tobacco (pounds)	Number of households	Share of total output (percent)
Large slave owners	16.9	£116	14	15%
Small slave owners	4.2	18	131	22
Servant owners	2.3	14	334	44
Small landowners	2.0	9	111	9
Tenants	1.0	6*	182	10
Total (or average)	2.5	£ 14	772	100%

NOTE: Income figures are based on output figures per worker in Table 7 and the assumption that tobacco was at a penny per pound.
*Tenants are assumed to have produced 1,500 pounds of tobacco per year. Rent reduced this income and their share of total output about 25 percent.
SOURCES: *AM*, vol. 25, p. 257 (adjusted); Inventories and Accounts, MHR. See also Table 7.

ping on the Eastern Shore meant that a significant portion of the returns from tobacco production were redistributed from the bottom to the top stratum of white society.[8]

Tobacco production generated considerable income. Crop reports from the inventories of both large and small farmers tell essentially the same story: output per male field hand averaged between 1,200 and 1,800 pounds of tobacco (worth £4 to £8); when the work force included female servants and slaves, output per laborer generally came to between 1,000 and 1,600 pounds of tobacco. Income per household averaged about £14 (see Table 8). Less is known, unfortunately, about the way the quality of a planter's land affected his income. If, as many eighteenth-century travel accounts and crop books report, a male field hand could tend two to three acres, yields per acre fell between 400 and 900 pounds of tobacco. Today, according to Department of Agriculture estimates, tobacco yields on Maryland farms run between 700 and 1,500 pounds per acre. Both sets of figures suggest that on some colonial farms output and income were double that on others simply because owners had better land

8. Inventories and Accounts, MHR; Wills, MHR; *AM,* vol. 54, p. 394.

with which to work. Productive land gave settlers a crucial advantage in trying to earn a living as tobacco planters.[9]

Not everyone, however, was equally committed to planting tobacco or dependent on market agriculture. If each householder, sharecropper, adult servant, and slave in Talbot County had cultivated tobacco, by the turn of the century the county's annual crop would have come to between 2.6 and 3.1 million pounds. Actually, much less than that was produced each year. Eastern Shore customs records indicate that even during the boom of 1697–1701, yearly exports from Talbot and Kent together amounted to no more than 1.8 million pounds of tobacco. Some of the shortfall between potential production and actual exports can be explained by infertile soil, poor harvests, and runaway and reluctant workers, but the difference in the figures also suggests that as committed as most of the region's planters were to the market crop, at least some remained outside the staple economy and others devoted less land and labor to tobacco than they might have done. The failure to maximize staple production reflected in part a persistent, sensible concern of immigrant English farmers to achieve self-sufficiency. This concern was heightened by the post-1680s growth in family size and the resulting need to raise more food for nonproductive, younger household members. In turn, the late seventeenth-century drop in tobacco prices made a movement away from market specialization, especially for those without investments in servant and slave field hands, a logical choice.[10]

9. See Tables 7 and 8. An excellent discussion of tobacco yields may be found in Gregory A. Stiverson, *Poverty in a Land of Plenty: Tenancy in Eighteenth-Century Maryland* (Baltimore, 1977), pp. 85–103. Current estimates can be found in USDA, *Soil Survey: Prince Georges County, Maryland* (Washington, D.C., 1967), pp. 141–149. In three hundred years, tobacco planting methods have changed little.

10. Production estimates are based on the data in Tables 7 and 8, and the trade estimate is calculated from data discussed more fully in Chapter 6. The discrepancy between export and production figures may reflect smuggling. In 1692 Edward Randolph, the most important customs official in the colonies, wrote to superiors that trade in Maryland was being disrupted by overland smuggling of Eastern Shore tobacco to Delaware. If smuggling was extensive, then household income from market production was higher than the export figures indicate. On smuggling, see Robert Noxon Toppan, ed., *Edward Randolph, Including His Letters and Official Papers . . . 1673–1703,* Publications of the Prince Society (Boston, 1899), vol. 28, p. 118; vol. 31, pp. 361–363, 371.

Export figures correspond to an average household income of £5 from to-

Little had occurred to change drastically the lot of English yeomen who moved to the Eastern Shore. In 1688, Gregory King estimated that English "freeholders of the better sort" had annual incomes before expenses of £13. Peter Bowden, working more recently and more carefully than King, put the value of the output of a thirty-acre seventeenth-century English wheat farm at around £40 to £50 annually. Talbot County landowners, if they sold meat, corn, and dairy products to lodgers and neighbors and rented some of their holdings, may have grossed £20 a year, but quite often a landed planter would be lucky if his farm returned half that much. The Chesapeake planter had fewer production expenses than a grain farmer and accordingly kept more to save or spend, but in total, his economic position was little better. Even the agricultural income of the richest planters with their large labor force was not significantly greater than that of a prosperous yeoman grain grower or sheep farmer. For the rural poor, the cottagers, artisans, and apprentices who left England and came to the Eastern Shore, the hope of becoming a landowner clearly offered the prospect of a markedly improved standard of living. For other immigrants, especially yeomen farmers, the adoption of tobacco planting promised only the same material rewards that hard work and good fortune might have brought in England.[11]

---

bacco, production figures to an income of £14. If tobacco brought in £5 yearly, then the crop made up in value 35 percent of household output (food production the other 65 percent). If tobacco brought in £14 annually, the staple accounted for 65 percent of household output. These estimates assume that an adult consumed 16 bushels of corn and 100 pounds of meat yearly and that farmers raised only enough food to feed the family. Data on family size, crop prices, and tobacco production come from the sources in Tables 7 and 8. For a stimulating discussion of some of the points raised in this paragraph, see James A. Henretta, "Families and Farms: *Mentalité* in Pre-Industrial America," *WMQ* 35 (1978): 3–32.

11. On English farming, consult Peter Bowden, "Agricultural Profits, Farm Profits, and Rents," in *Agrarian History of England and Wales*, ed. Thirsk, p. 593–695; and Peter Laslett, *The World We Have Lost: England before the Industrial Age* (New York, 1971), pp. 53–80. Bowden calculated the income of a yeoman farmer. Husbandmen and cottagers, the most numerous members of rural English society, made considerably less. Of equal importance, Bowden estimated that expenses reduced the gross income of the hypothetical arable farm he described from £42.5 to £14.5 net—about the amount for which a Talbot householder sold his tobacco crop.

Often, of course, those who came to the Eastern Shore depended as much on a trade as on farming to make a living. Especially in the grazing and dairying areas of England, large numbers of cottagers, pushed off the land by the farming population, found employment in the textile, leather, and metalworking trades. But even in the corn-growing areas of the country, many farmers earned some of their income as weavers, tailors, shoemakers, carpenters, and sawyers. Moreover, most rural English communities supported several small entrepreneurs—a village blacksmith, one or two millers, a butcher and brewer, and always a few innkeepers. The extent of industry differed greatly from county to county but was always significant. In Gloucestershire, for example, part of the hinterland that supported Bristol's colonial commerce, about 45 percent of the population engaged in some artisanal work, most frequently in the textile industry. In Oxfordshire, a more fully agricultural county, farmers made up perhaps 70 percent of the population, while those who practiced a craft during at least part of the year accounted for roughly a quarter of the area's inhabitants. In the great shipping towns from which people departed for the Chesapeake, skilled workmen were even more prevalent.[12]

Artisans accounted for perhaps one-fourth of the white male immigrants to the Eastern Shore. Some, particularly those in the textile trades, found no work as craftsmen in the region; others completed a term of service and departed; still others, a fortunate minority, acquired land and began to call themselves planters. Nonetheless, in late-seventeenth-century Talbot, one land-

---

12. On rural industry, see Joan Thirsk, "Industries in the Countryside," in *Essays in the Economic and Social History of Tudor and Stuart England*, ed. F. J. Fisher (Cambridge, 1961), pp. 70–88; A. J. and R. H. Tawney, "An Occupational Census of the Seventeenth Century," *EHR*, 1st ser., 5 (1934): 25–64; C. W. Chalkin, *Seventeenth-Century Kent: A Social and Economic History* (London, 1965), pp. 114, 246–247, 269–270; W. G. Hoskins, *The Midland Peasant: The Economic and Social History of a Leicestershire Village* (London, 1957), pp. 167–169; and L. A. Clarkson, *The Pre-Industrial Economy of England, 1500–1700* (London, 1971), pp. 86–97. On English ports, see, for example, D. V. Glass, "Socio-economic Status and Occupations in the City of London at the End of the Seventeenth Century," in *Studies in London History*, ed. A. E. J. Hollaender and W. Kellaway (London, 1969), pp. 573–589.

owner in seven listed himself as an artisan each time he signed an official document.[13]

Most of these planter-craftsmen were carpenters and coopers. They earned their wages by constructing and selling tobacco "hogsheads" (shipping containers) and by doing the more elaborate wood and metal work on the dwellings and barns of other settlers. Their business flourished because it required neither a large investment of capital nor full-time devotion to the craft. Between 1704 and 1710, for example, no one in Talbot County left an inventory listing tools valued at more than £8, and 45 of the 53 skilled planters who died during the period had less than £2 invested in tools. In Talbot, as in rural England, most artisans were also farmers, and their wealth consisted primarily of household furnishings and livestock.[14]

Artisanal entrepreneurs were far less common on the Eastern Shore than were carpenters and coopers. Before 1713, no Talbot resident found employment as a brewer or miller, and only four settlers made their living as tanners or blacksmiths. Thomas Robins, who left an estate of £1,400 in 1721, was by far the most prominent craftsman on the Eastern Shore. He had an inventory of £200 in leather goods and employed four servants as shoemakers in his tannery. Tristram Thomas, a rich shoemaker who died in 1685 with an estate of £514, had £54 invested in his craft and £107 in small debts owed him by his customers. In contrast, Clement Hopkins was relatively poor when he died in 1693 with a £77 estate, but his tanning operation, evaluated at £36, also represented a substantial investment. The only other artisan of note was a blacksmith who left a business worth £60 in 1712 as part of a £173 inventory.[15]

Why did so few settlers engage in these trades? Every English county had its substantial craftsmen, and undoubtedly some of them came to the Chesapeake. Here they found the same de-

13. Talbot County Land Conveyances and Talbot County Court Records, MHR.

14. Inventories and Accounts, MHR.

15. Inventories, vol. 2, p. 214 (Thomas Robins, 1721); Inventories and Accounts, vol. 9, p. 175 (Tristram Thomas, 1686); vol. 12, p. 112 (Clement Hopkins, 1693); Talbot Inventories, IB, no. 3, p. 164 (Thomas Bartlett, 1712); all in MHR. No additional names of artisan entrepreneurs turned up in the land or court records.

mand as in England for such goods as nails, shoes, and alcohol. But they also faced two problems. First, they had to raise enough money to establish and maintain business contacts. They had to sell on credit and were never in as strong a position to force payment or withstand refusals to pay as the English shippers against whom they competed. Second, they could seldom undersell those shippers. Reliable comparative prices are available only for cloth, but these indicate that goods produced in Talbot retailed for two or three times as much as material made in England, Ireland, or Germany. As a result, even such men as Robins and Thomas spent much of their time planting tobacco.[16]

Only the trade of shipbuilding thrived. By the 1690s, at least three major shipyards—one on the Third Haven under the direction of Ralph Fishbourn, a second operated by Solomon Sumers on Island Creek, and a third belonging to William Sharpe—were located in Talbot County, and at least one more was to be found on the Chester River in Kent County. The sustained demand for new vessels forced local builders to bring in skilled artisans from other colonies. At times the yards employed upward of twenty craftsmen, who turned out everything from 20-ton sloops to 350-ton ships. The industry attracted both local buyers and London and Liverpool shippers. The availability of large quantities of high-quality, low-cost lumber—especially oak—kept expenses down and allowed local builders to compete with London shipyards, while the settlement of several Quaker craftsmen with the skill to construct large vessels and with the contacts in England and Pennsylvania to find workers and buyers made the Eastern Shore the center of Chesapeake shipbuilding.[17]

While full-time artisans found fewer opportunities on the seventeenth-century Eastern Shore than they did in England, the same was not true of merchants. Merchants had long played

16. Clemens, "From Tobacco to Grain," Appendix I-C, p. 167, gives cloth prices taken from Talbot County inventories.

17. The extent of Eastern Shore shipbuilding can be gauged from records in *AM*, vol. 25, pp. 598–601; Maryland Commission Book no. 4012, MHR; and the Oxford Naval Office Records, C.O. 5/749, PRO (photocopies at the Library of Congress). See also a 1697 petition to the Talbot County court in the Talbot County Land Conveyances, A.B. no. 8, pt. 1, p. 285 (1697).

a central role in the economic life of English communities; the development of tobacco marketing in the Chesapeake would expand this role. English farmers, of course, had traditionally relied on town merchants to handle the sale of agricultural produce and to provide cloth goods and household necessities. But while the function of the trader was vital to England's rural economy, it was also limited. English traders dealt with an agricultural population whose chief concern was supplying itself with food. The surplus a farmer had left for sale gave him access to the market, but producing this surplus was not the chief goal of a farmer's endeavors. In this situation, changes in crop prices seldom induced farmers to grow more or less of a crop, and if the market did alter the farmer's behavior, he was as likely to cut production when higher prices let him maintain his standard of living with less work as he was to increase production in order to maximize profits. Put simply, the market gave the merchant little leverage over the farmer. Moreover, despite the growth of cities such as London, Bristol, and Norwich and the increasing effect of their markets on urban hinterlands, most English merchants continued to trade primarily in their own parish or county. There they faced competition from the face-to-face barter transactions by which rural villagers often supplied each other. Only in the late seventeenth century would an integrated, regionally specialized marketing system begin to take shape. In the Chesapeake, by contrast, settlers were from the beginning part of an Atlantic, urban-controlled commercial economy; they relied on the international market both in selling their tobacco and to obtain goods and credit, and they dealt with the market through local merchants.[18]

In the seventeenth-century Chesapeake, the term "merchant" covered various occupations: tobacco receiver (factor, agent)

18. For a sense of the chronology of the development of a national market, compare Hoskins, *Midland Peasant,* pp. 175, 190–192, 211–215, with E. A. Wrigley, "A Simple Model of London's Importance," *Past & Present,* no. 37 (1967), pp. 44–70. The most detailed treatment can be found in Alan M. Everitt, "The Marketing of Agricultural Produce," in *Agrarian History of England and Wales,* ed. Thirsk; pp. 466–588. I found particularly helpful Jan de Vries, "Peasant Demand Patterns and Economic Development: Freisland, 1550–1750," in *European Peasants and Their Markets: Essays in Agrarian History,* ed. William N. Parker and Eric L. Jones (Princeton, 1975), pp. 205–238.

for an English trader, shopkeeper, and shipowner. In Talbot County during the 1670s, when population was spread thinly along the banks of numerous bayside rivers, 45 men earned part of their living by collecting tobacco from and distributing goods to far-flung plantations, and even in the period 1680–1713, when families lived closer together and the economy was more efficiently organized, at least 60 merchants plied their trade in the county. Yet tobacco receivers, shopkeepers, and shipowners were no more common in Talbot than were merchants, mercers, innkeepers, and boatsmen in rural England; their function in the Atlantic economy distinguished Talbot merchants.[19]

Tobacco receivers had a central role in the initial organization of Eastern Shore trade. The receiver worked under contract and for a commission; he was not an independent merchant. For preparing cargoes for shipment and disposing of imports he generally received a 5 to 10 percent commission. Because each extra month in colonial waters cost English shippers £40 or more in seamen's wages, few hesitated to pay for speedy loadings. Disputes were common over the amount of the commission, over charges for storage, transport, and wastage, and over the proper rate for converting sales of goods valued in sterling into tobacco remittances. The most crucial decision was at what price to evaluate tobacco when planters exchanged the crop for goods. If the receiver had a large shipload of merchandise on his hands and was under pressure to load tobacco quickly, he might offer planters more than the market value for the crop. The English merchant would consequently receive less tobacco than he expected from his agent on the Eastern Shore. Lawsuits followed and most Maryland courts supported English merchants. Few receivers remained long in their work. If the receiver did his job well, the temptation to take the profits and return to England or invest in planting was too great; and if the receiver bungled his assignments, he quickly lost his English contacts.[20]

19. Merchants and the specific activity in which each engaged were identified from several sources. Occupations were generally listed when people were involved in land transactions and court cases. More detailed information on trade practices came from the Provincial Court Records (many volumes published in *AM*); the ship census listed in *AM*, vol. 25, pp. 598–601; and Inventories and Accounts, MHR.

20. For example, consult *AM*, vol. 49, p. 30; vol. 67, pp. 33–36, 169; vol. 68, pp. 62–65; vol. 69, pp. 303–308; vol. 70, pp. 278–279.

Some of those who began as agents for English merchants attempted to establish their own stores. Such a venture required capital and luck. To entice the planter away from the shipboard trade on merchant vessels, a storekeeper had to stock foods rich and exotic to the seventeenth-century palate—raisins, spices, cheese, and rice, for example—and plenty of good strong West Indian spirits. He needed all manner of pots, pans, and other household items, jewelry and fine pewterware, gloves, shoes, and other clothing for daily fieldwork, and, by far the most expensive merchandise, yards and yards of dowlass, holland, and broadcloth from the looms of Europe. If he hoped to deal with fifty planters, the storekeeper would need an inventory of £300 to £400, and few men in the tidewater could raise that kind of money. Understandably, London merchants had no special interest in financing competitors. When credit could be obtained, local merchants often went bankrupt because small planters were invariably poor credit risks. Only his year-round residence in a region and the greater ease with which he could procure molasses and rum from the West Indies gave him any advantage over ship captains who ran floating stores in the Great Choptank and Chester rivers while their merchant vessels took on tobacco. Under these conditions, few men opened stores in Talbot County until late in the seventeenth century. Jonathan Sybrey, who died in 1684, had one, and Edward Mann established another in the 1670s, but probably as a factor for William Orchard of Poole rather than on his own account.[21]

Less capital was required to enter the coastal trade, but hardly any Eastern Shore entrepreneurs did so. Many had sloops built, but only one locally owned vessel sailed for Barbados during the seventeenth century and none elsewhere. Instead, sloop owners used their vessels in the Chesapeake to move tobacco and goods around. For a £12 investment a man could obtain a craft that might rent for anywhere from £4 to £10 a month during the shipping season. The failure to use these sloops at other times of the year in trade with Barbados, Massachusetts, and New York

21. See sources cited in note 20. See also Inventories and Accounts, vol. 8, p. 441, MHR; *AM*, vol. 45, p. 545; vol. 57, p. 334; vol. 65, pp. 112–113; vol. 66, pp. 393, 437 (Jonathan Sybery); vol. 70, p. 321 (Edward Mann); and Talbot County Land Conveyances, GG, no. 3, pp. 151–173 (Robins family).

could be attributed in part to the fact that long voyages required more capital and West Indies goods could be obtained cheaply and with little worry from New England merchants. After the 1680s, when a number of planters first acquired the money to build and outfit sloops and raised enough corn to load these vessels, war made the risks too high. Moreover, those who wished to invest in shipping had the alternative of buying a share in an English merchant ship.[22]

Although ambitious traders, especially outport factors, continued to arrive in Talbot and Kent, the work of many tobacco receivers gradually passed into the hands of wealthy planters with mercantile connections. These merchant-planters steadily diverted funds from commerce into the purchase of labor and land, but in turn took advantage of their increasing command of the production of servants, slaves, and tenants to secure better terms when they sold tobacco. When rising staple prices warranted greater risks, many merchant-planters extended their operations by buying tobacco from their neighbors. They consigned their tobacco to London merchants and retailed goods they received in return. The procedure assured English ship captains of relatively quick loading while eliminating the recurring expenses and uncertainty that reliance on a tobacco receiver occasioned.[23]

In pursuing trade and farming, the merchant-planter symbolized the dominance of commercial agriculture on the Eastern Shore. This new agricultural economy brought significant changes from life in England: the replacement of a food crop (wheat) by a consumer product (tobacco), the measurement of

22. Hire rates are scattered through *AM*; see, for example, vol. 58, p. 43. Sloop costs are listed in *AM*, vol. 65, pp. 656–657; vol. 68, pp. 231–232; and in various inventories in Inventories and Accounts, MHR. I have used the Barbados Naval Office Records, C.O. 33/14, and the Jamaica Naval Office Records, C.O. 142/13, PRO (microfilm in the Alderman Library, University of Virginia), and found only one Eastern Shore sloop listed in the late seventeenth century. Shares in English ships are somewhat more commonly found in the inventories than outright ownership of sloops, but see *AM*, vol. 25, pp. 598–601.

23. The activities of these wealthy merchant-planters are discussed in Chapter 5. The importance of commercial wealth to the careers of some of the most prominent seventeenth-century Maryland leaders is underscored by the biographical information in Lois Green Carr and David William Jordan, *Maryland's Revolution in Government, 1689–1692* (Ithaca, N.Y., 1974), pp. 232–282.

income and wealth in terms of labor more than land, and the
growth of direct dependence on an Atlantic market, with the consequences described for the occupational structure. Yet the
similarities with the Old World were equally important. Farming
was still done by families and production organized by households. Land retained its importance in providing a material link
between generations; and grain cultivation, livestock husbandry,
and simple craftsmanship all persisted in the New World tobacco
economy.

ECONOMIC OPPORTUNITY AND INEQUALITY

The commercialization of agriculture offered much economically to the energetic and ambitious while it made inevitable
ever greater disparities in the positions of poor and rich. Few
English people, however, judged opportunity and inequality
solely in terms of the market. Most were still part of a world in
which families struggled simply to provide the same standard of
living for their children as they themselves enjoyed, and inequality resulted primarily from inherited status or from the
gradual pressure of population growth on limited community
resources. To be sure, in the seventeenth century, those with
access to capital demonstrated an increasing willingness to calculate in terms of profit and loss. Farmers experimented with new
cultivation techniques and crop rotation cycles, and merchants
extended urban trading networks farther into the countryside.
Simultaneously, many turned to law and the bureaucracy because the growth of the state and the market made these more
lucrative fields. Both characteristics—one of simple persistence,
the other of change and improvement—were integral to the lives
of the whites who settled the Eastern Shore.[24]

In Talbot and Kent counties, economic opportunity was
closely tied to the way wealth was passed from generation to
generation. As a rule, Eastern Shore planters followed the cus-

24. Two excellent discussions of social mobility in England are Lawrence
Stone, "Social Mobility in England, 1500-1700," *Past & Present*, no. 33 (1966),
pp. 16–55; and Alan Everitt, "Social Mobility in Early Modern England," *Past &
Present*, no. 33 (1966), pp. 56–73. See also the analysis in Wallerstein, *Modern
World-System*, pp. 227–260.

tom of partible inheritance and drew up their wills to divide equally among the male children that part of the estate not given to their wives and daughters. The practice of partible inheritance, by distributing property among numerous heirs, should have prevented extreme concentrations of wealth and have given each son the same chance in life. But during the first decades of settlement on the Eastern Shore, when planters could not always marry and life expectancy was short, the actual pattern of inheritance varied greatly from family to family. When a deceased planter had lived a long life and raised a large family, his estate had to be split among numerous sons and daughters; when the father died at an early age or had few children who lived as long as he did, there would be only two or three sons to inherit all the property. Less frequently, second-generation planters benefited from bequests from aunts or uncles who died without children of their own. As a result, a small number of native-born Eastern Shore colonists began their careers with all the assets of one or more families behind them while others had to be content with a fifth, sixth, or even smaller portion of the family holdings. Actually, most inheritances did not go directly from a planter to his sons but rather came under control of the planter's wife. In a society with many fewer women than men, a woman might remarry two or even three times, and in the process, if she selected her new husbands prudently, could accumulate large amounts of property. This property secured the economic position that her sons would someday occupy. Later, the marriage of these second-generation children and the eventual increase in family size would undermine the chances of many new immigrants and freedmen to move into the planter class.[25]

Opportunity, however, was also a function of the market. Between the early 1660s, when settlement of the Eastern Shore began, and 1680, tobacco prices dropped from over 1.5 pence per pound to 1.0 pence. But falling prices had been accompanied by expanding production because cheap servant labor and virgin land kept costs down. Then, in the 1680s, the price of

---

25. Wills, MHR. See, in addition, Lois Green Carr and Lorena S. Walsh, "The Planter's Wife: The Experience of White Women in Seventeenth-Century Maryland," *WMQ* 34 (1977): 542–571.

tobacco fell even further, to 0.7 pence per pound, and bottomed out. The supply of servants diminished, the cost of land increased, and the Eastern Shore's boom economy ground to a halt. Judging by the low, relatively stable prices of the period 1680–96, planters had pushed tobacco production to the breaking point and profit margins had become dangerously narrow.[26]

Not that opportunity ended in the 1680s. The struggle was always as much to capitalize on short-term increases in the price of tobacco as it was to accumulate wealth gradually. In such years as 1685 and 1697, peak prices encouraged investment by established planters and allowed poorer colonists to rent land and form households. But if prices rose enough to whet expectations, these expectations, especially for the propertyless, differed from what they had been before 1680. For in the earlier period, it was not unusual for servitude to be followed by tenancy and tenancy by landownership. After the 1680s, however, judging from the careers of servants who obtained their freedom in the last two decades of the seventeenth century, tenancy became a permanent condition. Over a farmer's lifetime, tobacco no longer provided enough income to allow tenants, who had to share their produce with a landlord, to accumulate the capital necessary to convert a leasehold into a freehold. And even free immigrants and the children of landowners found their battle with the staple economy more arduous. For while rising land prices and a decreasing supply of labor did not keep many planters from profiting during the boom years of the mid-1680s and late 1690s, the economic well-being of those who stayed in Talbot and Kent appeared as secure as it did only because those who could not compete—the disinherited and debt-ridden—left.[27]

26. Tobacco prices are given in the Appendix.
27. Economic opportunity for servants is discussed in Russell R. Menard, "From Servant to Freeholder: Status Mobility and Property Accumulation in Seventeenth-Century Maryland," *WMQ* 30 (1973): 37–64; and Lois Green Carr and Russell R. Menard, "Servants and Freedmen in Early Colonial Maryland," in *Essays on the Seventeenth-Century Chesapeake,* ed. Thad W. Tate and David L. Ammerman (Chapel Hill, forthcoming). My work with more than 200 post-1680 immigrant servants found virtually no evidence of freedmen acquiring land. Attempts to trace Talbot servants to Kent and Queen Anne's counties indicated that few, if any, became landowners.

The gradual contraction of opportunity appeared most noticeably in the struggle for land. A new planter needed between 50 and 100 acres to begin farming on the Eastern Shore. With this amount of land, he could cultivate tobacco, grow food crops, pasture livestock, and avoid deforestation. In the early 1660s, it was possible to purchase 50 acres of woodland for as little as 1,000 pounds of tobacco and to patent the same amount of land for somewhat less. As population growth increased the demand for land, and clearing and building increased the value of plantations, prices rose steadily. In 1680, a 50-acre tract cost about 1,700 pounds of tobacco, or the equivalent of a planter's annual production. By 1700, this price had doubled. The dual pressure of climbing land prices and the stagnating tobacco economy squeezed many poorer immigrants out of the land market.[28]

Except to the poor, however, landed society remained relatively open. Perhaps this fact can best be illustrated by the data in Tables 9 and 10, tracing the careers of those who owned over 1,000 acres in 1670, 1680, and 1706. Some 35 percent (14/40) of the large landowning families in 1670 and 47 percent (21/45) of those in 1680 maintained their position through 1706 or acquired even more land by that date. These families formed the core of an emerging planter elite that during the eighteenth century would engross huge tracts of land. But a majority of the large landowners in 1670 and 1680 died before 1706 without leaving a male heir or divided their estates into smaller properties by splitting them among their children. The large landowners of the early eighteenth century came in almost equal numbers from the ranks of newcomers, small planter families, and the established elite of two decades before.

Overall, almost three out of five of those who owned land in 1706 had settled in Talbot or Kent after 1680. Nevertheless, kinship connections among resident planter families played an increasingly important role in the distribution of land during the last decades of the seventeenth century. More and more often,

28. Land prices come from the Talbot County Land Conveyances, MHR. See also Graph 4 and Clemens, "From Tobacco to Grain," p. 169. The number of new land purchasers dropped every decade, from twenty-five per year in the 1680s to nine per year in the period 1700–1709.

Table 9. Family position in 1670 and 1680 of men who held over 1,000 acres in 1706, Talbot County

Family status before 1706	Number of families	
	1670	1680
Large landed family	20	23
Small landed family	7	17
Not yet settled	33	20
All large landowners	60	60

SOURCE: Lloyd Rent Roll of 1706, MS 2001, MHS.

planters first acquired land not through purchase but by marriage or inheritance. As the relative number of women and children in the region increased, estates tended more frequently to be divided among several heirs, and kinship networks that included several landowners became more common. By the end of the century, perhaps half of those who owned land on the Eastern Shore were linked by birth or marriage to some other landowner. Outsiders continued to settle in the region and buy land, but most were now relatively well-to-do immigrants—merchants, skilled craftsmen, or planters from other regions of the Chesapeake—who had little difficulty obtaining land, establishing a household, meeting interest payments, and weathering bad seasons.[29]

At the same time, settlers could, and often did, move away from the bayside. Even if credit remained a problem, land in the backcountry cost considerably less. The first major movement out of the older regions of Kent and Talbot came in the late 1680s. A more significant migration inland occurred during the 1697–1701 boom, when settlers pushed to the Tuckahoe in eastern Talbot and north to Kent, taking advantage of the expansion of the credit structure to begin households in the interior. In

29. Talbot County Land Conveyances, MHR; Lloyd Rent Roll of 1706, MS 2001, MHS. Of the more than 600 male landowners in Talbot in 1706, some 54 percent first acquired land by purchasing it; 23 percent began their careers as landowners through an inheritance; and 22 percent became landowners when they married the daughter or widow of a landowner.

Table 10. Position in 1706 of heirs of men who held over 1,000 acres in 1670 and 1680, Talbot County

Family status, 1706	Number of landowners with over 1,000 acres	
	1670	1680
Deceased, no heirs	18	14
Owned fewer than 1,000 acres	8	10
Owned 1,000 acres or more	14	21
All large landowners	40	45

SOURCE: Lloyd Rent Roll of 1706, MS 2001, MHS.

1706, as a result of this population shift, the provincial government established Queen Anne's County out of a section of Talbot and Kent.[30]

Consequently, it would be too simple to say that falling tobacco prices had by the 1680s ended opportunity on the Eastern Shore. Despite disadvantageous market conditions, advancement continued for some whites. Slavery spread and ever more land came into production. For other white inhabitants, especially former servants, tenancy and migration offered the greatest hope. The shrinking of opportunity left the Eastern Shore without real deprivation or enormous wealth, still a land of small planters. This point can be reinforced by comparing the social structure of Talbot County in 1680–87 and in 1704–10, with the aid of Tables 11–13.

Initially, most English farmers who settled on the Eastern Shore probably thought of themselves in terms that reflected their backgrounds as yeomen, husbandmen, cottagers, or even members of the gentry. But if such designations as "artisan" and "merchant" carried over to the Chesapeake, most others disappeared, to be replaced by the term "planter." In truth, virtually every free person who remained long in the Chesapeake became some sort of planter, and the distinctions that emerged among

30. Queen Anne's County Land Records and Kent County Land Records, MHR. Land prices for Queen Anne's County are given in Clemens, "From Tobacco to Grain," pp. 169–170. Migration patterns have been estimated from data given in Table 3.

Table 11. Social structure of free white population, Talbot
County, 1680–87 and 1704–10 (percent)

Status	1680s (N = 800)	1700s (N = 1,160)
Large slave owners	1%	1%
Smaller slave owners	9	11
Servant owners	26	29
Small landowners	14	10
Landless	50	49
All free whites	100%	100%

NOTE: Both sets of figures are estimates derived from data in court, land,
and probate records, but the 1700s figures have been adjusted in accordance
with the 1704 census. In Talbot in 1704, there were 590 landed householders,
182 tenants (for a total of 772 householders, of whom an estimated 60 were
women), and 388 free male nonhouseholders. In addition, there were an estimated 434 male servants and 460 male and female slaves. When the 60 female
householders are subtracted, the above figures add up to 1,994 taxables, the
number in the 1704 census and approximately the number of taxables listed in
the court records and included in Table 2.

SOURCES: Inventories and Accounts, MHR; Lloyd Rent Roll of 1706, MS 2001,
MHS; *AM*, vol. 25, pp. 256–58.

them must be looked for not in their titles but in their share of
the distribution of land and labor. On this basis the tables were
constructed.

Three significant facts about the Eastern Shore emerge from
the tables. First, despite a small yet significant increase in the

Table 12. Wealth of deceased tobacco planters who died
landless, Talbot County, 1680–87 and 1704–10

Inventoried wealth (pounds)	1680s (percent) (N = 35)	1700s (percent) (N = 64)
£0–5	0%	11%
6–20	31	41
21–40	20	27
41–80	23	19
81 and over	26	3
Total	100%	101%

SOURCES: Inventories and Accounts, MHR; Lloyd Rent Roll of 1706, MS 2001,
MHS.

Table 13. Wealth of deceased tobacco planters, by status, Talbot County, 1680-87 and 1704-10

Inventoried wealth (pounds)	Slave owners (percent)		Servant owners (percent)		Landowners (percent)	
	1680s (N = 14)	1700s (N = 27)	1680s (N = 31)	1700s (N = 44)	1680s (N = 16)	1700s (N = 2?)
£0-40	0%	0%	0%	11%	56%	31%
41-80	0	11	26	30	19	31
81-200	36	30	74	41	19	38
201-350	28	37	0	16	6	0
351 and over	36	22	0	2	0	0
Total	100%	100%	100%	100%	100%	100%

NOTE: Estate value does not include land or labor.
SOURCE: Inventories and Accounts, MHR.

relative number of planters with servants and slaves, the basic structure of free society changed little over the last decades of the seventeenth century. The class of free poor did not grow because most such people left. Second, in the 1680s the ownership of land and labor had yet to create a precise pattern of economic differentiation among the planters. Those, for example, with wealth of £20 to £60 were as likely to have land as not. Third, the degree of inequality increased with time. When economic growth stopped, the rich claimed an increasingly large share of the region's wealth and resources.[31]

By 1710, the largest planters in Talbot County had amassed far more property than their counterparts in the 1680s. Of the six men identified as large slave owners in the 1680s, five had between £780 and £1,300 and one had £4,020 of inventoried assets, excluding land and labor. For the period between 1704 and 1710, two wealthy planters possessed perhaps £10,000 in inventoried property, six had more than £2,000 but less than £6,000, and the rest had between £1,000 and £2,000.[32]

31. Compare Tables 11-13 with those in Russell R. Menard, P. M. G. Harris, and Lois Green Carr, "Opportunity and Inequality: The Distribution of Wealth on the Lower Western Shore of Maryland, 1638-1705," *MHM* 69 (1974): 169-184.
32. Inventories and Accounts, MHR; Lloyd Rent Roll of 1706, MS 2001, MHS. Some wealth figures are estimates based on the landholdings of planters.

At the other end of the scale, between 1680 and 1710 the landless became poorer and a gap between them and the small landowners appeared. During this period, the percentage of landless men in each wealth bracket under £40 grew, and in the early eighteenth century some men died with less than £5, a truly paltry sum (see Table 12). This change in economic status among the landless may be attributed to the disappearance of wealthy but landless merchants (factors), artisans, and innkeepers from Talbot society as well as to the growth of a stratum of almost destitute freemen. Unlike the situation in the 1680s, there was little overlap between these poor and the small landowners, almost 70 percent of whom had over £40 in personal property (see Tables 11–13).

In the middle range of wealth, however, distinctions remained blurred. Small planters often enjoyed much the same material comforts as the owners of servants and slaves. For half of the free whites on the Eastern Shore, economic equality prevailed. These small farmers, most with estates of £100 to £300, constituted the most numerous and productive class in Eastern Shore society. The labor, land, and livestock they had at their disposal clearly differentiated them from the immigrant laborers, husbandmen, and artisans that some of their parents had been, while their commercial orientation ranked them alongside the yeomen and lesser gentlemen farmers of rural England.

THE EARLY COLONIAL EASTERN SHORE: AN OVERVIEW

Both population and market conditions ended the economic boom on the early Eastern Shore. These conditions also explain the gradual transformation of Talbot and Kent from a predominantly male, immigrant, and fluid society to a more stratified one of family farmers. As early settlers acquired land, built up their estates through years of farming, and divided their property among their children, economic inequality naturally developed. For not only did the wide range in family sizes make it inevitable that there would be significant differences in the amount of property inherited by second-generation colonists, but the accumulation of such property by established planters set them off more and more distinctly from the great majority of freed servants and newly arrived immigrants. By the turn of the century, a core group of landed families had emerged in Talbot and Kent; these families, while by no means of equal economic status, were increasingly bound by ties of marriage and distinguishable from the more mobile, propertyless whites who settled after them. The kinship networks that marriages in the 1690s and 1700s began to form would provide the social basis for the farming economy of the eighteenth-century Eastern Shore.

Market conditions, however, also contributed to the growth of inequality in Kent and Talbot counties. The early years on the Eastern Shore had been ones of relatively high tobacco prices and inexpensive land. Not only were these auspicious conditions under which to establish oneself as a planter, but the opportunity these conditions provided drew to the Eastern Shore quite a few settlers with the capital to exploit their chances fully. With the deceleration of the Atlantic tobacco trade and the fall of local crop prices, new settlers found it increasingly difficult to duplicate the successes of earlier immigrants. Free immigrants, in fact, virtually stopped coming, and planters soon found they could not even compete effectively for servants. Under these conditions, only a small number of landowners, those who had already amassed large estates, were able to switch over to more costly slave labor or branch into the marketing of tobacco and the retailing of European trade goods to maintain their incomes. At the other end of the economic scale, some smaller planters opted out of tobacco production and direct dependence on the market and lived by arable farming and local exchange. Others joined freed servants in the continuing exodus from the tidewater Chesapeake.

By the turn of the century, the society these disheartened migrants left behind closely resembled the English village communities that had supplied so many Chesapeake immigrants. In England as well as the Chesapeake, the poor moved frequently, if not far, in search of work and land. Just as clearly, atop rural society both in England and on the Eastern Shore was a propertied elite. The English gentry, to be sure, made up a somewhat greater percentage of the population than did the merchant-planters of Talbot and Kent and were more secure in their control over the countryside. In addition, members of the English gentry owed their position more to the advantages of birth and the accumulation of land than did their Eastern Shore counterparts, who had begun their rise to power through the ownership of labor and exploits in trade. But against these distinctions must be balanced the fact that the English gentry itself was acquiring an ever more commercial character, and that, with time, the Eastern Shore merchant-planter class would grow to rival the English elite in wealth and prominence.[33]

More striking still was the importance of middling farmers in the economic life of both the Eastern Shore and rural England. In both societies, independent proprietors made up more than half of the householding population and accounted for most of the community's agricultural production. In both societies, roughly the same proportion of farmers supplemented their income through work at a trade, although in England artisanal entrepreneurs were more common. Chesapeake proprietors were more committed to a cash crop and more dependent on the market; unlike the English yeoman, they might own slaves, and by 1700 they were probably a bit more wealthy. Yet they remained family farmers and continued, through the cultivation of corn and the raising of livestock, to supply their own food even while growing tobacco.[34]

33. Especially useful for their discussion of English society are Chalkin, *Seventeenth-Century Kent*, pp. 191–217, 230–256; Alan M. Everitt, *The Community of Kent and the Great Rebellion* (Leicester, 1966), pp. 33–45; Margaret Spufford, *Contrasting Communities: English Villagers in the Sixteenth and Seventeenth Centuries* (Cambridge, 1974), pp. 46–117; Hey, *English Rural Community*, pp. 53–56; and Jan de Vries, *The Economy of Europe in an Age of Crisis, 1600–1750* (London, 1976), pp. 30–83. Robert Paul Brenner, "Commercial Change and Political Conflict: The Merchant Community in Civil War London," Ph.D. dissertation, Princeton University, 1970), contains a superb analysis of the impact of commercialization on the English social structure.

34. According to Laslett, *World We Have Lost*, pp. 53–80, especially p. 64, in the community of Goodnestone-next-Wingham in 1676, the gentry comprised 5 percent of all householders, the yeomen 42 percent, tradesmen 14 percent, and laborers and the poor 39 percent. In Myddle, about midway in the seventeenth century, the gentry made up 6 percent of householders, yeomen and husbandmen 42 percent, tradesmen 14 percent, and laborers and all others 38 percent; see Hey, *English Rural Community*, p. 53. The average wealth of free white male residents of Talbot County was, according to the inventories, £84 around 1685 and £74 around 1705 (see Appendix for a discussion of these figures). These estimates are a good deal above those of Hey, p. 55, for Myddle.

In retrospect, it is clear that the English settlers of the Eastern Shore preserved more of the economic life they had known in the Old World than did the seventeenth-century colonists of New England or the Caribbean. In New England, the abundance of land and the freedom such abundance secured helped to destroy attempts to re-create nucleated common-field villages, but the shift toward individual proprietorship did not end communal decision making or result in extensive market activity. Commercial agriculture did not create a provincial elite, and farming and trade tended to remain separate endeavors. In the West Indies, traditional patterns of economic life broke down completely. The prevalence of disease, the profits of large-scale sugar production, and the availability of slaves drove many whites, especially women and children, from the Caribbean and created a society of enormously wealthy planters and brutalized black laborers. With neither time nor land to raise food, West Indians lived entirely from Atlantic trade. Only in the seventeenth-century Chesapeake did family farming and market agriculture develop hand in hand.[35]

35. On New England communities, see Kenneth A. Lockridge, *A New England Town, The First Hundred Years: Dedham, Massachusetts, 1636-1736* (New York, 1970), especially pp. 69-75; but compare Lockridge's argument to that in Richard L. Bushman, *From Puritan to Yankee: Character and the Social Order in Connecticut, 1690-1765* (New York, 1970), and Charles S. Grant, *Democracy in the Connecticut Frontier Town of Kent* (New York, 1961). While Lockridge stresses the peasant characteristics of New England settlers and Grant and Bushman the entreprenurial characteristics of the immigrants, all three historians depict the region's agricultural economy in remarkably similar ways. Robert Zemsky, in *Merchants, Farmers, and River Gods: An Essay on Eighteenth-Century Politics* (Boston, 1971), analyzes the differences among regions in Massachusetts; his picture of New England society suggests that such communities as Dedham were fast becoming the exception rather than the rule. On life in the West Indies, see the meticulous description in Dunn, *Sugar and Slaves,* pp. 43-83, 263-299; and Richard B. Sheridan, *Sugar and Slavery: An Economic History of the British West Indies, 1623-1775* (Baltimore, 1973), pp. 105-107, 124-147, 208-233. Contrast the description of Sir Thomas Modyford's sugar plantation with that in this chapter of Henrietta Maria Lloyd's farms. At her death in 1697, Lloyd owned 237 cattle, 286 swine, and 137 sheep, and she left her children 11,500 acres of land.

PART II

Revitalization, 1713–76

In which we shall explore how Atlantic markets gave Eastern Shore whites a chance to improve their material lives. After a short discussion of the Anglo-Chesapeake economy, Chapters 5 and 6 focus respectively on continuity and change on the Eastern Shore. Chapter 5 presents an essentially static picture of the organization and operation of the tobacco economy in Talbot County; Chapter 6 analyzes the contrasting processes of agricultural diversification in Talbot and Kent.

Chapter 4

The Atlantic Economy

To the joy of Eastern Shore planters, the Atlantic economy began an immediate if modest revival after Queen Anne's War. By 1717, the import and reexport trades had both returned to average peacetime levels and over the next decade showed signs of renewed vitality. Between the end of Queen Anne's War and the beginning of the American Revolution, the tobacco trade grew 1.8 percent per year, from 36 million pounds of tobacco a year to 101 million pounds.[1]

Short-term cycles of boom and recession still characterized the Atlantic economy (see Graph 5). A modest increase in the price of tobacco led to rapid expansion of the crop's production. In turn, expanding production eventually forced the price down, and production leveled off at a plateau somewhat higher than the one at which the process began. Unlike the experience in the seventeenth century, however, at the end of each cycle of boom and recession the price of tobacco returned to a higher level than that at which it had been initially. While established customers bought little more than they had before, merchants nevertheless increased sales by expanding their market. Over

1. For background, see Jacob M. Price, *France and the Chesapeake: A History of the French Tobacco Monopoly, 1674–1791, and of Its Relationship to the British and American Tobacco Trades,* 2 vols. (Ann Arbor, 1973), vol. 1, pp. 509–543. The growth of the trade can be estimated by comparing the following figures for Chesapeake tobacco exports (in millions of pounds): 37 (1702), 36 (1709), 24 (1713), 41 (1721), and 50 (1727). The annual growth rate for 1702–13 was 0.1 percent; for 1709–21, 1.3 percent; and for 1721–27, 0.7 percent. For trade statistics, see Customs 3, Import-Export Ledgers, PRO.

Graph 5. The eighteenth-century revitalization of the tobacco economy: long-term movements of price, production, and population.

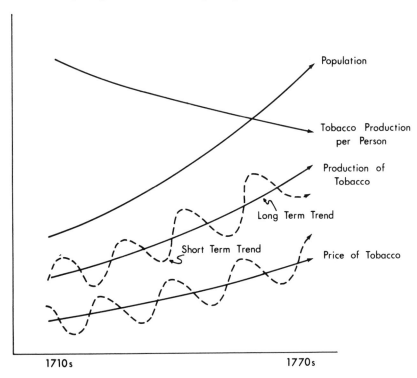

the long run, then, Chesapeake tobacco prices could rise (albeit gradually) despite a steady growth in production. Merchants made the trade even more profitable by organizing more efficiently the supply and distribution of tobacco.[2]

Reexports provided the major stimulus for the growth of the tobacco trade. In the early decades of the eighteenth century, English shippers reexported almost three-fourths of the tobacco they imported. After mid-century, reexports often amounted to 80 percent or even 90 percent of the sales of imported tobacco. Certainly the potential existed to expand the English home mar-

2. This paragraph is based on my analysis of tobacco prices and import-export figures, but see Gary M. Walton and James F. Shepherd, *Shipping, Maritime Trade, and the Economic Development of Colonial North America* (Cambridge, England, 1972), pp. 6-26.

ket as well, especially in light of steady population increases, sustained urban development at the Atlantic ports, improved standards of living in rural England, and the creation of interregional canal and turnpike systems. But the potential was never realized. Almost four-fifths of the reexports went to the Dutch and the French. The Dutch trade increased from 6 million pounds of tobacco annually in the early 1720s to 10 million pounds by the 1740s and to over 30 million by the early 1770s. Over the same period, the trade with France (and Flanders) grew from 5 million pounds to 15 million and then to 35 million. The Dutch trade was a continuation of a seventeenth-century pattern; the French trade created new opportunities for English merchants.[3]

West-coast merchants in large measure directed the expansion of the reexport trade. During this period, the newer Atlantic ports—Liverpool, Bideford, Whitehaven, and Glasgow—entered their golden age of commercial capitalism and urban development. Liverpool's tobacco imports, a mere half-million pounds annually in the 1680s, and but 2 million pounds a year during the first two decades of the eighteenth century, rose to an average of over 6 million pounds a year in the 1740s. Liverpool merchants reexported virtually all the tobacco they imported. While the growth of Liverpool's trade stopped at mid-century, that of Glasgow did not. From hardly a million pounds a year around 1720, Glasgow tobacco imports and reexports climbed to over 40 million pounds a year in the early 1770s. In total, the growth of outport trades over the same period accounted for two-thirds of the increase in British tobacco imports from the Chesapeake. A trade of but 14 million pounds annually in the 1720s had become a commerce of approximately 50 million pounds in the early 1770s. Demand in the reexport market fueled most of this expansion.[4]

Behind the rise of the outports lay several factors. First,

3. Statistics are given in Customs 3, Import-Export Ledgers, PRO, and Price, *France and the Chesapeake,* vol. 2, pp. 845–851.

4. On Liverpool, consult Paul G. E. Clemens, "The Rise of Liverpool, 1665–1750," *EHR* 29 (1976): 211–225; and Price, *France and the Chesapeake,* vol. 1, p. 590. For Glasgow's trade, see U.S. Department of Commerce, Bureau of the Census, *Historical Statistics of the United States, Colonial Times to 1957* (Washington, D.C., 1957), Series Z223–Z240, pp. 765–766.

chronologically, was the growth of the Irish reexport market. As early as 1665, Ireland took 1.8 million pounds of tobacco from England. By 1683 Irish imports totaled 2.8 million pounds, and before Queen Anne's War ended imports reached 4.0 million pounds. Thereafter the Irish trade stagnated, but Irish consumers had played a critical role in the early development of outport trade with the Chesapeake. Irish rural villages not only provided a market for tobacco but also supplied Atlantic-bound vessels with cargoes of linens, immigrants, and inexpensive provisions. This lessened the dependence of outport merchants on their London counterparts for trade goods. At the same time, their location on the west coast sheltered Liverpool, Whitehaven, and Bristol shippers from the worst ravages of the numerous wars that engaged seventeenth- and eighteenth-century European powers. The ability of outport merchants to get their ships safely to the Chesapeake and back allowed them to take advantage of the large differential that existed during wartime between the English and the colonial price of tobacco. Outport merchants also smuggled adeptly; they entered tobacco without paying the high import duties, and in wartime carried on illicit trade with belligerents.[5]

These steps set the stage for eighteenth-century expansion. At each outport, the development of Atlantic commerce led to population growth, labor specialization, and urban building. Merchants improved their harbor and transportation facilities and expanded their credit sources. They sent factors to the Chesapeake and established stores there to collect tobacco systematically and speed its shipment home. The growing efficiency of their trade went hand in hand with their ability to capture the French reexport business and draw on French buyers for capital to underwrite operations in Maryland and Virginia.[6]

5. On Ireland, consult L. M. Cullen, *Anglo-Irish Trade, 1660-1800* (Manchester, 1968), pp. 31-46. Material on wartime trade and smuggling can be found in *Reports of the Committees of the House of Commons*, vol. 1, pp. 603-634; Thomas Heywood, ed., *The Norris Papers* (Manchester, 1845), pp. 81-82, 99-100; and Price, *France and the Chesapeake*, vol. 1, pp. 126-133, 446-454.

6. For a brief discussion of port improvements, see Clemens, "Rise of Liverpool," and the sources mentioned there. The relationship of the French market, the outport store system in the Chesapeake, and the expansion of credit consti-

As early as the 1720s, the vigorous competition that outport merchants offered established London firms had an impact on the latter's trade. Micajah Perry's testimony in 1721 underscored this effect. Perry's report to a parliamentary committee investigating fraud in the tobacco trade began by bemoaning the fate of his father's business, which before 1719, he claimed, had netted the crown up to £100,000 annually in tobacco duties. Such a concern would have required fifteen ships of 200 to 300 tons, employed 300 mariners or more, and transported 5 million pounds of tobacco. With his father but three years in the grave, the son saw the empire collapsing. His shipping was down to five voyages annually, his vessels returned half freighted, and the selling price of his tobacco had fallen from 11.5 pence per pound of sweet-scented tobacco to 9.5 pence. Perhaps the son was not the merchant his father had been, but he realized that the rules of competition had been altered to his disadvantage.[7]

Scottish factors offered better terms to Chesapeake planters. At their Maryland and Virginia stores, Scots bought tobacco outright rather than, as London shippers did, accept it on consignment and remit the net proceeds. Moreover, backed by French capital, Glasgow factors generally gave the planter a higher price than London correspondents could. By dealing with Scottish storekeepers, Chesapeake planters gained the security of sure, quick sales. By not taking the risk of a consignment sale, they lost the more specialized services London merchants provided. In most cases, especially when small planters were involved, the Scots won. As their business picked up, Scots dumped increasingly large amounts of tobacco on the market for prices that Perry claimed were progressively lower, and London firms found themselves with less and less money to return to their Virginia customers. Scottish firms, Perry pro-

---

tute the focus of Jacob M. Price's extremely persuasive interpretation of the growth of the Chesapeake. See, for example, his articles "The Rise of Glasgow in the Chesapeake Tobacco Trade, 1707–1775," *WMQ* 11 (1954): 177–199, and "Capital and Credit in the British-Chesapeake Trade, 1750–1775," in *Of Mother Country and Plantations: Proceedings of the Twenty-Seventh Conference in Early American History,* ed. Virginia B. Platt and David Curtis Skaggs (Bowling Green, 1971), pp. 7–36.

7. *Journal of the House of Commons,* vol. 20, pp. 102–103.

tested, proceeded recklessly on their way, apparently oblivious of the economic havoc they created and mindless of the financial calamity that would inevitably befall them for buying high and selling low. Of course, this was only half the story, for Scottish houses and their Whitehaven and Liverpool counterparts sold as well as bought in the Chesapeake. By expanding their stores and factors into numerous tidewater counties, they made themselves the indispensable suppliers of trade goods. Moreover, by smuggling they actually cut their major expense, and in all likelihood made more profit than Perry's accounting indicated.[8]

The London trade, of course, did not collapse in the face of outport competition. Demand was increasing in the northern European market that London supplied, and consignment shipping proved too profitable to the large planters, especially those who dealt in high-quality tobacco, to be abandoned out of hand. Competition did, however, put a premium on efficiency and fraud, which further improved the position of English merchants in the European reexport market.[9]

The competition among English shippers and the spread of the store system in the Chesapeake gave planters more leverage in marketing their crops. The passage of comprehensive tobacco inspection acts in Virginia in 1730 and Maryland in 1747 enhanced this leverage. The acts were similar and partially successful. They controlled the grade of the staple shipped to England, designated specific sites at which the tobacco was to be inspected and shipped, mandated the destruction of poor-quality tobacco, and provided for the issuance and circulation of tobacco notes for quality crops delivered to inspection warehouses. While the

8. Ibid. See as well T. M. Divine, *The Tobacco Lords: A Study of the Tobacco Merchants of Glasgow and Their Trading Activities, c. 1740–90* (Edinburgh, 1975), pp. 55–99.
9. For the continuing role of London merchants in Maryland trade, see Edward C. Papenfuse, *In Pursuit of Profit: The Annapolis Merchants in the Era of the American Revolution, 1763–1805* (Baltimore, 1975), pp. 35–75; and Jacob M. Price, "The Maryland Bank Stock Case: British-American Financial and Political Relations before and after the American Revolution," in *Law, Society, and Politics in Early Maryland,* ed. Aubrey Land, Lois Green Carr, and Edward C. Papenfuse (Baltimore, 1977), pp. 3–40. Statistical confirmation of these points can be obtained from Customs 3, Import-Export Ledgers, PRO.

crop-reduction provisions clearly hurt small planters, who could not afford to lose any source of income, the acts also benefited them in ways other than merely improving the price of inspected tobacco. In 1730 Governor William Gooch of Virginia sent to English officials a carefully drafted discussion of these benefits of the act:

> Almost all the tobacco made by the common people, (and they make the best), is sold to the merchants in this country and the factors from the out-ports, for clothing and other necessaries which the planters want etc. Their manner of dealing hitherto hath been that if a planter wants but a pair of shoes at one of these stores, he must lay out a whole hogshead of tobacco, seeing the merchant will not receive a less quantity, neither will he deal at all, unless the tobacco lyes convenient to his receiver; and by this means the poor planter is often obliged to take goods that are of little or no use to him, and at what price his neighbouring storekeeper pleases to impose, because he cannot otherwise have what he really hath occasion for. This has indeed proved a discouragement to many industrious people, and must in time oblige them to leave off planting. . . .
>
> By this act the greatest encouragement is given to the common people . . . for after their tobacco hath passed inspection, they must take as many notes for it as they please; i.e., notes for fiftys or hundred pounds, dividing their tobacco into what parcels they think proper, the same as money . . . the planter will not henceforward be confined to one particular merchant, but will be at liberty to deal where he can meet with the best goods and best purchase. . . .
>
> As to the lessening the consumption by advancing the price, I can see no ground to apprehend such a consequence: for since the rich and even people of middling fortunes will ever be fonder of smoking good than bad tobacco, be the price what it will; so custom having made smoking as necessary as food to the labourer and mechanick.

Gooch underestimated the role credit would continue to play in maintaining dependence, but taken in conjunction with the successful efforts in both colonies during the middle of the eighteenth century to introduce paper money, the inspection acts gave the white inhabitants of the Chesapeake an incentive to remain tobacco planters as well as greater ability to try other crops and new merchants.[10]

The growth of the eighteenth-century tobacco trade was also a product of an increasing supply of labor in the Chesapeake. Natural population growth, among both blacks and whites, accounted for much of it, but the importation of African slaves also increased. The intensification of the slave trade was made possible by the growing scale of merchant capitalism at Bristol and Liverpool and by the willingness of merchant princes at these ports to shift their operations among the West Indies, South Carolina, and the Chesapeake as market conditions dictated. The increasing volume of the slave trade, especially in mid-century, may also have reflected the concentrated doses of capital supplied to particular merchants by French wholesale tobacco buyers. Such capital not only allowed merchants to run the higher risks of slave trading but also allowed them to extend more liberal credit to their Chesapeake customers. To the flow of slaves was added a trickle of white immigration that came increasingly from Ireland, Germany, and Scotland, rather than England, and suddenly reached enormous proportions as people began moving south from Pennsylvania into the Shenandoah valley in the 1760s and early 1770s.[11]

Tobacco production did not keep pace with Chesapeake population growth. In most areas, the growing proportion of young children in the population reduced average productivity.

10. No comprehensive study exists of eighteenth-century efforts to improve the tidewater economy, but see Carville V. Earle, *The Evolution of a Tidewater Settlement System: All Hallow's Parish, Maryland, 1650–1783* (Chicago, 1975), pp. 24–30; John C. Rainbolt, *From Prescription to Persuasion: Manipulation of Seventeenth-Century Virginia Economy* (Port Washington, 1974); and Joseph Albert Ernst, *Money and Politics in America, 1755–1775: A Study in the Currency Act of 1764 and the Political Economy of Revolution* (Chapel Hill, N.C., 1973). Virginia governor Gooch's discussion of the problem is quoted from *CSPCS, 1731*, p. 47. One of the best overviews of the period is given in John Hemphill, "Virginia and the English Commercial System, 1689–1733: Studies in the Development and Fluctuation of a Colonial Economy under Imperial Control," Ph.D. dissertation, Princeton University, 1964, pp. 98–148.

11. On white immigration, see Abbot Emerson Smith, *Colonists in Bondage: White Servitude and Convict Labor in America, 1607–1776* (Chapel Hill, N.C., 1947). The organization of the slave trade is discussed in Clemens, "Rise of Liverpool."

The inspection legislation further reduced the market output per person. Moreover, some settlers moved beyond the reaches of the tobacco economy and established subsistence farms. Others turned to new cash crops, especially grains. Fundamental changes in supply and demand conditions in Europe provided added incentives for English shippers to haul wheat and corn from the New World to the Old, and induced some Chesapeake planters to decrease their tobacco acreage and others to abandon the traditional staple entirely. Yet these developments, all of which occurred on the Eastern Shore of Maryland, hardly undercut and in some cases sustained the basic vitality of the eighteenth-century tobacco economy. If an eighteenth-century Talbot planter did not live in a boom economy, he at least expected to profit from tobacco and would probably live to see his children do likewise. If he found his economic world increasingly dominated by large merchants and wealthy landowners, he still could bargain for credit, labor, and favorable trading conditions. For many whites, the Eastern Shore promised as good a life as they would have known in England.[12]

12. The population of the Chesapeake grew from about 134,500 people in 1712 to at least 646,300 in 1773. Tobacco production per capita fell from 186 to 155 pounds. Information on population comes from Russell R. Menard, "The Growth of Population in Early Colonial Maryland, 1634–1712" (unpublished, 1972); Arthur Karinen, "Numerical and Distributional Aspects of Maryland Population, 1631–1840," Ph.D. dissertation, University of Maryland, 1958, pp. 202–203; and Evarts B. Greene and Virginia Harrington, *American Population before the Federal Census of 1790* (New York, 1932), pp. 141, 149–150.

Chapter 5

The Planters of Talbot County

The Eastern Shore of Maryland shared the prosperity that returned to the Chesapeake after Queen Anne's War. Through the remainder of the colonial era the region would have steady population growth, a bountiful rural economy, and a fixed social order. Talbot, Queen Anne's, and Kent, which numbered some 10,800 people in 1713, grew to a population of 37,800 by the time of the American Revolution. During the same period, the expansion of the Atlantic market increased the returns to tobacco planting and helped initiate the introduction of new cash crops. The natural increase of the black population added progressively to the wealth of white landowners, and as the labor force grew, the value of land rose accordingly. On this prosperity social stability was based. As long as the economy allowed a father to establish his children on their own farms, sons and daughters remained on the Eastern Shore, and with each new generation, ties of kinship and land among families multiplied.[1]

The economic benefits of life on the Eastern Shore, however, were not equally shared. While to most whites, residence in the

1. Eastern Shore population figures are from Tables 2 and 6, and Arthur Karinen, "Numerical and Distributional Aspects of Maryland Population, 1631-1840," Ph.D. dissertation, University of Maryland, 1958, pp. 202-203. For land prices, see Paul G. E. Clemens, "From Tobacco to Grain: Economic Development on Maryland's Eastern Shore, 1660-1750," Ph.D. dissertation, University of Wisconsin, 1974, pp. 169-174; and Eastern Shore land records, MHR. Between 1713 and 1773, the percentage of slaves in the Eastern Shore's population increased from 13 to 40 percent; see Chapter 2 as well as the Provincial Tax Lists of 1776 and the Maryland Assessment of 1783, MHR, for further details.

region promised an adequate income and a standard of living similar to that of their neighbors, trade and tobacco planting rewarded a few disproportionately and left many others almost destitute, with emigration as their only option. The problem is one of degree: how different were the circumstances of tenant and landowner and of agricultural laborer and merchant-planter? What proportion of the population fell into each of these classes? This chapter addresses these questions by examining the social structure, material life, and economic prospects of whites in Talbot County in the years before corn and wheat replaced tobacco as a market crop.

Since the seventeenth century, this analysis will demonstrate, Eastern Shore society had changed in three respects. The number of middling family farmers, the importance of slave labor, and the power of the merchant-planters all had grown. In the continuing predominance of small farmers who mixed production for home and the market, the Eastern Shore shared much with the Middle Colonies and still resembled rural England. In their growing reliance on slaves, Eastern Shore planters followed a path previously taken in Virginia. And in the coming of age of third-generation merchant-planter families, the Eastern Shore acquired an elite that rivaled the landlords of New York's Hudson Valley, the great sugar planters of the West Indies, and the gentry of England.

THE TRIUMPH OF THE
MERCHANT-PLANTER CLASS

No man better symbolized the Eastern Shore merchant-planter class than Richard Bennett III. Bennett's great-great-grandfather, a prosperous tanner, lived during the late sixteenth century in Wivelscombe, in Somerset County, England. Three of his sons, coming of age opportunely as England began its assault on Spain's New World empire, moved to London and became engaged in the colonization and commerce of the fledgling colony of Virginia, where they obtained land in Isle of Wight County. Edward, the youngest, probably taking advantage of his father's connections with the English gentry, married well, established himself as a city merchant, and stayed in London. A second brother, Richard, also became a merchant, but emigrated with the third brother, Robert, to Virginia. When Richard and Robert died in the mid-1620s, Edward continued in the tobacco trade. He entrusted his business in the colony more and more to a young nephew, who came to be known as Richard Bennett I.[2]

The nephew did well and became a leader in the small but influential Puritan community in Virginia. When Oliver Cromwell took power in England, he commissioned Bennett to obtain the submission of the recalcitrant governments of Virginia and Maryland and later appointed him governor of Virginia. Bennett further assured his station in the colony by marriage to Mary Anne Utie, either the daughter or widow of Colonel John Utie, late of the Virginia Council; despite his Puritan politics, Bennett survived, with his position and influence intact, the restoration of Stuart rule in England in the 1660s. In the meantime, his son, Richard Bennett II, had moved to Maryland, settled among Puritans on the Severn River, and married Henrietta Maria Neale, the daughter of an influential friend of the Catholic proprietary family. Born in 1667, Richard Bennett III could hardly have known either his grandfather or father, both of whom died in the mid-1660s. They left him the bulk of their property and placed him in the care of his mother.[3]

Henrietta Maria was soon remarried, to Philemon Lloyd, a Talbot County merchant. The marriage united two of the greatest family fortunes in the Chesapeake, for Lloyd was probably the richest man in Maryland. His death in 1685 left young Bennett the oldest male in the household. For the next twelve years, Bennett and his mother carried on Philemon's trading adventures, and in 1697 he and Robert Graison, a prominent local merchant, commissioned Thomas Skillington of St. Michael's River to construct a ship large enough for use in the Atlantic tobacco trade with England. After his mother's death in 1697, Bennett married Elizabeth Rousby and thereby secured large inheritances from her father, James, and her uncle, Peter Sayer.

2. John Bennett Boddie, *Seventeenth-Century Isle of Wight County, Virginia* (Chicago, 1938), pp. 266–288; Mary N. Brown, "Governor Richard Bennett," *MHR* 9 (1914): 307–315.

3. Boddie, *Seventeenth-Century Isle of Wight County,* and Brown, "Governor Richard Bennett."

With the marriage he converted to the Roman Catholic faith of his wife and thus forfeited his right to hold office in Protestant Maryland. Free from political obligations, he settled into a life of farming and trade in Queen Anne's County, where he and Elizabeth had moved shortly after the wedding.[4]

Between 1733 and 1746, the only period for which shipping records are extant, Bennett purchased six sloops and had at least two in operation every year. He had mercantile connections in the West Indies, Philadelphia, Boston, Virginia, and London. The *Hopewell*, a forty-ton vessel that frequently stopped at the port of Oxford in Talbot during the 1740s, was typical of those he owned. Until 1744 the *Hopewell* went to Barbados with barrel staves and corn and returned with rum and sugar; then Bennett shifted the voyages to Boston, probably because he feared French privateers. On the New England trips he exchanged wheat for manufactured goods and rum. These voyages could not have been as profitable as previous ones, for at the height of the war with France, Bennett sent the *Hopewell*, unarmed and undermanned, back to Barbados. Disaster followed: the French captured the vessel; the English recaptured it; and Robert Pringle, a Charleston, South Carolina, merchant, claimed the sloop for Bennett in an admiralty court. Pringle disposed of its wheat cargo for a low price in Philadelphia, took a share of the proceeds, and sent the *Hopewell* back to Maryland, where it arrived shortly before Bennett's death in 1747.[5]

His West Indian connections were of particular importance to Bennett. Trade with Jamaica, Barbados, and the Leewards allowed him to ship slaves to the Eastern Shore, a highly lucrative business for the few Chesapeake merchants who had suffi-

---

4. Inventory of Philemon Lloyd, Talbot Inventories, J.B. no. 1, pp. 322–331 (1685), MHR; Inventory of Henrietta Maria Lloyd, ibid., pp. 388–399 (1697). On Rousby and Sayer, see Wills, vol. 6, p. 166; vol. 7, p. 334, MHR. On the marriage, see Frederic Emory, *Queen Anne's County, Maryland: Its Early History and Development* (Baltimore, 1950), p. 537. For Bennett's early shipping concerns, consult *AM*, vol. 25, p. 600.

5. Ships Bennett had constructed are listed in the Maryland Commission Book no. 4012, MHR. Information on Bennett's shipping endeavors is in the Oxford Port of Entry Books, MHR and MHS. See also Walter B. Edgar, ed., *The Letterbook of Robert Pringle*, 2 vols. (Columbia, S.C., 1972), vol. 1, pp. 385, 393, 413; vol. 2, pp. 609, 653, 778, 846.

cient capital for it. In one shipload during the 1730s, Bennett landed eighty slaves from the Caribbean at Oxford, probably the largest such undertaking ever conducted with local money. While grain and slaves brought profits, perhaps even more came in from the tobacco trade. Bennett handled the Eastern Shore business of John Hanbury and William Anderson, London consignment merchants; dealt extensively with Robert Morris, the local agent for Foster Cunliffe of Liverpool; ran two stores, one at Bennett's Point and one at Wye Town; and, in the 1740s, had a 140-ton vessel built so he could avoid the expense of consigning tobacco on English-owned shipping. As a creditor, Bennett lent more money to more people than any other inhabitant of the Eastern Shore.[6]

Bennett was also a planter. In 1733, the only year for which comprehensive data were collected, he owned 6,760 acres in Talbot County. Some land he rented; other land he left wooded, so it could appreciate in value; and some land, in the Wye area, he farmed with slave labor. While most of his holdings were in Queen Anne's County, to the north, Bennett had in Talbot alone five tobacco plantations and over thirty field hands. His commitment to tobacco and slavery, his simultaneous involvement in trade, and his fortuitous inheritances and wise marriage all marked Bennett as a merchant-planter.[7]

However wealthy, Bennett was not alone at the top of Talbot society. In the 1730s, fifteen other men and one woman in Talbot each held at least 1,000 acres of land and ten adult slaves. They formed the core of the merchant-planter class. In most cases, their wealth and family position had developed together.

6. On Bennett's handling of slaves, see the Oxford Port of Entry Books, MHR and MHS. Bennett's dealings with English merchants and local planters can be traced in the Inventories, MHR. For his connection to Morris, see Oswald Tilghman, *History of Talbot County, Maryland, 1661-1861*, 2 vols. (Baltimore, 1915), vol. 1, pp. 164-165; and the Callister Papers, MHS.

7. All subsequent statements about the ownership of land and slaves rely on the Talbot County Tax List of 1733, MHS; Talbot County Rent Roll of 1733, MHR; and Talbot County Debt Book of 1738, MHR. The analysis in this section owes a debt to Aubrey C. Land's "Economic Base and Social Structure: The Northern Chesapeake in the Eighteenth Century," *JEH* 25 (1965): 639-654, and "Economic Behavior in a Planting Society: The Eighteenth-Century Chesapeake," *Journal of Southern History* 33 (1967): 469-485.

Long-standing friendships, marriages, shared inheritances, and business partnerships reinforced bonds that wealth alone would not have made so strong. All dealt with the same London merchants; most had careers in law, politics, commerce, or religion as well as managing plantations; all were major creditors of the other planters in the region; and all had made or inherited some of their wealth from the tobacco trade.[8]

Only the Lloyds occupied as dominant a position as Richard Bennett. The first Lloyd to settle in the Chesapeake was Edward, who probably came to Virginia in the 1630s. In 1645 he sat in the House of Burgesses from Lower Norfolk County; four years later he led Puritan settlers from Virginia to the Severn River in Maryland and immediately became embroiled in the politics of Lord Baltimore's strife-torn province. During his first years in Maryland, politics brought Lloyd into contact with Richard Bennett I, and in 1658 their friendship may have helped Lloyd gain appointment to the provincial council. About three years later, Lloyd moved to the Eastern Shore and established a plantation on the Wye River. He remained there until about 1666, when, leaving his twenty-year-old son, Philemon, in charge of his property, he returned to England to become a London tobacco merchant.[9]

Philemon Lloyd lived two more decades at the Wye plantation. When he died in 1685, he left 7,430 acres of land and an estate valued at £4,624 to his stepson, Richard Bennett, and three sons and four daughters from his marriage with Henrietta Maria Neale. His eldest son, Edward, became one of the most powerful figures in Maryland; he served on the council from 1701 until his death in 1719 and managed the Eastern Shore consignment trade of several London merchants. At his death Edward II owned 3,813 acres of land, thirty slaves, sixteen servants, and over £9,000 in other property. Another son, James, married the daughter of Robert Grundy, a wealthy Oxford merchant, and

8. Talbot County Tax List of 1733, MHS, and Talbot Debt Books, 1733 and 1738, MHR, give information on the property holdings of the merchant-planters. More general points about their careers are discussed below.

9. Tilghman, *History of Talbot County,* vol. 1, pp. 132–144. Lloyd's activities in London trade are detailed in the London Port Books, E.190/58/1 and E.190/68/1, PRO.

devoted most of his life to commerce. James died in 1723, leaving an estate of £3,244 and 2,156 acres of land. A third son, who lived until 1732, spent much of his life in Annapolis, where he was drawn by marriage and his career in provincial politics.[10]

In 1733 the Lloyd family's fortunes rested in the hands of Edward Lloyd III. His father and uncles were dead, his brothers and cousins were still quite young. At age 22, Edward had come into possession of over 3,000 acres of land in Talbot County and ten adult slaves. Over the next thirty years he became the most prominent creditor and shipper in the region. He married Anne Rousby, the daughter of a wealthy Calvert County planter and a relative of Richard Bennett's wife, and in 1743 he followed his father on the Maryland Council, a position he held until 1767. In developing Eastern Shore trade with Philadelphia and Southern Europe, Lloyd used his contacts with Robert Morris, a Philadelphia speculator and merchant (whose father, a Liverpool factor, had been a business partner of both Lloyd and Richard Bennett). When Lloyd died in 1770, his estate, including 160 slaves, came to almost £100,000, making him perhaps the richest man who ever lived in colonial Maryland.[11]

Unlike the Lloyds, Samuel Chamberlaine dated his residency on the Eastern Shore only from the early eighteenth century. He came to Oxford for the first time in 1714 as a seventeen-year-old apprentice seaman on the *Elizabeth* of Liverpool, captained by his brother. After his brother died in 1721, Samuel settled in Oxford and married Mary Ungle, the daughter of Robert Ungle, an Oxford merchant. Ungle was at this time an important figure in local politics, notorious for his crude humor and exces-

10. See the information on the Lloyd family given by Christopher Johnson, "Lloyd Family," *MHM* 7 (1912): 420–430, and Oswald Tilghman, "Lloyd Family," *MHM* 8 (1913): 85–87. The family connections with the Hanbury firm in England are mentioned in the Calvert Papers, MS 174, no. 1028, MHS. Additional information comes from the Talbot Inventories, J.B. no. 1, pp. 322–331 (1685); Maryland Inventories, vol. 3, pp. 1–40 (1719); vol. 4, pp. 107, 223 (1720); vol. 10, pp. 309, 330 (1724); vol. 11, p. 253 (1725), MHR. Landowning figures were compiled from the Lloyd Rent Roll of 1706, MHS, and the Talbot County Land Conveyances, MHR.

11. See the sources cited in note 10 and Oxford Port of Entry Books, MHS and MHR. The Lloyd Collection, MS 2001, MHS, gives his complete inventory.

sive drinking, but impressively rich; Chamberlaine's marriage to Ungle's daughter undoubtedly eased the newcomer's entry into Talbot society. During his first years in the county, Chamberlaine worked as a factor for Foster Cunliffe of Liverpool, handled the trade of his Liverpool relatives, and bought and built on numerous lots in Oxford. His marriage and his success as a businessman probably influenced his appointment in 1724 as justice of the peace, an indication that the proprietary government and his friends had recognized Chamberlaine as one of the leaders of Talbot County after a residence of only a few years. His wife died in 1726 and three years later Chamberlaine married Henrietta Maria Lloyd, the orphaned daughter of James Lloyd the merchant. In 1733, thanks in some measure to his wife's dowry, Chamberlaine owned 2,686 acres and seventeen adult slaves. In 1756 the Talbot debt book listed over 5,300 acres in his name, and at his death in 1770 he had 4,169 acres and an estate worth £5,717. Chamberlaine's career in Talbot proved the value to immigrants of mercantile connections with English trading centers.[12]

Between 1757 and 1761, Samuel Chamberlaine's two sons married the daughters of George Robins. These marriages were doubly significant. Not only did they follow the conventional pattern of uniting Eastern Shore fortunes, but all four of the young people involved could claim Philemon Lloyd as their great-grandfather. Robins's wife, Henrietta Maria, was the daughter of Richard Tilghman of Queen Anne's County and Anna Maria Lloyd (see the Genealogical Chart). The Tilghmans could be traced back to the gentry of Kent County, England, and at least two Tilghmans, Samuel, a ship's captain in the tobacco trade, and Richard, a London doctor, patented land in Talbot County. Richard made his money as sheriff of the county, his

12. Tilghman, *History of Talbot County,* vol. 1, pp. 531, 552; Talbot County Debt Books of 1733 and 1770, MHR; Talbot Inventories, vol. 6, pp. 279, 290, 574, MHR. Chamberlaine's connection with Liverpool merchants is mentioned in the Talbot County Land Conveyances, PF no. 13, pp. 68, 82 (1723), MHR. Cunliffe had a store in Oxford as early as 1722; see Maryland Inventories, vol. 11, p. 440 (1722), MHR. Chamberlaine's purchases of Oxford property can be traced in the Talbot County Land Conveyances from the 1720s.

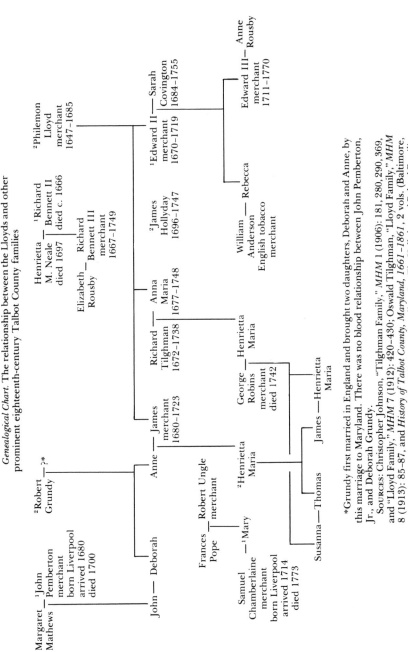

Genealogical Chart. The relationship between the Lloyds and other prominent eighteenth-century Talbot County families

*Grundy first married in England and brought two daughters, Deborah and Anne, by this marriage to Maryland. There was no blood relationship between John Pemberton, Jr., and Deborah Grundy.

SOURCES: Christopher Johnson, "Tilghman Family," *MHM* 1 (1906): 181, 280, 290, 369, and "Lloyd Family," *MHM* 7 (1912): 420–430; Oswald Tilghman, "Lloyd Family," *MHM* 8 (1913): 85–87, and *History of Talbot County, Maryland, 1661–1861*, 2 vols. (Baltimore, 1915), vol. 1, pp. 132–163, 531–552; James Bordley, Jr., *The Hollyday and Related Families*

son achieved the same commanding position in Queen Anne's, and his granddaughter married Robins.[13]

George Robins came from a family of adventurers, planters, and artisans. In the 1660s his grandfather had moved to Talbot County from London to oversee an elaborate trading enterprise, but he eventually settled into the life of a planter. George's father, Thomas, styled himself a gentleman because he sat on the Talbot bench, but he made his money from shoemaking, grain, and tobacco. When Thomas died in 1721, he left his son seventeen slaves, a large herd of livestock, four farms that produced bountiful crops of corn, tobacco, and wheat, and his inventory of leather goods. George Robins spent the next two decades building a commercial fortune by trading with the West Indies and handling the accounts of John Hanbury and Samuel Hyde of London. At the time of his marriage to Henrietta Maria Tilghman, in the early 1730s, Robins had fourteen adult slaves and 4,624 acres, and when he died in 1742, his inventory was valued at over £16,000.[14]

The Robins family was also linked to the Goldsboroughs. Nicholas Goldsborough, the first member of this family to live on the Eastern Shore, had left behind his mercantile business in Blandford, England, in 1669 and taken passage to Barbados. From there he went to New England, and then finally settled on Kent Island, where he died in 1670. His children grew up in the home of their stepfather, George Robins. The eldest son, Robert, married the daughter of a wealthy Anne Arundel County landowner and provincial court justice. He followed his father-in-law into the law, holding county offices and appearing in the local court until 1705, when he received appointment to

13. On the Tilghmans, see Christopher Johnson, "Tilghman Family," *MHM* 1 (1906): 181, 280, 290, 369. The connection between the Lloyds and Robinses can be traced in the works listed in note 10. The position of the family in the county is demonstrated by the wealth and slave-owning figures in the Maryland Assessment of 1783, Talbot and Queen Anne's counties, Returns of Property, MHR.

14. For the early career of the Robins family, see Talbot County Land Conveyances, GG no. 3, pp. 151–173. The growing family wealth can be traced in the Maryland Inventories, vol. 2, p. 214; vol. 8, p. 22; vol. 34, p. 88, MHR; and the Talbot County Inventories, IG no. 4, pp. 33–51, MHR. Robins's shipping concerns can be followed in the Maryland Commission Book no. 4012, MHR, and the Oxford Port of Entry Books, MHR and MHS.

Myrtle Grove, Talbot County. The smaller structure was constructed in 1724 by Robert Goldsborough; the larger wing was added in 1790. The house is on Goldsborough Creek, off the St. Michael's (Miles) River. Photo by Paul G. E. Clemens.

the provincial bench. From 1719 until retirement at the age of eighty, Robert Goldsborough was chief justice of the colony's highest court. He also invested in agriculture, and in 1733 owned some 1,941 acres, twenty-six adult slaves, and a magnificent plantation home, Ashby. His son, Nicholas, also did well enough for himself to be included among the merchant-planters, and at least two of his brothers followed Robert in careers as planter-lawyers. The Goldsboroughs probably owed more of their wealth to agriculture and office and less to commerce than any of their equally prominent contemporaries, but marriage of two of Robert Goldsborough's children to children of George Robins (the eighteenth-century merchant) and the marriage of his brother Charles into the Ennalls family, then the wealthiest merchants in Dorchester County, united the profits of agriculture, office, and commerce.[15]

In 1733, four other members of the merchant-planter class had ties to the Lloyd family. Frances Ungle, who had inherited twelve adult slaves and 1,200 acres of land when her husband, Robert, died, was Samuel Chamberlaine's mother-in-law. James Hollyday, who lived near the Lloyds in Island Hundred and owned sixteen adult slaves and 1,075 acres of land, had married Sarah Covington, the widow of Edward Lloyd II. In the 1670s, Hollyday's father had come to Talbot County as a factor for an English tobacco merchant, and the family maintained close business and personal connections with the London merchant community until the American Revolution. The link between the Lloyds and the Reverend Henry Nicols, who had acquired eleven slaves and 1,514 acres since taking over an Anglican parish in Talbot County, was through the minister's son, Jeremiah, who married a daughter of the merchant James Lloyd, and became a business partner of one of Samuel Chamberlaine's sons. Colonel Mathew Tilghman Ward, the county's largest slaveowner—he held thirty-two adult slaves in 1733—and one of its largest landowners with 3,844 acres, could also claim

15. Eleonora Goldsborough, *The House of Goldsborough*, 6 vols. (unpublished manuscript, 1932); a typed copy is at MHS. Mrs. John Donoho of Myrtle Grove Plantation allowed me to look at family papers that reconfirmed my opinion that the Goldsboroughs seldom engaged directly in trade.

Ratcliffe Manor, Talbot County. Henry Hollyday built this brick mansion on the Tred Avon River shortly after marrying Anna Maria Robins in 1749. Both the Hollyday and Robins families belonged to the merchant-planter class. Photo by Thomas J. Waterman, Historic American Buildings Survey, Library of Congress.

Wye House, Talbot County, was the late-eighteenth-century home of the Lloyd family, and the most elegant mansion on the Eastern Shore. Photo by Jack E. Boucher, Historic American Buildings Survey, Library of Congress.

membership in the small circle of families allied to the Lloyds, although only through his wife's brother.[16]

No contemporary of the Lloyds would have been surprised at how little chance there was for an aspiring immigrant to join the Eastern Shore elite. It was not the children and grandchildren of England's rural poor who rose to power in Talbot County. Through the varied careers of the merchants, officeholders, lawyers, and ministers who battled their way to the top of Talbot society there runs a common theme: all made their fortunes in a business world where connections and reputation were required. A lawyer's clients, a merchant's trading partners, or a provincial official's appointments came to him because of who he was and whom he knew. It is true that few of the immigrant adventurers who founded the most prominent Eastern Shore families arrived with great wealth in hand; even fewer, however, arrived poor. Many faltered along the way; others died without children. If the seventeenth century witnessed the rise of the elite from among the ranks of ambitious entrepreneurs, the eighteenth century saw this elite consolidated through marriage and enriched through trade, office, and estate management.[17]

Commerce, coupled with careful investment in agriculture, provided the most common, but not the only, path into the elite. The Hollydays and Goldsboroughs began as lawyers and their success was followed by appointment to lucrative provincial offices. Richard Tilghman, one of the wealthiest seventeenth-century residents of Talbot, benefited from his brother's involvement in the tobacco trade, but his long-running appointment as county sheriff counted more. Furthermore, while such men as Robert Ungle and Samuel Chamberlaine never abandoned

16. See notes 7 and 10. On the Hollydays, consult James Bordley, Jr., *The Hollyday and Related Families of the Eastern Shore of Maryland* (Baltimore, 1962). William Anderson of London and Talbot County served as the family link with the English merchant community.

17. The best example of a rise from real obscurity to wealth was the case of the Edmondson family. John Edmondson, the founder, land speculator and merchant, immigrated as a servant and after a hectic entrepreneurial career died in debt. His grandsons became large landowners, substantial slave owners, and local officeholders, and one of them was wealthy enough to be considered a merchant-planter.

their work as storekeepers and commission merchants, their positions in the customs office not only brought them a substantial salary but did no harm to their trading careers.[18]

What established the power of the merchant-planters and most clearly set them apart from elites in other colonies was the diversity of their activities. In New England, for example, where farming had little connection to Atlantic commerce and rural people seldom amassed great estates, the economic elite rose chiefly from among land speculators and urban merchants. The merchants made their wealth either by shipping goods between other colonies or by marketing the fish and timber with which northern New England was abundantly supplied, but they had little contact with the farming population. In the West Indies, in contrast, sugar and slaves created the fortunes that brought the planter class to power, and merchants, however well off, played a secondary role in the agricultural economy. New York presented still a different picture: along the Hudson Valley were both commercial farmers, whose extensive property holdings simply underwrote grain marketing and milling enterprises, and a landlord class, which lived handsomely from rents. The merchant-planters of the Eastern Shore combined all these characteristics, for most made their money in as many ways as they could.[19]

---

18. Most of the information on officeholding and its profits comes from the Talbot County Court Records, MHR. See also the excellent studies by Donnell M. Owings, *His Lordship's Patronage: Offices of Profit in Colonial Maryland,* Studies in Maryland History, no. 1 (Baltimore, 1953); and Alan F. Day, "A Social Study of Lawyers in Maryland, 1660–1775," Ph.D. dissertation, Johns Hopkins University, 1976. Day's work (pp. 197–247, 687–699) is especially valuable for its information on the Goldsboroughs.

The Lloyd family's progress as landowners gives the best example of the elite's gradual accumulation of assets. When the first Edward died, he held 1,400 acres. His son died in 1685 with 7,340 acres. In 1707 the three sons and four daughters of Philemon held almost 12,400 acres, virtually all in Talbot County. In 1733 the Lloyds held 17,600 acres, about evenly split between Talbot and Queen Anne's, and by 1766 they had obtained 7,800 acres in Kent and doubled their total Eastern Shore holdings. Between 1733 and 1766, the value of the land owned by the Lloyds increased from £8,100 to £43,000. See the Lloyd Rent Roll of 1706, MHS, and the Debt Books and Rent Rolls from the three central Eastern Shore counties, MHR.

19. The role of commerce in creating an elite in New England is explored by

The Bennetts, Lloyds, and Goldsboroughs of the Eastern Shore
came of age economically in the early eighteenth century. For
decade after decade, enterprise and wealth brought them influence, prestige, and a refined standard of living. But what of the
humbler sort? To what life could other whites in Talbot County
aspire? Many well-to-do tenants and small landowners, the great
bulk of the region's white population, lived much like Isaac Cox.

Isaac Cox grew up in Thirdhaven Hundred. His father was a
prosperous farmer and his grandfather had been a seventeenth-century settler. In the 1730s, land was given to all the family's
sons, and Isaac received 93 acres along Tuckahoe Creek, many
miles from the Chesapeake Bay. By the 1740s he had married,
bought a second farm of 100 acres, and built a 30-by-18-foot
dwelling house, two stories high (of 12 foot pitch) and with a
brick chimney. Alongside he constructed a 16-by-16-foot framed
wooden kitchen with a brick chimney—both the separate kitchen
and the brick chimneys, while not uncommon, were signs of
some affluence—as well as a stable and smokehouse, and he
planted a small apple orchard.[20]

Bernard Bailyn in *The New England Merchants in the Seventeenth Century* (Cambridge, Mass., 1955); but Robert Zemsky, in *Merchants, Farmers, and River Gods: An Essay on Eighteenth-Century American Politics* (Boston, 1971), argues convincingly that provincial political power in Massachusetts rested chiefly in the hands of professional politicians who were more likely than not to be of noncommercial background. The relationship between wealth and occupation receives careful attention in Gloria Lund Main, "Personal Wealth in Colonial America: Explorations in the Use of Probate Records from Maryland and Massachusetts, 1650–1720," Ph.D. dissertation, Columbia University, 1972, pp. 234–298. For other colonies, see Richard B. Sheridan, "The Rise of a Colonial Gentry: A Case Study of Antigua, 1730–1775," *EHR* 13 (1960–61): 342–357, and "The Wealth of Jamaica in the Eighteenth Century," *EHR* 18 (1965): 292–311; and Sung Bok Kim, *Landlord and Tenant in Colonial New York: Manorial Society, 1664–1775* (Chapel Hill, N.C., 1978), pp. 142–161.
20. Talbot County Debt Book of 1748, MHR; Talbot County Land Conveyances, vol. 18, p. 226 (1754), MHR; Lloyd Rent Roll of 1706, MHS. Eighteenth-century land records contain numerous descriptions of plantation layout and buildings. These descriptions are not in deeds of conveyance but in evaluations of orphans' estates. Such evaluations were made to ensure that guardians would take proper care of estates put in their trust. About 200 evaluations survive from Queen Anne's and half as many from Talbot.

Lamb's Meadow, Kent County, was built in 1733 by Pearce Lamb, a Quaker. The house is located near the Sassafras River. From an etching by Don Swann. By permission of S. Donovan Swann, Jr.

Cox could afford to furnish his home adequately if simply. He had some twenty pieces of furniture to fill the three or four rooms into which the house was divided:

	£	s	d		£	s	d
Best bed	7	0	0	4 leather chairs	0	14	0
Second bed	6	0	0	5 old wooden chairs	0	7	6
2 additional beds	5	5	0	Old chair	0	0	6
Old chest of drawers	3	10	0	Old table	0	8	0
2 old chests	0	9	0	Old desk	2	5	0
Small trunk	0	4	0	Total	26	3	0

For the kitchen, Cox procured sixty pounds of pewterware, sixty pounds of ironware, seven pieces of old earthenware, and a dozen finer delftware dishes and plates. In addition, the kitchen contained punch bowls, an iron skillet, six old knives and forks, cooking irons, and numerous storage containers. While the list of kitchenware was long, there was nothing in it to suggest that the family had anything but the most useful and least expensive pots, pans, and utensils. Cox also owned a small amount of personal property: perhaps two changes of clothing and a few garments of a little quality, a gun, some old books, a looking glass, a few fancy clasps and a silver belt buckle, and an old saddle.[21]

When Cox ran into unexpected trouble, he could always ask his kin for help. Thomas Salmon could not. Salmon was the first and last person of that name to live on the colonial Eastern Shore. He arrived sometime in the late 1720s and acquired lodging with Pearce Flemond, a slaveowner in Tuckahoe Hundred. Salmon lived as a laborer. His inventory in 1735 was:

	£	s	d
Clothing	0	10	0
Horse and saddle	5	0	0
2 hoes, 1 ax	0	6	0
424 pounds of tobacco	2	13	0
Currency	1	4	0
Total	9	13	0

21. Inventories, vol. 57, p. 323 (1753), MHR; Accounts, vol. 37, pp. 152–154 (1755), MHR.

The 424 pounds of tobacco represented either wages or a crop share paid him by Flemond. He owned only his own clothing, a few simple tools, and a horse. The horse was his most important purchase because it allowed him to look for work or to escape debts by leaving the area.[22]

William Sharp, who died in 1771, was considerably more prosperous than Isaac Cox or Thomas Salmon. His family can be traced to the 1650s, when Peter Sharpe arrived in Calvert County. Peter's son, William, moved to Talbot County in the 1670s and settled on land his father had patented during the previous decade. By the 1680s William had acquired 1,000 acres of land, bought some slaves, and entered the coastal trade, but he never managed to reach the ranks of the merchant-planter class. His sons became landowners and slaveowners, and one of his grandsons, William, was the prosperous mid-eighteenth-century planter with whom we are concerned.[23]

Sharp resided near the Chesapeake Bay. He lived in a 36-by-17-foot clapboard house framed with brick, buttressed inside and out by brick chimneys, and supported by a brick cellar that ran half the length of the house. The house and an adjacent 20-by-8-foot shed were covered by whitewashed, feather-edged shingles and weatherboard, and the floors were made of clapboard planks. He had also constructed a shingled 10-by-22-foot barn for livestock and the storage of grain and a similar structure for hanging tobacco. Around the farm he put up several sheds and 3,500 panels of fencing; planted apple, cherry, and peach trees in a small orchard; and, elsewhere on the 430 acres he owned in Talbot County, erected quarters for four tenant families.[24]

Sharp's plantation home, although comfortable, was minimally furnished. He had in it a chest of drawers, two beds, two desks, four tables plus a special but inexpensive tea table, a cup-

22. Talbot County Inventories, JB no. 2, p. 65 (1735), MHR; Talbot County Tax List of 1733, MHS.
23. Lloyd Rent Roll of 1706, MHS; Inventories and Accounts, vol. 19½A, p. 132; Wills, vol. 6, p. 289; Patents, vol. 17, pp. 182, 390; all in MHR. A short biography of the first William Sharpe (1655–99) is in Lois Green Carr and David William Jordan, *Maryland's Revolution of Government, 1689–1692* (Ithaca, 1974), pp. 277–278.
24. Talbot County Land Conveyances, vol. 20, p. 494, (1775), MHR.

Troth's Fortune, Talbot County, was built by William Troth after he moved to Maryland with other Virginia Quakers in the late seventeenth century. Photo by E. H. Pickering, Historic American Buildings Survey, Library of Congress.

Tobacco barn, Calvert County. The date of construction is unknown, but the barn may have been built in the late eighteenth century. The building approximates in size and shape the barns of colonial Eastern Shore landowners. Photo by E. H. Pickering, Historic American Buildings Survey, Library of Congress.

board, and an old chest. In the kitchen one found indications of a higher standard of living: separate teakettles and coffeepots, two dozen china custard cups, a dozen fruit dishes, and six fabric tablecloths as well as such standard items as pewterware, iron pots, knives and forks, and various canisters and serving dishes. In Sharp's personal property there were other signs of wealth—£10 of wearing apparel, seventeen yards of country-made cloth, an expensive looking glass, three globe maps, several guns with a powder flask, a watch, and four books—the *Book of Common Prayer,* Montesquieu's *Spirit of the Laws,* a dictionary, and a volume entitled *The Way to Health and Happiness*—perhaps reflections of worldly concerns, political inclinations, and respectable Anglican beliefs.[25]

What most set Sharp apart from Cox and Salmon was that he owned two families of slaves: one slave of seventy years, two male field hands and their wives, and seven children. His farming, which was more diversified and run on a larger scale than Cox's, required the use of a plow and several carts to bring in the wheat crop. His livestock included eight cows, a bull, two steers, six calves, three hogs, two sows, twenty-seven shoats, and fourteen ewes with lambs. Additionally, Sharp possessed the numerous small tools that every householder needed to clear land, plant, sow, weed, reap, and harvest. Still, if William Sharp was richer than Isaac Cox, his inventory, excluding the value of slaves, was modest.[26]

To understand more fully the structure of the society in which such men as Cox, Salmon, and Sharp lived, we must turn to the Talbot County tax list of 1733. The constables of each hundred in Talbot County compiled the list by walking around their districts and noting each home. At every household, the constable obtained only the information he needed to levy the correct head tax, that is, the name of the head of the family, the names

25. Maryland Inventories, vol. 126; pp. 14–15, 20–24 (1773); Accounts, vol. 74, pp. 97–101 (1777); Talbot County Debt Books, vol. 50, p. 63 (1768); all in MHR. For comparative discussions, see Cary Carson, "Doing History with Material Culture," in *Material Culture and the Study of American Life,* ed. Ian M. G. Quimby (New York, 1978), pp. 41–64; and Lois Green Carr, "'The Metropolis of Maryland': A Comment on Town Development along the Tobacco Coast," *MHM* 69 (1974): 124–145.

26. Maryland Inventories, vol. 126, pp. 14–15, 20–24 (1773), MHR.

Cottage, Talbot County. This brick dwelling of a small landowner is located in the Tuckahoe region. Photo by E. H. Pickering, Historic American Buildings Survey, Library of Congress.

of other white males sixteen years of age or older, and the names of black slaves sixteen or older. The constable did not note free women unless they were black (and therefore taxable) or the heads of households. Using data from the 1733 tax list and from listings (rent rolls) made in 1733, 1738, and 1756 of the county's landowners, one can develop a picture of Talbot's social structure.[27]

In 1733, four features distinguished that social order: the small number of large slaveowners, the large number of landowners without slaves, the prevalence of small landowners and tenants, and the numerical predominance of servants, laborers, and slaves (see Table 14). Relative to the seventeenth century, Talbot's economy now supported a greater number of householders in an area that had been appreciably reduced by the loss of land to Queen Anne's County in 1706. These householders, in turn, relied more on the labor of slaves, servants, and hired workers and less on their own families than had seventeenth-century tenants and landowners.[28]

The black population remained enslaved and hence at the bottom of the social structure. For blacks themselves, however, slavery in 1733 was not quite the same as it had been for the first African immigrants to the Eastern Shore. One critical change was demographic: sometime after 1720 natural population growth began (as it had for whites about 1700). The number of blacks, added to as well by the continuation of the slave trade, grew rapidly, but even more important, the ratio of blacks to whites and the proportion of native-born blacks in the population both increased. Learning from childhood to cope with enslavement and supported by parents and an ever increasing number of kin, young blacks growing up in eighteenth-century Talbot probably found more manageable the oppression they faced than had the first people forced into bondage by Eastern Shore planters. A second significant change was economic: as farmers devoted more attention to grain crops, vegetables, and

27. See the sources listed in Table 13. An alphabetized, typed copy of the 1733 Talbot Tax List has been placed at the Maryland Hall of Records. In addition to the 1733 list, I used the 1722 and 1776 Talbot tax records, MHS.
28. See Table 13.

Table 14. Social structure of Talbot County in the 1730s: landownership, holding of adult slaves, and householder status (number of adult white males)

Land owned (acres)	Adult slaves owned			Householder without slaves	Non-householder	Total
	10	9–6	5–1			
1,000	16	4	12	0	1	33
999–200	2	7	53	68	11	141
199–1	0	0	45	151	0	196
Unspecified	1	1	8	1	25	36
No land	1	0	20	400	787	1,208
Total	20	12	138	620	824	1,614

Summary of data

Householders	Men	Women*
Land and slaves	149	23
Land only	220	11
No land	421	14
All householders	790	48
Nonhouseholders	824	—
All whites	1,614	—
Adult slaves	436	316

*These figures not included elsewhere in the table. Only wealthy women long remained unmarried and the heads of households.

Sources: Talbot County Tax List of 1733, Lloyd Collection, MS 2001, MHS; Talbot County Debt Books, Talbot County Land Conveyances, Maryland Wills, MHR.

fruits, blacks were undoubtedly better fed but driven harder in the fields.[29]

Adult whites, of course, did not face slavery, but most were not independent farmers. They did not head a household and in

29. On the timing and causes of the beginnings of natural population growth among blacks, see Russell R. Menard, "The Maryland Slave Population, 1658 to 1730: A Demographic Profile of Blacks in Four Counties," *WMQ* 32 (1975): 29–54; and Allan Kulikoff, "A 'Prolifick' People: Black Population Growth in the Chesapeake Colonies, 1700–1790." *Southern Studies* 16 (1977): 391–428. On the slave family, consult Allan Kulikoff, "Afro-American Society in Tidewater Maryland and Virginia, 1700 to 1790," *WMQ* 35 (1978): 226–259. In Talbot the number of black taxables increased from 300 in 1710 to 750 in 1733, and then to 1,695 in 1776. The ratio of white to black taxables fell over this same period from

some way depended on a planter who did. Of some 820 nonhouseholders on the 1733 list, perhaps 170 were servants, another 190 were kin of the householder with whom they lived, and the remaining 460 men earned their livings as sharecroppers, laborers, and tradesmen. While men in the first two groups had hardly any property—and what they did have, in fact, belonged to their parents or masters—sharecroppers and laborers, such as Thomas Salmon, had little more. Seldom did they own much beyond their clothing, a few agricultural and trade tools, and a horse. Quite a number did not even own a horse. Some had substantial amounts of tobacco and corn in their inventories, which could easily push their estates to around £20, but in a typical year most of their crop payments had to be returned to creditors. Most important, sharecroppers and laborers seldom owned livestock, which ensured that merely for survival they had to depend on the planter population.[30]

In contrast to Talbot's sharecroppers and laborers, the county's large population of tenants exercised some degree of economic independence. In 1733, tobacco planting supported more than 400 nonlanded heads of households, some of whom were older sons whose parents had given them possession but not title, some guardians of the estates of young heirs, and a few overseers for nonresident owners; but most were tenants who had obtained a standard short-term lease from a neighboring farmer. The majority rented around fifty acres of land, a small clapboard dwelling, a tobacco barn, and a shed or two. Virtually all of them owned several beds and other less expensive furniture, some earthenware and ironware for the kitchen, a few simple agricultural and artisanal tools, and some livestock and poultry—generally the ubiquitous dunghill fowl. The tenant's short-run outlook, then, was relatively good. He had a home, a

---

3.3 (1710) to 2.2 (1733) and then to 0.8 (1776). Around 1700, the black population had more men than women (men/women = 1.35) and fewer children than adults (children/adults = 0.74). After natural population growth began, the sex ratio should have approached unity and the number of children per adult should have increased. These trends appeared in the 1720s. By the 1770s, the sex ratio was 1.00 and the number of children per adult slave 1.08. Data come from *AM,* vol. 25, pp. 256–258 (adjusted); Eastern Shore Tax Lists of 1722, 1733, and 1776, MHS; and Maryland Inventories, MHR.

30. See sources listed in Table 13.

little personal property, and enough cattle, swine, and chickens to provide food. He was generally married and had relatives in the area. While a tenant had fewer assets than such landowners as Isaac Cox, he had much more personal property than such laborers as Thomas Salmon.[31]

The large tenant population in Talbot County points to the numerical importance of small planters in the region. Among the 400 landowners on the 1733 list, only 9 percent were classified as large owners (1,000 acres or more) and 38 percent as owners of between 200 and 1,000 acres, while 53 percent had under 200 acres. About one-third of Talbot's landowners worked 100 acres or less, or, in other words, farmed on about the same scale as tenants. In 1756, when proprietary agents made an extremely thorough search for people who owed Lord Baltimore quitrents, the list they drew up again clearly demonstrated how prevalent small landowners were: 341 people (53 percent of all landowners) held under 200 acres. Small planters, of course, controlled a small percentage of the land. In 1756, the 341 owners with under 200 acres held only 16 percent of the land in Talbot while the 35 people with 1,000 acres or more held 38 percent of the land. Even so, most small owners had ample land on which to raise tobacco and food crops and to pasture livestock. A small holding did not affect a planter's immediate prospects as much as it did his or her ability to provide land for children. From the unprovided-for heirs of small planters came many of those who quit the Eastern Shore.[32]

The layout of a small plantation reflected a landowner's station in the agricultural economy. Buildings on 50- and 100-acre plantations were likely to be few, simply constructed, and crude. Typically, the small landowner lived in a 20-by-15-foot clapboard home with a dirt floor; the structure was generally separated into two rooms and heated by fireplaces with wooden

31. See Table 13. The evaluation of orphans' estates contains data on the layout of tenant farms. The farms are listed under the names of the owners. By way of comparison, in the period 1730–39 the average inventory estate value of a nonhouseholder was £12; of a tenant, £51; of a landowner without slaves, £107; and of a slave owner, £344. Tenants averaged 5 head of cattle and 13 swine apiece; landowners, 13 cattle and 25 swine; and slave owners, 24 cattle and 44 swine (Maryland Inventories, MHR).
32. Talbot County Debt Books, 1733, 1738, and 1756, MHR.

chimneys. Neither glass windows nor brick construction were common, and notched logs occasionally replaced clapboards. To the side of the house would be found a 30- or 40-foot tobacco barn and several sheds in which to store corn and keep hens and chickens. Occasionally planters constructed milkhouses— although this was clearly the exception among small landowners —and there might be an apple orchard of two or three dozen trees on the property. More prosperous landowners, of course, constructed larger and more substantial homes and operated more diversified plantations with more buildings for crops and livestock.[33]

Landed planters owned much the same kind of personal property as tenants, but simply owned about twice as much. Like tenants, most had clothing, beds and bedding, household furniture, kitchen utensils, farm tools, a riding horse, cows, swine, and sheep. In addition, during the 1730s, about one of every two landowners had the aid of servants in running the plantation. The fifty nonslaveholding landed planters who died during the decade had working for them seventeen male servants, seven female servants, and ten children who were in service.[34]

Slave owners generally lived somewhat better. The 1733 tax list identified 170 white men and 23 white women who owned adult slaves. The great majority (80 percent) held no more than five adult slaves and found themselves in much the same position as William Sharp. They had spacious brick homes, separate kitchens, and plentiful orchards. Pewterware and silver plate replaced earthenware on their tables. They planted several market crops, had gardens and orchards, and leased out some of their land. Twice as wealthy as most other landowners (excluding the value of slaves), still half owned fewer than 200 acres.[35]

33. See, for example, the following plantation descriptions: Talbot County Land Conveyances, vol. 18, p. 116 (Rowland Hadaway, 1752); p. 215 (William Parrot, 1754); p. 297 (Terrance Connolly, 1755); and p. 307 (Benjamin Sylvester, 1755), MHR.

34. Maryland Inventories, MHR.

35. See Table 14. The evaluations of orphans' estates give the impression that by mid-century whites who owned at least two families of slaves generally had brick homes and the other comforts described in the text. For typical descriptions of plantations, see Talbot County Land Conveyances, vol. 18, p. 201 (William Harrison, 1753); pp. 236–237 (William Edmondson, 1754); p. 465

Whether or not they owned slaves, the shared experience of family farming, as well as ties of kinship, bound together most of Talbot's white householders. In the 1730s, the core of this white community was a group of some 800 landowners and tenants, chiefly second- and third-generation residents of the Eastern Shore, who owned or rented the 200,000 acres of land between the Wye and Great Choptank rivers. Most managed well but were certainly not rich. Most had gotten a good start as farmers because their parents had prospered before them. Not as dependent on their own labor as seventeenth-century colonists had been, they nonetheless took a more active part in day-to-day fieldwork than did planters in the West Indies, South Carolina, and tidewater Virginia. In the size of their farms, the number of their livestock, and the simple nature of their accommodations, they led lives much like those of the grain farmers who settled the Middle Colonies.[36]

But Talbot was also a society characterized by stark differences in the position of poor and rich. The lawyers, merchants, agricultural entrepreneurs, and provincial officeholders—the thirty men with at least half a dozen adult slaves—who dominated Talbot in the 1730s held an average of slightly more than £2,700 apiece in wealth. A mere 2 percent of the nondependent population, these men controlled some 45 percent of the property in the county; in contrast, the 460 sharecroppers, laborers, and tradesmen who made up the bottom third of the white economic hierarchy held but 2 percent of the wealth in the county; and the 750 adult slaves in Talbot had no possessions that could not be taken from them. In this contrast between poor and rich, Talbot resembled England and the plantation colonies to the south.[37]

(Daniel Powell, 1758); and vol. 19, pp. 18–20 (William Dickinson, 1760), MHR.

36. In addition to the sources listed in note 19 above, see James T. Lemon, *The Best Poor Man's Country: A Geographical Study of Early Southeastern Pennsylvania* (Baltimore, 1972), pp. 150–183; Thomas J. Wertenbaker, *The Planters of Colonial Virginia* (Princeton, 1922); and Edmund S. Morgan, *American Slavery, American Freedom: The Ordeal of Colonial Virginia* (New York, 1975), pp. 338–362.

37. Few of the richest planters on the Eastern Shore left inventories, and in the absence of evidence indicating exactly how wealthy these men were, calculations of the percentage of wealth held by the richest free males in the region are not accurate enough to permit precise comparison with other colonies. For the

THE PROFITS OF TOBACCO PRODUCTION

Talbot County householders made a good living from the tobacco economy. Some did so as slave owners, some worked the
fields with indentured servants, and others supported themselves and their families with their own labor. To analyze how
successfully Talbot County planters grew tobacco, I shall focus
first on the slave owners and then extend the discussion to the
use of servant labor and the operation of small farms by families
without servants or slaves. Determining the profitability of tobacco
production in eighteenth-century Talbot requires measuring the
productivity of black and white workers, the expenses of maintaining a field hand, the investment in land and labor, and the
time during which a planter received returns on the capital laid
out. But even with these figures and modern accounting for-
mulas at our command, difficulties remain in determining what
profitability meant to the farmer on the colonial Eastern Shore.

In the early eighteenth century, a typical field hand did not
produce as much tobacco as had servants and slaves in the late
seventeenth century. On smaller farms, householders still grossed upwards of 1,600 pounds of tobacco per male worker, and
crops of 2,000 pounds per field hand were not unknown. But on
larger Talbot County plantations, output per field hand declined progressively from around 1,600 pounds of tobacco in the
1690s to 1,200 pounds in the 1720s, and then to 1,000 pounds in
the 1740s. Soil exhaustion is an improbable explanation for this
decline in productivity, given the generous land–labor ratio in

---

calculations in the text, for example, I estimated Richard Bennett's wealth at
£20,000 (excluding land), but he may have owned twice as much. If Bennett's
estate came to £40,000, then the richest 2 percent of the free male population
held almost 51 percent of the property in the county. In addition to Bennett,
four others of the thirty large and medium slave owners had more than the
£2,700 average, but the exact amount of wealth held by only two of them is
known. For an earlier attempt to estimate wealth distribution, see Paul G. E.
Clemens, "Economy and Society on Maryland's Eastern Shore, 1689-1733," in
Law, Society, and Politics in Early Maryland, ed. Aubrey C. Land, Lois Green Carr,
and Edward C. Papenfuse (Baltimore, 1977), p. 106. Comparative data are given
in Main, "Personal Wealth in Colonial America," and Jackson Turner Main,
"The Distribution of Property in Colonial Connecticut," in *The Human Dimension
of Nation Making: Essays on Colonial and Revolutionary America,* ed. James Kirby
Martin (Madison, Wis., 1976), pp. 54-104, especially p. 60.

Talbot and the fact that the decline did not occur on small farms. The explanation for the lower returns may be in the difficulty large planters had in managing unacculturated or recalcitrant African laborers, but more likely the reason lies in the initiative wealthier residents took in changing the crop mix on their holdings. In any case, a planter who cleared 1,600 pounds of tobacco before expenses had gotten a good year's work from a field hand.[38]

Talbot County slave owners put a substantial amount of their proceeds into clothing and supervising their field hands. With the cold Chesapeake winters and the chilly evenings in the fall and spring, common sense dictated that planters dress their slaves adequately. Each year field hands received new shoes, stockings, shirts, and breeches or enough fabric with which to make their own clothing. Over longer periods, slave owners distributed additional items, such as hats, coats, bedding, and tools. From harvest to harvest and plantation to plantation, as Table 15 indicates, the expenses incurred by landowners varied, depending chiefly on the relative price of English merchandise and Talbot County tobacco. During the middle decades of the eighteenth century, a careful planter could probably get by with an outlay of 360 pounds of tobacco per field hand (£1.5 in 1720s prices). In addition, he paid yearly provincial, county, and parish taxes, amounting to between 100 and 150 pounds of tobacco per adult slave. On the larger plantations, the owner often hired an overseer. The overseer generally contracted for a share of the crop (rather than a wage), amounting in most cases to the average output of a male field hand. In a year, 600 or 700 pounds of tobacco could easily be expended to keep a male slave working (see Table 16).[39]

---

38. Output figures for male field hands were constructed by the method discussed in Table 7. I explored the theme of this section under various assumptions in "The Operation of an Eighteenth-Century Tobacco Plantation," *Agricultural History* 49 (1975): 517–531. The best treatment of profitability in the seventeenth century can be found in Lorena S. Walsh, "Charles County, Maryland, 1658–1705: A Study of Chesapeake Social and Political Structure," Ph.D. dissertation, Michigan State University, 1977, pp. 262–275. Walsh's discussion of Robert Cole's plantation is based on Testamentary Proceedings, vol. 6, pp. 118–147, MHR.

39. In addition to the sources listed in Table 15, consult the James Hollyday

Table 15. Clothing costs for a male slave field hand, 1722 and 1774

	£	s	d		£	s	d

John Pemberton's farm, 1722

(tobacco at 1d per pound, expenses of 370 pounds of tobacco per field hand)

	£	s	d
5 yds. country cloth @ 2s	0	10	0
1.5 yds. kersey @ 2s/6d	0	3	9
8 yds. brown linen @ 1s	0	8	0
1 pair shoes @ 5s	0	5	0
1 pair country-made stockings @ 2s	0	2	0
Expenses in making	0	2	0
Total	1	10	9

William Martin's farm, 1722

(tobacco at 1d per pound, expenses of 420 pounds of tobacco per field hand)

	£	s	d
2 shirts @ 3s	0	6	0
2 linen breeches @ 3s	0	6	0
1 woolen breech @ 6s	0	6	0
1 waistcoat @ 9s	0	9	0
1 hat @ 3s	0	3	0
1 pair shoes @ 5s	0	5	0
Total	1	15	0

Edward Lloyd's farm, 1774

Account 1 (maximum)

(tobacco at 3d per pound, expenses of 180 pounds of tobacco per field hand)

	£	s	d
7 yds. osnaburg @ 1s/4d	0	9	4
1.5 yds. white cloth @ 3s	0	4	6
3 yds. fine cloth @ 4s	0	12	0
coat @ 3s	0	3	0
breeches @ 2s/6d	0	2	6
2 shirts @ 2s	0	4	0
1 pair shoes @ 7s/6d	0	7	6
stockings @ 3s	0	3	0
Total	2	5	10

Account 2 (minimum)

(tobacco at 3d per pound, expenses of 100 pounds of tobacco per field hand)

	£	s	d
7 yds. osnaburg @ 1s/4d	0	9	4
2 shirts @ 2s	0	4	0
1 pair shoes @ 7s/6d	0	7	6
stockings @ 3s	0	3	0
Total	1	3	10

SOURCES: Accounts, vol. 6, pp. 245–248, 376–377, MHR; Lloyd Plantation Account Book, Lloyd Collection, MS 2001, MHS.

Account Book, MS 454-454.1, MHS; the Robert Lloyd Crop Book, Lloyd Collection, MS 2001, MHS; and the Goldsborough Crop Book, Myrtle Grove, Easton, Maryland. Among the numerous listings in the inventories, see in particular Talbot Inventories, IB no. 3, p. 316 (Thomas Beswick, 1718, food for overseer and slaves); Accounts, vol. 16, p. 331 (Thomas Studham, 1738, harvesting crop of wheat, oats, and tobacco); Talbot Inventories, vol. 6, pp. 561–568, and Accounts, vol. 65, p. 139 (Standley Robins, 1767–68, reaping and clothing expenses); and Kent Inventories, vol. 6, p. 320, and Kent Accounts, vol. 5, p. 148 (Christian Adair, 1769, expenses for slaves and hired help). Tax rates were determined from the Talbot County Court Records, MHR; Eastern Shore Parish Records, MHR; and, for provincial taxes, *AM*.

Table 16. Annual net return from a male field hand employed in tobacco production on a self-sufficient farm, with and without overseer, c. 1720

Pounds of tobacco	Without overseer	With overseer
Production per worker	1,600	1,600
Expenses: taxes and clothing	500	500
Overseer's share	—	200
Net return	1,100	900
Value of net return (@ 1.05d/lb.)	£4.8	£3.9

NOTE: The overseer's share is the amount he would claim per field hand on a farm with eight field hands. Most overseers worked with groups of eight to ten slaves, and their share came to between one-tenth and one-eighth of the output of a single male slave.
SOURCES: Inventories, MHR.

Almost as much had to be spent on female slaves. The government levied the same tax on slave women as on men, and overseers insisted that crop shares be adjusted so that they made as much when in charge of female as male workers. (Women were counted for half or two-thirds of a crop share, and the overseer received a full share.) Moreover, clothing for women cost only slightly less than for men. On the Lloyd estate in 1774, where the maximum spent on a male slave was £2.25, the maximum spent on a female slave—for six yards of osnaburg, five yards of white cloth, stockings, a petticoat, a jacket, two smocks, and a pair of shoes—came to about £2.[40]

During the middle decades of the eighteenth century, a typical planter, after deducting expenses for clothing, taxes, and, when necessary, an overseer, could expect to clear annually between £4 and £5 from the employment of a male slave in tobacco production. This assumes that the field hand brought in a crop of 1,600 pounds that could be marketed at a little more than a penny per pound. If in good years, when prices jumped 10 or 20 percent, production could be pushed as high as 2,000 pounds

40. Lloyd Plantation Account, Lloyd Collection, MS 2001, MHS.

Table 17. Annual net return and internal rate of return
from investment in a male field hand and 20 acres of land,
c. 1720

	Tobacco output (pounds)	Price (pence)	Annual net return (pounds)	Internal rate of return (percent)
Low price, limited output	1,200	0.90	£2.6	4.5
Average price and output				
No overseer	1,600	1.05	4.8	11.5
Overseer	1,600	1.05	3.9	9.0
High price, large output	2,000	1.25	7.8	20.0

NOTE: The net return (*A*) has been calculated as in Table 16. The internal
rate of return (*IRR*) was determined by solving

$$P/A = \sum_{t=1}^{n} \frac{1}{(1 + IRR)^t}$$

where *P* (the initial investment) = £38.4 and *n* = 25, to represent an investment
that yields *A* annually for 25 years. Once *P/A* was determined, *IRR* was found
in a handbook of compound interest and annuity tables.
SOURCES: Inventories, MHR. See also Tables 15 and 16.

per field hand, the planter could net as much as £8. On the other
hand, when prices fell by an equivalent amount and planters
allocated less time to market production, a short crop of 1,200
pounds per male slave represented no more than a return of £2
to £3 after expenses (see Table 17). To the planters themselves,
this simple calculation of profit was probably the most important
indication of how well they were managing tobacco and slaves.[41]

These earnings can be converted by accounting techniques
into a rate of return on the initial investment in land and labor.
In the 1720s, a planter who wished to increase tobacco production by purchasing a young male field hand had to lay out £38.4
for a worker and an adequate amount of farmland. No fewer
than twenty acres sufficed if the planter hoped to rotate his crop
fields and keep his land fertile. Both tobacco and corn, the principal food crop, drew nutrients quickly out of the soil, and after
two or three acres had been used for a few years, this land

41. See Tables 16, 17, and the Appendix. Between 1720 and 1745, the average real price of tobacco was 1.05 pence per pound. This price was determined
by averaging tobacco prices (given in the Appendix) and dividing by 1.2.

required a decade or two before it could be as profitably used again. With time, investment costs rose, but through the 1730s, the expenses of buying land and labor increased no more than the general price index and actually a little less than the price of tobacco. Only after 1740 did diversified agricultural production and rising population density push costs up more quickly than the price index.[42]

The rate of return the planter made depended on the number of years he was able to work a field hand. If a planter purchased a male slave eighteen years of age, he could hope for twenty-five years of labor from him. But the rigors of fieldwork and the diseases spread by tidewater swamps, local epidemics, and passengers off ships from England took a heavy toll from the labor force. If in the middle decades of the eighteenth century white life expectancy at age twenty was thirty years, it is not unreasonable to assume that slaves, who were worked harder and fed, clothed, and housed less well, lived somewhat shorter lives.[43]

Over the course of twenty-five years and under average conditions, the planter could expect a rate of return of about 11.5 percent (see Table 17). This rate corresponds to a situation in which a person places £38.4 in a bank, where the account earns 11.5 percent annually, and makes twenty-five annual withdrawals of £4.8 each, which exhaust the bank balance. The calculation assumes that the field hand's production averaged 1,600 pounds of tobacco a year and that the price of the crop held at 1.05 pence per pound. But conditions were critical to the planter's prospects, for the rate of return varied significantly with changes in output and price. Judged against the standard borrowing

42. A price index, measuring inflation during the years 1724-44, is given in the Appendix. Land prices come from the Talbot County Land Conveyances, MHR, and slave prices from the Maryland Inventories, MHR. Investment costs of £38.4 in the 1720s rose as follows (current money prices): £45.5 (1730s), £59.6 (1740s), £66.0 (1750s), and £77.8 (1760s). The figure of 20 acres is based on the assumption that a planter allotted 2.5 acres per field hand every three years and allowed land, once used for three years, to lie fallow for at least 20 years. In Chapter 6 the land-labor ratio will be discussed more fully.

43. See the discussion in Chapter 2 of white life expectancy and, in particular, Lorena S. Walsh and Russell R. Menard, "Death in the Chesapeake: Two Life Tables for Men in Early Colonial Maryland," *MHM* 69 (1974): 211-227; and Kulikoff, "A 'Prolifick' People," 391-428.

rate on the eighteenth-century Eastern Shore—8 percent of a loan repaid in tobacco—investment in land and labor for tobacco production was profitable for the planter as long as the crop's price remained around a penny per pound or above and production averaged at least 1,500 pounds per fieldhand.[44]

The profitability of using slaves in tobacco production may also be viewed in the context of other options planters had. Most planters put some of their money into land. Through appreciation, land returned its purchaser no more than 2 to 4 percent annually, and if it were resold, the mortgage earned the original buyer 8 percent a year. At the other end of the scale, a mercantile investment, in a coastal vessel or in retail goods for local sale, probably earned upwards of 15 to 20 percent annually. The amount required to begin trading often proved prohibitive, however, and the risks involved discouraged others from investing.[45]

Buying servants offered yet another investment opportunity. Contract terms—the number of years to be worked in relation to the price—frequently were not attractive, however. Moreover, few newly arrived servants adjusted quickly enough to the climate or agricultural routine of the Chesapeake to be as useful as they would become later. While the same could be said of slaves, over the short contract period of a servant the loss of production mattered far more. When the four, five, seven, or occasionally fourteen years of service ended, the planter owed the freedman a barrel of corn, a suit of clothes, and some agricultural tools

44. See Table 17. For a concise discussion of the internal rate of return, see Robert C. Higgins, *Financial Management: Theory and Applications* (Chicago, 1977), pp. 47–51, 95–108; and Robert W. Fogel and Stanley L. Engerman, "The Economics of Slavery," in *The Reinterpretation of American Economic History*, ed. Fogel and Engerman (New York, 1971), pp. 311–341.

45. Returns from the appreciation of land calculated from prices in the Talbot County Land Conveyances, MHR. There are no records from which to calculate returns on investments in coastal vessels or retail merchandise, but factors for English merchants earned a 5 to 15 percent commission for handling purchases and sales. Yearly profit depended, however, not only on the commission rate but also on the volume of business. For a discussion of profits in English trade see Ralph Davis, "Earnings of Capital in the English Shipping Industry, 1670-1730," *JEH* 17 (1957): 409–425; and Richard Grassby, "The Rate of Profit in Seventeenth-Century England," *English Historical Review* 84 (1969): 721–751. Some data on the scale of business of an Eastern Shore merchant may be found in the Robert Morris Ledger Book, MHR.

(worth no less than £1.5 in 1720s prices). Under these constraints, only low-cost (£10) or long-term (seven years and up) servants promised to return to the planter more than he had laid out. While in the seventeenth century such laborers had been readily available, in the eighteenth century the only real sources of supply were the occasional shipments of English convicts to the Eastern Shore. Felons from London and Bideford jails, excaping long confinement or death in England, served terms of at least seven years in the colonies.[46]

Planters also could rent their land. Here again, however, actual profits fell short of potential returns. Although most planters had little difficulty renting some land, at least until mid-century, few could rent all they owned. In other words, the planters often chose not between buying labor and land but between purchasing a slave and letting land lie idle. Only after 1750 was population density on the Eastern Shore high enough to assure tenants to most landowners, and by that time, rising land prices had significantly reduced the rate of return from rents. Moreover, to get a tenant, planters generally had to lay out some of the capital to help the renter start a household, and returns on such a loan were low. Finally, the tenant, through improper tillage, could reduce the long-term earnings potential of the holding. All of these reservations aside, however, the figures in Table 18 suggest that the rentier occupied a favored position in Talbot's economy.[47]

Quite likely, planters made only the crudest attempts to calculate profitability. They knew prices and could estimate profits but seldom computed a rate of return; they knew the value of what a field hand produced in a given year and could estimate

46. On the method of comparison, see the note to Table 18. Contract terms under which servants worked are often found in the Talbot County Court Records, MHR; and the Inventories, MHR, list the value of servants with various numbers of years left to serve. Information on convict laborers comes from the English court records transcribed in the Queen Anne's County Land Records, MHR.

47. In the 1760s, the internal rate of return on 50 acres of land yielding 600 pounds of tobacco in rent was about 11.0 percent, while an investment in a slave and 20 acres of land gave 16.0 percent if annual net production came to 1,100 pounds of tobacco for twenty-five years. In the 1720s, however, the figures had been 19.0 percent (rent) and 11.5 percent (slave). Eighteenth-century population growth is discussed briefly in the conclusion.

Table 18. Returns from an equal investment on servants, slaves, and land, 1720–45

Type of investment	Net present value in 1720
Servant (5-year term, £14 cost)	£−2.2
Slave	14.4
Servant (5-year term, £10 cost)	22.0
Servant (8-year term, £14 cost)	27.4
Land	34.9

NOTE: The net present value (NPV) is calculated by converting all future cash flows from an investment into their current (or discounted) value and then summing the inflows and outflows. The estimates in the table are for investments of equal scale (£38.4) and 25-year duration. In the case of servants and slaves, the initial investment includes 20 acres of land per field hand, and the returns are from tobacco produced on this land by the worker. In the case of land, returns come from a rent of 600 pounds of tobacco per 50 acres.

In order to calculate the NPV on various investments, I used two standard indexes whose values can be determined in a handbook of compound interest and annuity tables: $P/A,d,n$—present value, at a discount rate of d percent, of annual year-end payments of £1 for n years:

$$P/A,d,n = \sum_{t=1}^{n} \frac{1}{(1+d)^t}$$

and $P/F, d, n$—present value, at a discount rate of d percent, of a payment of £1 at the end of year n:

$$P/F,d,n = \frac{1}{(1+d)^t}$$

For an investment of £38.4 in a slave and 20 acres of land, with an annual return of £4.8 (1,100 pounds of tobacco at 1.05 pence per pound) for 25 years, then, with a discount rate of 8 percent,

$$NPV = 4.8(P/A,0.08,25) - 38.4 + 9.8(P/F,0.08,25)$$

where the last term allows for the fact that the planter retains the 20 acres of land after the twenty-fifth year and that the real value of the property has risen from £6.6 to £9.8.

For servants with five-year terms, several adjustments were necessary. First, the average annual net return was set at 940 pounds of tobacco (£4.1 at 1.05 pence per pound) rather than at the 1,100 pound figure used for a slave. I have assumed that in the servant's first year in the Chesapeake, he was only half as productive as he would be thereafter, and that net production came to only 300 pounds of tobacco $\left(\frac{1,600}{2} - 500 \right)$. The figure of 940 pounds represents the average of one year with net output of 300 pounds and four years with 1,100 pounds. (Because of the discounting employed, using the average rather than the actual figures slightly distorts the final answer.) Second, replacements, at a cost of £14, had to be bought every five years through year 20. Then, at the end of each five-year period, freedom dues of £1.5 were paid. The net present value of the initial investment in a servant and 20 acres of land (£14 + £6.6 = £20.6) came to what it cost to raise a slave, but lacked a yardstick by which to measure future earnings against present costs. The profitability of using slave labor to grow tobacco helps to explain why the system endured and why the Eastern Shore's large landowners lived as well as they did, but long-run profitability cannot have been the key to the way the planters themselves thought about the system. They lived in a world of limited choices. As long as land remained abundant and tobacco the only crop that could be readily sold, the price of the crop served as a simple but adequate barometer of the advisability of buying more laborers, continuing as before, or withdrawing from market production. This situation would change only when new marketing arrangements gave planters options they had not previously had and the growth of population forced landowners to make choices with which they had not earlier been confronted.

While the majority of householders did not own slaves and were seldom able to obtain servants, they too had to decide how extensively to engage in market production. Through mid-century, according to the inventories, most small farmers produced about as much tobacco as they could. Production on family-operated farms was about 2,000 pounds of tobacco per year and occasionally went as high as 3,000 pounds. At the end of a typical planting season, a family with two children would

---

$$\text{NPV} = 4.1(P/A,0.08,25) \quad \begin{array}{c} \text{initial} \\ \text{outlay} \\ -\pounds20.6 \end{array} \quad \begin{array}{c} \text{replacement expenses} \\ -14[(P/F,0.08,5) + (P/F,0.08,10) + \ldots \end{array}$$

$$\begin{array}{c} \text{freedom dues} \\ + (P/F,0.08,20)] - 1.5[(P/F,0.08,5) + (P/F,0.08,10) + \ldots + (P/F,0.08,25)] \end{array}$$

$$\begin{array}{c} \text{land recovered} \\ + 9.8(P/F,0.08,25) = -1.2 \end{array}$$

Finally, the result was multiplied by $\frac{38.4}{20.6}$ to set the scale of the initial investments in servants and slaves equal.

For eight-year servants, the average annual net return was assumed to be 1,000 pounds of tobacco. Replacements had to be bought twice and freedom dues paid three times. The net present value was calculated for twenty-four years (an adjustment that does not greatly affect the comparative value of the final figure).

For rents, returns were assumed to be 600 pounds of tobacco for each 50 acres held. This much land initially cost £16.5 and had a real money value of £24.5 after twenty-five years.

SOURCES: See Tables 15, 16, and 17.

clear £3 to £6 from a 2,000-pound crop after taxes were paid
and clothing was purchased. In other words, the family as a whole
netted about as much as a slave owner did by the addition of a
single field hand to his labor force.[48]

What standard of living did the income from a family farm
provide? Certainly there was enough money to buy household
furnishings or make repairs on farm buildings, and there was
probably enough left over to purchase a little hard liquor,
Madeira wine, or fine linen. Investment was another matter. If
a farmer did without housewares and alcohol and put all his
money into improvements, he had enough to obtain about fifteen acres of land or two head of cattle. If, in addition, he was
willing to gamble on what was going to happen to tobacco prices,
and put off buying land and livestock for two years, he could
accumulate sufficient capital to contract for a servant. At each
step he had to balance the immediate comfort and security of his
family against the potential of making more money—and given
the risks and sacrifices this trade called for, it is not surprising
that the small farmer long remained the typical white resident of
the Eastern Shore.[49]

Tenancy moved the householder down a notch; that notch
was what he had to give up in rent. Some leases ran for many
years and planters made a formal entry of the contract in the
county land records. Most landlords, however, did not give tenants written leases, and planters and their renters renegotiated
terms each year. Generally leases gave tenants an entire farm
(certainly no less than fifty acres), limited the amount of land
that the tenant could clear and plant to what was needed for a
new tobacco crop (about three acres), called for the tenant to
make improvements on the property, and specified a rent of
between 500 and 600 pounds of tobacco a year. At best, then,
leasing cut the income of a small family farm by a third and
made it that much harder to save. Moreover, leasing limited the

48. See note 39. For a family of four, annual clothing expenses came to about
840 pounds of tobacco and taxes to 140 pounds, which left 1,020 pounds (worth
£4.5) from a 2,000-pound crop.
49. Comparative costs determined from Inventories, MHR; and Maryland
Inventories, MHR.

ability of a family to engage in nonmarket production in years of low tobacco prices.[50]

A tobacco economy that endured for over one hundred years, not surprisingly, benefited the white householders who controlled it. The benefits were limited, however, and the extent of the benefits differed greatly—as the tenant who was left with less than £3 at the end of a harvest knew well. A typical Talbot planting family probably cleared no more than £5 annually, and the average slaveowner around £15 to £20. These income figures were similar to ones in late-seventeenth-century Talbot; the only real change was in the number of householders the economy now supported.

By way of comparison, a Pennsylvania grain farmer, without slave labor, marketed an average of £20 in crops a year. The grain farmer put fifty or more acres into production; the tobacco planter generally less than ten per field hand. If the Chesapeake planter thus lagged somewhat behind his Pennsylvania contemporary in terms of income, he did so because he lived in a region where the market did not yet provide him a way to use his land. At the other end of the comparative scale were the plantation owners of the Caribbean. Only Talbot's merchant-planters could match their enormous incomes, often upwards of £2,000 a year; and in Talbot such money had never been made from staple agriculture alone.[51]

Persistence and Economic Mobility

Clearly, neither expectations nor opportunity were the same for all Eastern Shore whites. Everyone was not equally concerned with economic advancement or permanent residency in the region, and not everyone had the same ability to improve his situation. If there was a shared desire, it was probably for family,

50. Three-year leases were occasionally recorded in the Talbot County Land Conveyances, MHR. Other information on rents comes from the evaluations of orphans' estates in the same land-conveyance records.

51. For the West Indies, see the articles by Richard B. Sheridan listed in note 19. The figure for Pennsylvania comes from Lemon, *Best Poor Man's Country*, pp. 180–181, but I have adjusted Lemon's estimate to take into account price changes between the 1720s and 1790s.

land, and independence—householder status—but the specific way people defined and sought this goal surely varied from settler to settler depending on how great a stake a person already had in society, how readily he accumulated capital, and how strongly he was tied by family loyalties to other whites in the area.

The poor had the most to gain and least to lose by leaving Talbot. For the disinherited and distressed, migration had long been a way of life. The poor of rural England moved often, some coming all the way to the New World. In the colonies, the landless continued to migrate from place to place in search of security. Thus many of Talbot's sharecroppers and laborers had moved before. Moreover, most were like Thomas Salmon and without attachments to other people in the county; most were also like Salmon in that their small incomes made it difficult to get a start on the Eastern Shore. All could hope that in a less settled area they would have the opportunity, generally denied them in Talbot, to marry and become independent farmers. As a result, the majority of those poor whites who came to the Eastern Shore soon emigrated, and those who did stay usually did so because they had been able to lease land and a home.[52]

For only one period, 1722-33, can the magnitude of the exodus from the Eastern Shore be measured. During these years, as indicated by Table 19, 176 (65 percent) of the nonhouseholders in Bollingbroke and Thirdhaven hundreds either died or left Talbot County. Unless mortality was exceptionally high in the 1720s, death claimed no more than seventy to eighty of the nonhouseholders in Bollingbroke and Thirdhaven, meaning that by 1733 one out of every two survivors had simply moved away from the county. Among the emigrants were some sons who left home; but not surprisingly, the great bulk of

52. For comparative data on geographical mobility, see David Hey, *An English Rural Community: Myddle under the Tudors and Stuarts* (Leicester, 1974), p. 200; Lemon, *Best Poor Man's County*, pp. 71-97; especially pp. 83-85; and Stephanie Grauman Wolf, *Urban Village: Population, Community, and Family Structure in Germantown, Pennsylvania, 1683-1800* (Princeton, 1976), pp. 64-94. The best discussion of economic and geographic mobility in the eighteenth-century Chesapeake is in Allan Kulikoff, "Tobacco and Slaves: Population, Economy, and Society in Eighteenth-Century Prince George's County, Maryland," Ph.D. dissertation, Brandeis University, 1976.

emigrants were rootless agricultural workers. At the same time, of those poor who stayed in Talbot through 1733, two of every three acquired households and rented or bought land. (Among sons of established planters, the rate was three out of four.) Put a different way: householder status was the essential attribute of community membership in Talbot; unless a person could obtain it, he generally left.[53]

Once he became a tenant, a planter's situation changed. High land prices made it difficult to become a proprietor; a foothold in the economy and attachments to kin, if only through one's wife, made it hard to leave. The tenant's problem, as we have seen, was how to accumulate capital and still provide for a family. If he could not do both, the latter was clearly more important. We can illustrate this point by following the careers of leaseholders on the 1733 Talbot tax list: by 1748, only 25 of the 400 tenants on the tax list had become landowners, and of these 25, 18 had first leased land from their parents and then bought the property. But denied the opportunity to become landowners, most renters did not emigrate. Again, the only figures come from 1722–33 and they pertain to small farmers (tenants and nonslave-owning proprietors), not just renters, but the trend is clear: compared with the figure of 65 percent for nonhouseholders, some 55 percent of the small farmers in Bollingbroke and Thirdhaven either died or left Talbot during the 1720s. When the deaths are subtracted, the emigration rate for small farmers was but half that for the poor.[54]

As death, migration, and economic mobility drew people from each stratum of white society in Bollingbroke and Thirdhaven hundreds, immigration replaced those who were lost. A quarter of the slave owners, a quarter of the landowners, half the tenants, and almost two-thirds of the agricultural laborers and servants in the area in 1733 entered Bollingbroke or Thirdhaven after 1722 and had no direct ties to the families that had inhabited the hundreds at the beginning of the 1720s. The new slave

53. See Table 19. Most nonhouseholders were young, a fact that suggests that the death rate among them was relatively low and that out-migration was very common.
54. Talbot County Tax List of 1733, MHS, and Talbot County Debt Books of 1733, 1738, and 1748, MHR. See also Table 19.

Table 19. Persistence and economic mobility, Bollingbroke and Thirdhaven hundreds, Talbot County, 1722–33

Status in 1733	Slave owner	Other householder	Non-householder	Total
		Status in 1722		
Still in area				
Slave owners	23	12	3	38
Other householders	1	64	42	107
Nonhouseholders	0	11	23	34
All still in area	24	87	68	179
No longer in area				
Moved within Talbot	5	15	28	48
Relations remain*	22	57	50	129
Completely disappear	8	67	126	201
All no longer in area	35	139	204	378
Total	59	226	272	557
Percent persist	41%	38%	25%	–
Percent disappear	14%	29%	46%	–
Number upwardly mobile	–	12	45	–
Percent mobile of those still in area	–	14%	66%	–

*Members of immediate family.

SOURCES: Talbot County Tax Lists of 1722, MHS; Talbot County Tax List of 1733, Lloyd Collection, MS 2001, MHS.

owners were by and large wealthy, English by birth, and merchants or ministers by occupation. Their settlement in the region underscored the continuing importance of capital brought to Talbot by immigrants. Among the new landowners were at least some residents from nearby counties, and among the poorer immigrants were approximately 100 servants, mostly convicted English felons and Irish paupers. But the remaining people, almost 200 in number, although probably of Chesapeake and not English origin, simply cannot be traced, and their presence in Bollingbroke and Thirdhaven testifies to the remarkable movement of people that characterized the eighteenth-century tobacco economy.[55]

For the established planter, the final step was to become a

55. See Table 19 for sources.

slave owner. Buying a slave was essentially a market decision made to improve the purchaser's economic position. While no planter ignored the market when acquiring land, his first goal was to assure his family food and security. When he bought a slave, however, the goal was profit. Between 1722 and 1733, the number of slaves and slave owners in Talbot increased, but the slave-owning class itself remained relatively restricted. Most new slave owners were either well-to-do immigrants or the children of slave-owning families. While the 1720s were not depression years, neither were they overly prosperous. Under these conditions, slaves tended to remain in the hands of the large planters on whose farms they had been born or on whose vessels they had been brought from the Caribbean.[56]

In the late 1730s this situation changed dramatically. A propitious conjunction of demand and supply conditions spread slave ownership in much the same way that the 1697–1701 boom had given many small planters their first opportunity to buy servants. On the demand side, the introduction of inflationary paper money by the Maryland government in 1734 put cash in the hands of planters, and the expansion of the tobacco reexport trade in the late 1730s and early 1740s initiated a rapid rise in staple prices. On the supply side, problems in the West Indian and Carolina slave markets worked to the advantage of Chesapeake landowners. The West Indian slave trade, dependent on the vitality of the sugar market, ebbed in the mid-1730s, and the outbreak of war between France and England in 1739 —war that immediately spilled over into the Caribbean—made continued trade between the West Indies and Africa risky. In South Carolina, the assembly acted in 1739, after the Stono rebellion, to prohibit further importation of African and West Indian slaves. These circumstances left the Chespeake the prime market for English slavers.[57]

56. In 1722 there were 59 slave owners in Bollingbroke and Thirdhaven; in 1733 there were 72. Of these 72, 23 had owned slaves in 1722; 17, though not slave owners in 1722, were the children of slave owners; 16 were wealthy immigrants; and 16 neither had owned slaves in 1722 nor were related to anyone who did.

57. On paper money, consult Kathryn L. Behrens, *Paper Money in Maryland, 1727–1789,* Johns Hopkins University Studies in History and Political Science 41, no. 1 (Baltimore, 1923). Conditions in other colonies are covered in Richard

In Talbot County between 1734 and 1739, inflation drove up the cost of a slave 25 percent. Over the same period, however, tobacco prices rose 100 percent. As soon as laborers became available, planters began purchasing an unprecedented number. During the peak years, 1739–43, Oxford merchants sold some 600 slaves and a like number of servants (twice the number they had sold during the previous decade and a half). By late 1743, when the economic boom finally collapsed, most landowners in the county had become slave owners. This step, coupled with the continuing rise of property prices, drove a wedge between tenants and other small farmers, and further sharpened lines of economic distinction on the Eastern Shore.[58]

Talbot planters surely never thought about what the inhabitants of Bremen, Dublin, or Amsterdam were doing. Yet in the eighteenth century, much as in the seventeenth, the Atlantic economy linked the fortunes of Eastern Shore producers to the actions of European consumers. Tied to the reexport market by the outport merchants who brought ships to the Great Choptank River and to the English home market by the connections between local merchant-planters and London consignment shippers, Talbot farmers profited year after year from the general improvement in the Atlantic economy. Most householders lived a life of simple comfort and modest affluence, while a small class of entrepreneurs wrested enormous wealth from agriculture, commerce, and politics. At the same time, those whose lack of capital and credit denied them access to the land and those whose color denied them freedom gained little or nothing economically from laboring on the Eastern Shore. The whites tended to leave; blacks did not even have this choice.

Despite the growth of slavery, eighteenth-century Talbot had little in common with the West Indies, where an extremely large

---

B. Sheridan, *Sugar and Slavery: An Economic History of the British West Indies, 1623–1775* (Baltimore, 1973), pp. 422–433, 496–497, 502–503; and Peter H. Wood, *Black Majority: Negroes in Colonial South Carolina from 1670 through the Stono Rebellion* (New York, 1974), p. 325.

58. Slave prices from Maryland Inventories, MHR. Tobacco prices are given in the Appendix. The details of the 1730s boom are discussed in Clemens, "From Tobacco to Grain," pp. 127–130.

proportion of the whites who stayed accumulated estates of hundreds of slaves and many thousands of pounds sterling in other property. Nor did Talbot resemble the homogeneous, unstratified communities still to be found in sections of New England, where the market had yet to penetrate and land scarcity yet to force the young to leave. The lives of Talbot whites, in fact, paralleled most closely those of the rural proprietors of the Middle Colonies and the English countryside. Talbot, with its small, enterprising elite, its large population of simple householders, and its numerous class of geographically mobile poor whites shared with those societies both an economic system based on family farming and an increasingly stratified social order. Slavery, to be sure, distinguished the Eastern Shore in harsh, unreconcilable terms. But the wealth and intermarriages of the merchant-planters, the mixed market agriculture of the householders, and the rootlessness of poorer whites made the Eastern Shore a world very much like the farming regions of England and the Middle Colonies.[59]

59. See the works cited in notes 19 and 36.

Chapter 6

Agricultural Diversification

For a century after its settlement in the 1660s, the Eastern Shore remained primarily a tobacco-producing region. At least for the planter class, the staple economy paid well enough to allow improvement in the quality of material life and to justify further investment. The white inhabitants of Talbot, Kent, and Queen Anne's complained often, to be sure, about the low price they received for tobacco. The market for the crop was generally little better and often worse than it had been during the settlement period in the mid-seventeenth century. The tobacco economy offered little promise to the propertyless, and the recessions that periodically disrupted the market proved troublesome even to the wealthiest farmers. Yet no fundamental crisis ever struck the economy or threatened the dominant position of the region's landed planters. Diversified agriculture did not develop in response to problems in the traditional tobacco economy; rather, diversification came to the Eastern Shore gradually as local farmers capitalized on opportunities to increase their profits and decrease their dependence on a single market crop. Many of the merchants and planters who took the lead in introducing cash grain farming long continued to derive a substantial part of their income from tobacco.

But others did not. By the 1760s, some Eastern Shore residents had abandoned tobacco planting. Especially in the north, in Kent County, wheat farming came to dominate the local economy. There are consequently two questions that must be answered: Why did planters diversify? And why did some go further and replace tobacco with wheat? Historians have recognized that long before the American Revolution, corn and wheat became market crops in many parts of the Chesapeake. Moreover, recent studies have made clear that disastrous wheat harvests in the Mediterranean during the mid-1760s and a subsequent rise in European wheat prices greatly accelerated the spread of wheat farming in Maryland and Virginia. Beyond these two generalizations, however, little is known, particularly about when corn and wheat became significant cash crops; why this development occurred when it did; and what role local planters and entrepreneurs played in helping to meet the growing demand for grain products throughout the Atlantic economy.[1]

Planters adopted diversified agriculture, I shall argue, in response to two factors. The first was the growth in demand for grains. This growth in demand led to the development of new wheat- and corn-marketing networks and assured planters that they would get an adequate price for their crops as they increased output. Second, they diversified because they found they could grow more wheat and corn without reducing the amount of land and labor they devoted to tobacco. As population increased, however, and the land–labor ratio fell, planters eventually reached a point where they had to decide whether to use their land for tobacco or grains. They shifted to wheat because it brought better returns than tobacco. Kent farmers began the move toward wheat specialization, but tobacco production also fell in Queen Anne's and Talbot.

1. On diversification, I found particularly valuable David Klingaman, "The Significance of Grain in the Development of the Tobacco Colonies," *JEH* 29 (1969): 268–278; Ronald Hoffman, *A Spirit of Dissension: Economics, Politics, and the Revolution in Maryland* (Baltimore, 1973), pp. 60–91; Edward C. Papenfuse, *In Pursuit of Profit: The Annapolis Merchants in the Era of the American Revolution, 1763–1805* (Baltimore, 1975), pp. 35–75; Gregory A. Stiverson, *Poverty in a Land of Plenty: Tenancy in Eighteenth-Century Maryland* (Baltimore, 1977), pp. 85–103; and Carville V. Earle and Ronald Hoffman, "Staple Crops and Urban Development in the Eighteenth-Century South," *Perspectives in American History* 10 (1976): 7–80.

The analysis in this chapter ideally should include livestock husbandry. Livestock, as noted in Chapters 3 and 5, was important to the household economy of the Eastern Shore. The inventories, however, offer little evidence of an increase during the century in the number of livestock per household, and there are no records from which to determine if meat exports (or local sales) increased. Statements about income in this chapter exclude the value of livestock products.

Eastern Shore Tobacco and Grain
Production

Grain production did not eliminate completely the planting and marketing of tobacco on the colonial Eastern Shore. In fact, more tobacco was shipped from the region during the two and a half decades before the American Revolution than during the first quarter of the eighteenth century. But after the 1740s, the traditional staple came to play an increasingly smaller role in the diversified agricultural economy of Talbot, Queen Anne's, and Kent counties.

Between the 1690s and the 1740s, the tobacco trade of the Eastern Shore had increased fourfold. Most tobacco was exported from the port of Oxford, located in Talbot County where the Tred Avon flows into the Great Choptank River. To the north, however, in the area of the Chester and Sassafras rivers, shippers generally found it more convenient to cross the Chesapeake Bay and pay their customs fees at Annapolis than make their way south around Kent Island to Oxford. At both Annapolis and Oxford, customs were paid on the number of tobacco hogsheads put on board. While throughout the colonial period the hogshead remained the basic shipping container for tobacco, the amount of tobacco packed in a hogshead increased from around 500 pounds at the turn of the century to some 1,000 pounds by the 1740s. Accordingly, Eastern Shore customs records must be adjusted to take into account the extent of Annapolis exports and the changing weight of hogsheads. When these adjustments are made, the records indicate that over the first half of the eighteenth century the tobacco trade grew from 1.8 million pounds annually to 7.9 million pounds (see Table 20).

After about 1750 the tobacco trade declined, but this decline must be kept in perspective. Following the passage in 1747 of a tobacco inspection act, the government required that planters destroy rather than sell poor-quality crops. Almost half the tobacco grown in some western shore areas of the Chesapeake Bay, one historian has argued, could not pass inspection, and as a result, Annapolis trade fell off sharply, although the price of exported tobacco rose. On the Eastern Shore, enforcement of

Table 20. Annual average tobacco exports from the Eastern Shore, 1696–1773

Period	Hogsheads exported			Tobacco weight of hogsheads	Total weight (millions of pounds)
	Oxford	Annapolis Eastern Shore	Total		
1696–99	2,640	(1,000)	(3,640)	500	1.8
1717–19	2,890	4,050	6,940	600	4.2
1720–29	2,890	2,730	5,620	700	3.9
1730–39	2,920	3,300	6,250	800	5.0
1740–49	5,630	2,240	7,870	1,000	7.9
1750–59	4,530	(1,500)	(6,030)	1,000	6.0
1760–69	3,200	(1,500)	(4,700)	1,000	4.7
1770–73	3,990	(1,500)	(5,490)	1,000	5.5

NOTE: figures in parentheses are estimates.
SOURCES: *AM,* vol. 42, p. 66 (revenue statistics that can be converted to export totals); Calvert Papers, MS 174, nos. 192–1030 (revenue statistics); Oxford and Annapolis Port of Entry Records, MHS and MHR; Colonial Naval Office Records, C.O. 5/749, PRO. Hogshead weights from Maryland Inventories, MHR.

the act did not have such drastic consequences, but warehouse inspectors may have rejected up to a third of the region's crop. If the act had never been passed, the Eastern Shore tobacco trade from Oxford and Annapolis probably would have been maintained at the level reached in the 1740s.[2]

Estimates of tobacco production tell much the same story as export statistics: the output of tobacco on the Eastern Shore rose through the 1740s and declined during the next three decades (see Table 21). These estimates were constructed by multiplying the average output per taxable worker by the number of taxables on the Eastern Shore. They represent the potential size of the region's annual crop. As in the seventeenth century, the region's potential crop size was a good deal larger than the

2. On the inspection act, see Charles A. Barker, *The Background of the Revolution in Maryland* (New Haven, 1940), pp. 69–116, especially pp. 88–93 and 100–103; John W. Tyler, "Foster Cunliffe and Sons: Liverpool Merchants in the Maryland Tobacco Trade, 1738–1765," *MHM* 73 (1978): 246–277; and the very important discussion in Carville V. Earle, *The Evolution of a Tidewater Settlement System: All Hallow's Parish, Maryland, 1650–1783* (Chicago, 1975), pp. 24–28, 95–100.

amount actually exported (compare the last columns in Tables 20 and 21). Exports, if smuggling is allowed for, may actually have been higher than these figures suggest, however, while the passage of the inspection act helps to explain why after the 1740s, planters did not ship all of the tobacco they grew. In any case, the production figures reinforce the picture of the rise and decline of the Eastern Shore tobacco trade.

In 1696, when the tobacco trade of Oxford reached a million pounds, three small vessels, the largest but sixteen tons, left the port carrying grain cargoes in the coastal trade. Thirty years later, when a depression gripped the Eastern Shore, the coastal commerce in grain from Oxford consisted of fifteen or more ships annually. Gradual and limited as this growth was, it marked a fundamental reorganization of the staple economy of Talbot, Queen Anne's, and Kent. By the early 1740s, about two dozen sloops were involved each year in the export of grains from Oxford; two decades later the number of ships in the coastal trade had doubled. After the early 1760s, Oxford's trade declined as more and more vessels cleared directly from a new naval office located on the Chester River in Kent County. After years of incremental growth, corn and wheat exports from the Eastern Shore peaked in the late 1760s at over 150,000 bushels a year. By this time, wheat had replaced corn as the chief grain export (see Table 22). While missing reports and unrecorded trade through Annapolis make a full recounting of the history of the grain trade impossible, the growing commitment of Eastern Shore planters to grains in general and wheat in particular is obvious.[3]

The inventories provide a second measure of grain production on the Eastern Shore. These crop reports (summarized in Table 23) indicate a steady growth from the 1720s on in the production of wheat and corn and allow an estimate of the total annual output on the Eastern Shore of surplus grains (not locally consumed). To determine the surplus output of grains, local consumption must be estimated. Numerous records, discussed in Chapter 5, indicate that adult farmers on the Eastern Shore

---

3. Oxford Port of Entry Records, MHS and MHR; Chestertown trade records in Annapolis Port of Entry Records, MHS.

Table 21. Tobacco production per field hand, Talbot and Kent counties, and potential annual Eastern Shore tobacco output, 1701–69

Period	Production per field hand		Eastern Shore taxable population (thousands)	Estimated total output* (millions of pounds)
	Talbot	Kent		
1701–13	1,570	–	2.1	3.3
1720–24	1,460	1,280	5.1	7.0
1733–37	1,440	1,100	7.1	9.0
1740–45	1,420	1,440	8.5	12.1
1766–69	820	150	12.6	6.2

NOTE: Production figures were arrived at by the method described in Table 7.

*Output was calculated by multiplying the average of the Talbot and Kent production figures by the taxable population of the Eastern Shore (Talbot, Queen Anne's, and Kent counties). Because not all taxables were adult males, the output figures are biased upward.

SOURCES: Inventories, MHR; Paul G. E. Clemens, "From Tobacco to Grain: Economic Development on Maryland's Eastern Shore, 1660–1750," Ph.D. dissertation, University of Wisconsin, 1974, pp. 172–173; Arthur Karinen, "Numerical and Distributional Aspects of Maryland Population, 1631–1840," Ph.D. dissertation, University of Maryland, 1958, pp. 198, 201–206.

consumed fifteen bushels (three barrels) of grain annually and used another bushel to fatten hogs. If we assume that three people had to be fed by each taxable laborer, local consumption requirements came at most to forty-eight bushels of grain per taxable per year. When we allow for the food that went to the local population, we find that Talbot, Queen Anne's, and Kent counties produced a marketable grain surplus of 28,000 bushels a year in the 1730s, 314,000 bushels in the 1740s, and 832,000 bushels in the 1760s. As was the case with tobacco, planters could have grown much more corn and wheat than they sold in the export market. The discrepancy between grain production and export figures, however, was enormous (compare Tables 22 and 23).[4]

Clearly, direct overseas trade did not provide the only market for Eastern Shore grains. As early as the 1740s, Eastern Shore

4. For the consumption of corn, see, for example, Robert Lloyd Crop Book, Lloyd Collection, MS 2001, MHS.

Table 22. Wheat and corn exports from Oxford and Chestertown, 1743–74 (in thousands of bushels annually)

| Period | Oxford | | Chestertown | | |
	Wheat	Corn	Wheat	Corn	Total
1743–46	11	8	–	–	19
1760–66	31	48	–	–	79
1767–70	38	31	44	8	121
1771–74	10	26	43*	22*	101

*Incomplete data.
SOURCES: Oxford Port of Entry Books, MHR and MHS; Chestertown trade reports in the Annapolis Port of Entry Records, MHS.

merchants turned their eyes northward. Increasingly they sent wheat, and less often corn, to Annapolis and Baltimore, or hauled grain overland to the Delaware and had it shipped up to Philadelphia. One contemporary survey of annual grain production on the Eastern Shore during the years 1770–75 indicated that 720,000 bushels annually left Talbot, Kent, and Queen Anne's (500,000 wheat and 220,000 corn)—a figure that corresponds approximately with the estimate from the 1760s in Table 22.[5]

By mid-century, in short, the Eastern Shore economy had reached a turning point. Before 1750, both tobacco and grain exports rose, decade after decade; subsequently, tobacco shipments from the Eastern Shore fell, but the grain trade, both from local ports and overland, grew enormously. On the Eastern Shore as a whole, wheat took the place of corn as the second most important cash crop, and in Kent County, wheat actually replaced tobacco as the principal market product.

MARKETS AND DEMAND

The growth of traditional grain markets and the opening of new ones made possible the profitable expansion of Eastern Shore corn and wheat production. Only as demand grew could farm-

5. Hoffman, *Spirit of Dissension,* pp. 63–66; Edward C. Papenfuse, Jr., "Economic Analysis and Loyalist Strategy during the American Revolution: Robert Alexander's Remarks on the Economy of the Peninsula or Eastern Shore of Maryland," *MHM* 68 (1973): 173–193.

Table 23. Wheat and corn produced per adult taxable male, Talbot and Kent counties, and total annual surplus grain output on the Eastern Shore, 1720s–1760s

| | Production per taxable male (bushels) | | | | Eastern Shore taxable population (thousands) | Estimated total grain surplus* (thousand bushels) |
| | Talbot | | Kent | | | |
Period	Wheat	Corn	Wheat	Corn		
1720s	4	45	4	20	5.1	–
1730s	5	45	19	35	7.1	28
1740s	4	90	37	40	8.5	314
1760s	24	70	89	45	12.6	832

NOTE: See Table 7 for the method used to calculate production figures.

*Output was calculated by multiplying the taxable population of the Eastern Shore by the average of the Kent and Talbot grain production figures minus 48 bushels (the quantity that went to local consumption, assuming that each laborer had to feed three people). For example, in the 1760s, the calculation was $12.6 \times \left(\dfrac{24 + 70 + 89 + 45}{2} - 48 \right) = 832$.

SOURCES: See Tables 21 and 22.

ers increase supply and make as much or more for a bushel of grain as they had before. Actually, in the long run, increases in demand and supply more or less kept pace with each other, and before the 1760s diversification occurred with little rise in the real price of corn and wheat. Planters increased their profits from grains not because they got progressively better prices for their crops but rather because they were able to increase production without forcing prices down. This fortuitous situation they owed to the expansion of the Atlantic market. Just as important, diversification took place without a permanent or long-term improvement in the price of wheat or corn relative to the price of tobacco. In certain periods, to be sure, tobacco prices fell disastrously and induced planters to diversify in order to break their dependence on a single, unpredictable market crop, but in general, farmers in the 1760s could expect about the same relative returns from tobacco and wheat as an earlier generation of planters had gotten in the 1720s.[6]

6. The following discussion draws on Maryland Naval Office Records, 1689–1701, C.O. 5/749, PRO; Oxford Port of Entry Records, MHS and MHR; "Thomas Chamberlaine Account . . . at Oxford, Maryland, 1753–1754," Gift Collection, G 801, MHR; Oxford District Revenue Records for 1731 and 1733,

Trade between New England and the Caribbean first provided Eastern Shore farmers with markets for their grains. During much of the seventeenth century, New England shippers supplied West Indian planters and their slaves with lumber and provisions, and returned to Boston, Salem, and Newport with rum and molasses. The early boom in the staple economies of Barbados and Nevis, followed by the rapid development of Antigua and St. Christopher's and the gradual exploitation of Jamaica's vast cane-producing interior, kept the demand for provisions growing steadily, but the disruption of New England's rural economy during King Philip's War of 1675–76 and the spread of wheat blight forced New England merchants to alter their pattern of trade with the Caribbean. Massachusetts and Rhode Island shippers turned to the Chesapeake for supplies of corn for the West Indies, while they imported increasing amounts of wheat from Maryland and Virginia to feed the merchant and artisan population of New England's seaports. In turn, local Chesapeake merchants sent out their own ships carrying wheat north and corn south. Not surprisingly, the Eastern Shore's grain trade followed the general pattern. In 1744, a typical year in terms of the distribution of trade, fourteen coastal vessels cleared from Oxford—three each for Boston, Salem, and ports in Rhode Island, three to take on cargoes in Virginia, one for Bermuda, and one for Barbados. New England provided the only market for Eastern Shore wheat and took almost as much corn as any other trading region.[7]

In the 1740s, however, a major structural change began in the Eastern Shore's grain trade. Local farmers found new outlets for their crops in Annapolis and Philadelphia, and by mid-century

Calvert Papers, MS 174, nos. 912, 914 MHS; Chestertown trade records in the Annapolis Port of Entry Records, MHS; Barbados Naval Office Records, C.O. 33/14, PRO; Jamaica Naval Office Records, C.O. 142/13, PRO; and Customs 14, Colonial Import-Export Records for 1768–72, PRO. The location of microfilm copies of PRO records is noted in the bibliography.

7. While my analysis depends primarily on colonial trade records, see also Richard S. Dunn, *Sugar and Slaves: The Rise of the Planter Class in the English West Indies, 1624–1713* (Chapel Hill, N.C., 1972); Richard B. Sheridan, *Sugar and Slavery: An Economic History of the British West Indies, 1623–1775* (Baltimore, 1973); Charles Carroll, *The Timber Economy of Puritan New England* (Providence, 1973), especially pp. 75–97 and 137–142; and Bernard Bailyn, *The New England Merchants in the Seventeenth Century* (Cambridge, Mass., 1955).

the shipment of grain to these ports from the northern Eastern Shore may have reached 100,000 bushels a year. Some of the surplus grain crop simply left via Annapolis as part of the traditional coastal trade of Chesapeake merchants, but much of the wheat found its way in the form of flour to the head of the Chesapeake Bay, was then carted the short distance to the Delaware River, sent to Philadelphia, and reexported. By this time Philadelphia rivaled Boston among colonial ports. But while Boston maintained its position in the Atlantic economy by carrying the produce of other colonies, Philadelphia's success depended on the development of trade networks linking the city with the surrounding wheat-producing countryside. In the 1740s, the quest for additional grain supplies began to take Philadelphia merchants beyond Delaware and eastern Pennsylvania, and opened sustained overland trade with Anne Arundel, Cecil, and Kent counties in northern Maryland. The willingness of these merchants to buy Eastern Shore grains stimulated further agricultural diversification in the region.[8]

Southern Europe and the Caribbean supplied most of the demand for the wheat and corn grown in Pennsylvania and indirectly affected demand on the Eastern Shore. At the end of the third decade of the eighteenth century, Southern Europe may already have provided the most important market for Pennsylvania wheat, and over the next twenty years the tonnage of ships trading with Spain, Portugal, and Madeira doubled, then doubled again by the time of the American Revolution. Ultimately, Southern European ports also became the chief outlet for corn exported from Philadelphia, but in the early part of the eighteenth century, the demand for corn probably came more from the West Indies, and this market, chiefly because of the expansion of the sugar industry in Jamaica and St. Christopher's, grew steadily between the 1730s and 1770s. By the early 1770s, Philadelphia's annual grain exports to Southern Europe and the Caribbean had reached an average of 220,000 bushels.[9]

8. Hoffman, *Spirit of Dissension,* chaps. 2 and 4; James T. Lemon, *The Best Poor Man's Country: A Geographical Study of Early Southeastern Pennsylvania* (Baltimore, 1972); and Arthur L. Jensen, *The Maritime Commerce of Colonial Philadelphia* (Madison, Wis., 1963), pp. 52–69, 292–293.

9. See references in note 8 and H. E. S. Fisher, *The Portugal Trade: A Study of Anglo-Portuguese Commerce, 1700–1770* (London, 1971), especially pp. 69–70;

Despite the increasing importance of the Philadelphia market in the 1740s and 1750s, Oxford's trade retained essentially the same pattern in the early 1760s that it had had for decades. During 1761, when over 100,000 bushels of grain were exported, forty-three of the fifty-two vessels and 85 percent of the corn and wheat that cleared Oxford went to northern ports of call, most in Massachusetts, Rhode Island, and New York. Change came in 1765. In that year, two ships sailed directly for Lisbon. Two years later, the Chestertown naval office opened and direct trade with both Southern Europe and the Caribbean increased; by 1769, a new marketing pattern had been established. During the greatest boom in the history of the colonial Eastern Shore, fifty-one vessels set sail from Oxford and Chestertown with cargoes of grain—sixteen for Southern Europe, fourteen for the West Indies, and twenty-one for ports on the American mainland. They carried 12,600 bushels of corn to Cadiz, Lisbon, and Oporto; 12,900 bushels to Barbados, Jamaica, and the Leewards; and 13,700 bushels to Boston, Philadelphia, New York, Newport, and other northern stops, as well as the extraordinary total of 99,200 bushels of wheat to Portugal, and only 19,500 bushels to the traditional markets north of the Chesapeake. Through the early, prewar months of 1775, Southern Europe and the Caribbean provided Eastern Shore farmers an expanded market for their corn and wheat.[10]

The relationship of the Philadelphia and Southern European markets to the Eastern Shore's grain economy can be charted in the movement of prices. Through the mid-1730s, wheat prices, on which our discussion focuses, fell in response to an ever increasing local supply of the crop. This process continued until the price had fallen enough and West Indian demand for food had grown enough to make it profitable for Philadelphia merchants to begin purchasing Eastern Shore wheat for reexport. For the next two decades, through about 1760, local price fluctuations paralleled those in the Philadelphia grain market (see

---

James F. Shepherd and Gary M. Walton, *Shipping, Maritime Trade, and the Economic Development of Colonial North America* (Cambridge, England, 1972), pp. 214–225; and Customs 14, Colonial Export–Import Ledgers, 1768–1772, PRO.

10. See note 6.

Graph 6), and, in fact, the movement of grain prices in both localities followed the general pattern of booms and recessions in Atlantic commerce. Grain prices rose when the primary economies—sugar, rice, and tobacco—prospered, because prosperity went hand in hand with the importation of slaves and increased demand for provisions. Grain prices fell when war disrupted staple markets and increased shipping costs. These periodic fluctuations in wheat prices, however, did not add up to a general upward or downward trend in the market. Through the 1740s and 1750s, demand and supply grew together, and the real price of the crop, however high it jumped or low it fell, returned to around 30 pence per bushel. The initial increase in Eastern Shore wheat production consequently occurred without a significant long-term rise in the price of the crop.[11]

In the late 1750s, the demand for grain in Southern Europe became the major determinant of Eastern Shore prices. The relationship between prices in Oporto and Lisbon and prices in Talbot and Kent counties, however, was not direct. The price of wheat in Southern Europe depended primarily on the harvest in the Mediterranean; the price on the Eastern Shore depended both on local harvest conditions and on the demand for flour in New England and the Caribbean. Because some of these factors that affected price on the Eastern Shore operated independently from those that determined price in Spain and Portugal, the short-term movement of wheat prices in the two regions (see Graph 7) followed different paths. At the same time, rising prices in Southern Europe during the 1760s and 1770s were the major cause of the general increase on the Eastern Shore of the wheat price level.[12]

The post-1750s spurt in grain prices cannot have induced farmers to switch from tobacco to wheat, however, because dur-

11. For prices, see the Appendix and Graph 6. On the sugar and slave trades, consult Sheridan, *Sugar and Slavery*, pp. 487–506. The trade of Philadelphia is discussed in Jensen, *Maritime Commerce*.

12. For Southern European wheat prices, see Vitorino Magalhaes Godinho, *Prix et monnaies au Portugal* (Paris, 1955), pp. 76–77, 81–82; R. Romano, *Commerce et prix du blé à Marseille au XVIIIe siècle* (Paris, 1956), pp. 91, 184–185; Earl J. Hamilton, *War and Prices in Spain, 1651–1800* (Cambridge, Mass., 1947), pp. 181–186, 247–251. Note also the careful discussion in Hoffman, *Spirit of Dissension*, pp. 60–91, of the factors affecting Eastern Shore grain prices.

Graph 6. Philadelphia and Kent County wheat prices, 1720-74

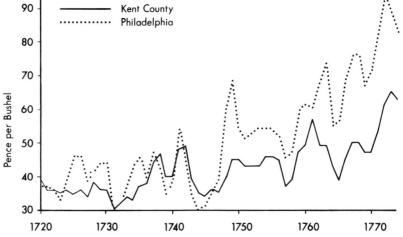

SOURCES: Anne Bezanson, *Prices in Colonial Philadelphia* (Philadelphia, 1935), pp. 422-423; Inventories, MHR.

ing this period, tobacco prices rose as well. The general relationship between the prices of the two crops can be seen in Graph 8. The index numbers plotted there indicate the ratio of wheat to tobacco prices relative to the ratio in the years 1745-49. Index numbers over 100 indicate that wheat prices had risen relative to tobacco prices. Index numbers under 100 indicate that wheat prices had fallen relative to tobacco prices. The graph demonstrates that through 1740, wheat prices fell almost continuously relative to tobacco prices, suggesting that the market supplied little incentive to farmers to diversify production. Over the next thirty years, however, wheat prices held their own but did not improve relative to tobacco prices.

While there was no long-term improvement in wheat prices relative to tobacco prices, wheat may nevertheless have been a better short-term, recession crop. Wheat and tobacco prices generally fluctuated together: when wheat prices rose, so did tobacco prices; when wheat prices fell, so did tobacco prices. But tobacco prices were more volatile, rising faster and falling

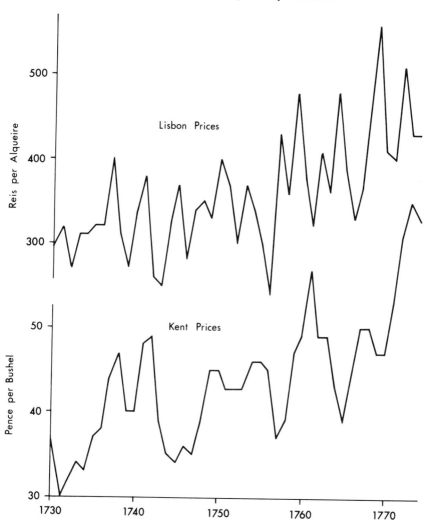

Graph 7. Lisbon and Kent County wheat prices, 1730–74

SOURCES: Vitorino Magalhaes Godinho, *Prix et monnaies au Portugal* (Paris, 1955), pp. 76–77; Inventories, MHR.

Graph 8. Relative prices of wheat and tobacco in Kent County, 1720–74.

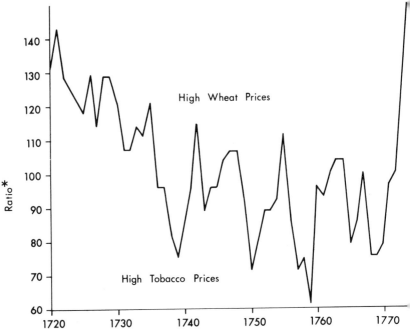

*The price ratio (wheat–tobacco) for any given year was divided by the ratio for the period 1745–49 and then multiplied by 100. During the period 1745–49, the price of a bushel of wheat was 28 times the price of a pound of tobacco.
SOURCE: Inventories, MHR.

sooner and farther. Between 1747 and 1750, for example, the Kent current money price of wheat went from 35 pence per bushel to 45 pence and the current money price of tobacco from 1.15 pence per pound to 2.30 pence per pound. Over the same period, the ratio of wheat to tobacco prices fell about 33 percent. The Kent tobacco market contracted quickly, however, the price falling to 1.70 pence per pound in 1752 and bottoming out at 1.50 pence per pound in 1755, while grain prices remained reasonably high until 1756. As a result, the price ratio climbed by the mid-1750s to its 1747 level. During each boom in the Eastern Shore's economy, tobacco prices tended to rise more quickly than wheat prices; during subsequent recessions, wheat prices tended to hold up longer and fall less.

Wheat prices held up better in recessions because of the way the crop was marketed. Most recessions coincided with wars; in wartime, merchants could get their ships to Massachusetts and the Caribbean more easily than tobacco exporters could get their produce across the Atlantic and then to continental Europe. Moreover, whatever problems Atlantic privateering and blockades created for coastal vessels were partially offset by illicit trade with the French West Indies and by increased demand for military provisions.[13]

In summary, during the 1740s and 1750s, when diversified agriculture first became common, recessions provided farmers with an incentive to grow more wheat and corn. In the 1760s and 1770s, when grains became major market crops, rising prices made diversification more profitable. But throughout the era—and this point is of critical importance—tobacco prices generally kept pace with grain prices. While the market pushed farmers toward grains, it did not pull them away from tobacco.

THE CHANGING RURAL SECTOR OF THE EASTERN SHORE ECONOMY

The large picture—the growth of demand for grains, the spread of wheat farming, and the decline in tobacco exports—does not show us how individual planters responded to conditions in the 1740s, 1750s, and 1760s. Was the tendency of the individual planter more often simply to diversify production—perhaps growing a little less tobacco and a lot more wheat—or was the tendency more often to shift from one staple to another, abandoning tobacco completely? How readily could tobacco planting and wheat farming be conducted simultaneously? Who took the lead—the slave owners or small farmers—in diversifying production? The following discussion of these questions rests first on plantation accounts and journals, one from Virginia and the remaining three from Maryland's Eastern Shore, and then on Talbot and Kent inventories, which do not give the same de-

13. On war and trade, see chaps. 1 and 4, and Richard Pares, *War and Trade in the West Indies, 1739–1763* (Oxford, 1936).

tailed information as the plantation accounts but do provide, because of their numbers, a firmer empirical basis on which to rest the analysis.

Landon Carter was born in 1710, the son of Robert "King" Carter, one of Virginia's greatest tobacco planters. After a London education, Landon followed his father into farming, and between the 1750s and his death in 1778 compiled a remarkable diary in which he recorded his efforts to manage several dozen slaves and a large landed estate. In keeping his diary, Carter left an unparalleled description of the month-to-month routine on a plantation committed to diversified agriculture.[14]

The planting season, Carter noted, began in February or March, when his slaves prepared the fields. Between April and early June, depending on the weather, the corn crop went in the ground. Through the fall harvest, Carter occasionally had to have the fields weeded. Corn was a fickle crop: while seed requirements were small, yields varied greatly from year to year, ranging from as little as 18 barrels to as much as 70 barrels per worker. More important, corn could be picked at leisure between November and early February, when other jobs were not pressing; it could be stored easily and for long periods of time; and it could be used not only as a market crop but also as a staple in the diet of members of the plantation and as food for livestock.[15]

In his diary in 1763, Carter noted that "tobacco planting I see is an art to be learned not more by practice than by reasoning justly upon things," and by his own account, Carter did better at tobacco planting than many of his wealthy neighbors. The entire planting process had to be carefully timed to avoid frost. The tobacco season began in April, after the corn had been started. Through the long summer days of June, July, and August, Carter's slaves had to weed constantly, and top, prune, and stem the plants. In winter they dried, pressed, and prized the tobacco before taking it to a shipping point. On several occasions, Carter believed, the malice of his workers cost him numerous ruined

14. Jack P. Greene, ed., *The Diary of Colonel Landon Carter of Sabine Hall, 1752-1778*, 2 vols. (Charlottesville, Va., 1965).

15. Ibid., vol. 1, pp. 251, 299, 317-318, 389, 394, 522, 567, 586, 678; vol. 2, p. 709.

plants and resulted in reduced crops, but in a typical crop year he averaged 1,500 pounds of tobacco per field hand, a good return by eighteenth-century standards.[16]

Corn and tobacco were the standard crops of the Chesapeake planter; wheat, as a market crop, was another matter. How well did wheat fit into the agricultural routine on Landon Carter's plantation? Carter sowed winter wheat in September, October, or November, well after the corn and tobacco had been planted but often before the corn had been picked. The July reaping, however, had to be done quickly, and occasionally he had to pull workers from the tobacco fields. Despite the labor requirements in July and September, farming winter wheat did not interfere in any fundamental way with the planting of tobacco and corn.[17]

Other grains, cattle, and vegetables all played a role in Landon Carter's farming both because of their food value and because of their use in assuring good yields of corn, tobacco, and wheat. Carter employed numerous methods to sustain soil quality: he rotated crops, sowing wheat in tobacco fields after the fall harvest and then introducing oats for twelve months. Carter also followed the practice of abandoning tobacco lands after three years—actually a type of long-term rotation rather than a wasting of land. He penned his livestock and shifted the cattle and sheep pens each year to prepare new ground with manure for spring planting. Carter complemented the use of animal fertilizer by the planting of vegetables, especially turnips and peas, that enriched the soil or held down weeds. In addition, he grew for home consumption onions, cabbages, radishes, broccoli, and lettuce.[18]

In September 1770 Carter listed in his diary the tasks at which his field hands were employed. Eleven were gathering hay, sixteen were picking peas, and three were helping with plowing. Four others were topping plants in the tobacco fields and five were preparing a tobacco house where the crop would be weathered. His remaining field hands were in their cabins, ill. Carter, like other Chesapeake planters, found that only two tasks, trans-

16. Ibid., vol. 1, pp. 149, 244, 357–358, 501–502, 519, 534; vol. 2, p. 729.
17. Ibid., vol. 1, pp. 132–134, 162, 187, 243, 317–318, 481.
18. Ibid., vol. 1, pp. 137–138, 140, 150, 155–156, 163–164, 204–205, 207, 212, 226, 319, 481, 549; vol. 2, pp. 697, 846, 1038.

planting tobacco plants and harvesting wheat, might require the labor of virtually all of his slaves. During the remainder of the year, diversified agriculture did not force Carter to curtail production of specific crops to devote time to other aspects of farming; rather, his commitment to numerous crops kept Carter and his slaves profitably employed throughout the growing season. After a good crop year, Carter grossed from grains and tobacco alone about £12 per field hand, of which at least 70 percent came from corn and wheat.[19]

The earliest Eastern Shore plantation record comparable to Carter's account dates from 1703 and ends in 1731. The crop book, compiled by Robert Goldsborough, contains only the most basic information—the size of the crop, the number and names of the hands, the overseer's share, and the merchant to whom the tobacco was consigned—but this is enough to permit us to evaluate the effect that changes in the number of field hands and the introduction of diversified farming had on productivity. In 1703 Robert Goldsborough probably owned only two slaves, a man and a woman, but by 1706 he employed six slaves—he called them servants but did not list their names—and had hired an overseer to manage tobacco planting. Between 1706 and 1717, Goldsborough never had more than seven or fewer than five people working for him; in a typical year, five slaves and an overseer tended the crop. In 1718 he added two slaves, and for the first time since 1703 he listed the names of all of his workers, indicating that of the eight people he mentioned, four were male slaves, three were female, and one was a white male overseer. From 1718 to 1730, Goldsborough used at least eight hands annually to grow tobacco and averaged nine workers per year over the period. As the number of workers rose from an average of six between 1703 and 1717 to an average of nine between 1718 and 1730, productivity fell from 2,140 pounds of tobacco per hand to 1,360 pounds per hand, but total production remained fairly constant at about 12,500 pounds annually. Six times before 1717 but only twice thereafter did Goldsborough's slaves produce as much as 2,000 pounds of tobacco apiece, and twice, both times before 1717, they brought in the extraordinary

19. Ibid., vol. 1, pp. 317–318, 496.

amount of 3,000 pounds of tobacco each. The decline in productivity must consequently be held in perspective: before 1717, Robert Goldsborough's field hands, both men and women, had been among the most efficient workers in the Chesapeake.[20]

In 1721 Goldsborough made a second major adjustment in the way he ran the plantation: he began to grow large amounts of corn. In his first year he harvested 233 barrels; production fell to 141 barrels in 1723 and to 56 barrels the year after, but in 1727, when the crop book again lists tobacco and corn, production had more than doubled, and over the next three years, his hands brought in an average of 230 barrels per year. To tobacco and corn Goldsborough added wheat in 1730, the last full year of the crop book, and harvested 190 bushels. To what extent had the increase in the labor force, the shift to diversified farming, and the drop in tobacco production per worker been related?

As the above data demonstrate, a general correlation existed on Robert Goldsborough's plantation between an increase in the labor force, the introduction of grain farming, and a decrease in the production of tobacco per worker. But the data do not all point in this direction: production per worker did not fall abruptly; it actually went up a little in 1717, when two new hands began working, and in 1719, when with eight workers on the plantation Goldsborough obtained 19,800 pounds of tobacco or 2,475 per hand—an extremely good return. Thus while it seems likely that productivity fell somewhat on Goldsborough's plantation in response to an increase in the scale of production, at least some of the reduction may have been voluntary. In any case, with more workers after 1716 than before, Goldsborough's total income was not reduced. Diversification seems even less closely related to the level of tobacco production because there was a five-year lag between the drop in productivity in 1716 and the introduction of corn as a cash crop in 1721.

Rather, Goldsborough diversified in response to the market. The first planting of corn followed a poor tobacco crop in 1720 and a plunge in the price of tobacco caused by the South Sea

20. For Robert Goldsborough, see the Goldsborough Crop Book, Myrtle Grove, Talbot County, Maryland (a microfilm copy has been placed on file at MHR).

Bubble panic in Europe. Similarly, the initiation of wheat farming in 1730 came during the most severe depression during the
eighteenth century. What the entire crop book suggests is that
Goldsborough was making market decisions: he was looking for
a way to offset short-term drops in the price of tobacco and to
break his dependence on the traditional staple. In the process,
he raised his gross income from about £50 yearly before 1721 to
around £125 annually after that date. This jump represented a
gain in the productivity of his labor force, from £9 to £14 per
hand—a little better than Landon Carter made in the 1760s.

Unlike Goldsborough, Robert Lloyd compiled his crop book
in the 1750s and 1760s after diversified farming had become a
way of life on the northern Eastern Shore. Lloyd lived from
1712 to 1770, establishing himself in the mid-1730s on Hope
Plantation in Queen Anne's County. Between the years 1756
and 1762, he kept detailed agricultural records.[21]

Lloyd, one of the greatest slave owners on the Eastern Shore,
put as many people to work as possible. Whether planting tobacco, sowing wheat, or husking corn, women worked alongside
men and older children worked with their parents. Along the St.
Michael's River in the 1750s, on one of Lloyd's five holdings, for
example, lived an overseer, Jonathan Garey, three adult male
slaves, three boys between the ages of fourteen and eighteen,
four women, a ten-year-old girl, and four children between the
ages of three and six—in all, fifteen slaves who had to be fed and
clothed, of whom eight cared for the crop of corn, tobacco, and
wheat. On each of Lloyd's estates, youth, the disabilities of old
age, or the responsibilities of child rearing left about half of the
slaves out of the agricultural routine. Among the eighteen men,
twenty-three women, and twenty-four children he owned in
1756, Lloyd had thirty-five workers.

During the seven-year period 1756–62, tobacco was the chief
cash crop. Production fluctuated between 28,900 pounds and
36,800 pounds. On different parts of the farm and in different
years, output per worker varied greatly, going from as little as

21. For Robert Lloyd, see the Robert Lloyd Crop Book, Lloyd Collection, MS
2001, MHS. See also James Hollyday Account Book, MS 454–454.1, MHS, for
another description of diversified agriculture.

640 pounds of tobacco per slave to as much as 1,220 pounds, but the average, roughly 900 pounds, was not as good as that which Landon Carter got on a larger plantation or Robert Goldsborough got on a smaller one.

Low tobacco yields per worker could not be attributed to concentration on wheat or corn, for in many years Lloyd grew no grains at all on two or three of the five quarters at which he planted tobacco. Rather, the problem lay in the soil, according to Lloyd: "In the quantity of ground in tillage for corn this year" (sixty acres), he wrote in disgust of the 1761 crop, ". . . there was not more than twelve acres in the whole but what might be called much worn old corn ground." By his own standards—he was pleased with forty-one barrels of corn and eighty-seven bushels of wheat per worker—his land seldom returned enough grain for the labor expended. When growing grains, Lloyd's field hands averaged twenty-six barrels of corn and fifty bushels of wheat apiece—which fell 40 percent short of his expectations; but because most of his workers planted only tobacco, Lloyd generally grew but 350 barrels of corn and 600 bushels of wheat.

Was Lloyd correct in blaming the soil? Properly managed, tobacco fields, as already discussed, could remain productive indefinitely. But if farmers insisted on planting grains on old tobacco fields or in using the fields over and over without an extensive fallow period, then their productivity naturally dropped. As long as grains remained secondary crops, the tendency existed to sow seeds on old tobacco fields rather than clear new land and rotate crops. Lloyd had probably overworked his land.

Lloyd's income fluctuated greatly. In 1756, a good year for the tobacco crop and an average year for the grain harvest, he grossed £450; in 1757, without much money from wheat or corn, his earnings before expenses fell to £203. Seventeen-fifty-nine was his best year: with three fields under cultivation and twenty-four slaves at work, a good grain harvest pushed his income to about £600. In an average year, Lloyd's crop had a market value of £390, or a return of £11 per worker.

Edward Lloyd IV did even better than his uncle. This Lloyd, who lived from 1744 to 1796, was chiefly remembered on the Eastern Shore for his political leadership during the revolutionary era, but he was also an accomplished farmer. When his

Table 24. Tobacco and grain production on nonslave farms, Talbot and Kent counties, 1760s

| | Talbot County | | | | | Kent County | | | |
	Number	Wheat (bushels)	Corn (barrels)	Tobacco (pounds)	Number	Wheat (bushels)	Corn (barrels)	Tobacco (pounds)
Tobacco farms	18	0	19	1,470	2	0	6	1,100
Wheat farms	0	–	–	–	14	147	17	0
Wheat-tobacco farms	8	65	30	2,020	4	139	22	790

NOTE: Figures are for average output per household (not per field hand).
SOURCE: Inventories, MHR.

father died in 1770, Edward Lloyd IV took possession of dozens of holdings spread over thousands of acres, scattered throughout Talbot and Kent counties, and some 200 slaves. In the years between 1772 and 1777, the market value of the tobacco, wheat, and corn produced by each field hand on the Lloyd estate came to between £15 and £26; with over ninety workers at his command, Lloyd could easily gross £2,000 annually from his farms. Ranking among the true elite of Eastern Shore society, Lloyd demonstrated that the diversified farming practiced south of the Chester River—with more emphasis on corn and tobacco than on wheat—could be extremely profitable for large slave owners.[22]

One cannot be sure how typical the experiences of Edward Lloyd, Landon Carter, Robert Goldsborough, and Edward Lloyd IV were. Some tentative conclusions, however, can be drawn about the commitment of large slave owners to diversified agriculture. These slave owners probably turned to wheat and corn as new market crops before the 1740s. Following the decision to diversify, agricultural income per field hand rose to around £14 a year and went as high as £25. While tobacco remained a significant cash crop on each of the four farms, occasionally accounting for more than a third of the total income, workers generally produced less than field hands had in the seventeenth and early eighteenth centuries. As large slave owners introduced grains on their farms, they generally, but not always, planted smaller tobacco crops. Planters most likely reduced the size of their tobacco crops in order to save soil fertility and establish a three-crop rotation system. The labor requirement for grains does not seem to have necessitated cutting back the amount of tobacco planted. If the same processes were at work among the less wealthy neighbors of these large slave owners, evidence of the extent of diversification on small farms should have been left in the crop reports in Eastern Shore inventories.

These reports show that diversification did not always entail smaller tobacco crops. In Table 24, nonslave farms, committed

22. Edward Lloyd Plantation Books, Lloyd Collection, MS 2001, MHS.

to wheat, tobacco, and mixed farming, have been compared. In Talbot, families that grew both wheat and tobacco averaged better tobacco yields than those that specialized in tobacco. Still, as late as the 1760s, most small farmers had not turned to wheat. In Kent, in contrast, small farmers shifted away from tobacco. Rather than strike a balance between the new and the old staple, they often abandoned tobacco completely.[23]

The failure of small farmers in Talbot to embrace wheat production wholeheartedly put them behind their contemporaries in Kent in the 1740s and left them there in the 1760s. Nevertheless, in both counties, gross agricultural income on small farms rose substantially. In Talbot, income went up from £12.8 to £20.3, a rise of almost 60 percent. In Kent, average yearly income for nonslaveholders climbed from £16.9 to £24.1, a jump of over 40 percent. Kent farmers had boosted their incomes by limiting tobacco production and harvesting larger wheat crops. In the early 1770s, after the shift to wheat was well under way, they reaped an additional benefit from their decision because Mediterranean demand pushed local grain prices to extraordinary levels. In Talbot, farmers brought in smaller tobacco crops in the 1760s than they had in the 1740s, but rising prices allowed them to gross about the same amount from tobacco in the later period as they had in the former. At the same time, they increased their total farm income by growing a good deal more corn and a little more wheat.[24]

The spread of grain culture occurred perhaps even more rapidly among the slave owners than it did among small farmers. In Talbot between the 1740s and the 1760s, the percentage of slave owners who raised significant quantities of wheat increased steadily, as did the average wheat output on those farms. The new interest in wheat did not lead to an abandonment of tobacco

23. Except as noted, the following discussion is based on crop reports in the Inventories, MHR. Some of the data discussed in this section are presented in Tables 24 and 25 and Graph 9.
24. The analysis in this paragraph uses crop and price data from the periods 1740–45 and 1763–72. The income figures for the two periods reflect a substantial rise in tobacco prices in both counties and a large jump in Kent wheat prices. In Talbot, two-thirds of the increase in income was attributable to a new crop mix and one-third to higher prices. In Kent, higher prices and a new crop mix contributed equally to the increase in income.

production, but wheat farming did bring with it significantly smaller tobacco crops (see in Table 25 the output figures and the statistics on the relative number of farms being used for wheat and tobacco production). As a result, by the 1760s, the typical Talbot slave owner received roughly equal amounts of income from the three major market crops—corn, wheat, and tobacco (see Graph 9). In Kent, on the other hand, not only did tobacco production decline markedly on those farms that continued to be used for tobacco as well as for wheat, but, by the 1760s, most slave owners stopped marketing the traditional staple. In the decade before the American Revolution, almost four-fifths of the gross agricultural income that slave owners in Kent received came from wheat and most of the remainder depended on the sale of corn.[25]

Strikingly, slave owners in Talbot and Kent, while changing their farming practices in different ways, benefited equally in terms of income. From the 1740s to the 1760s, gross income per field hand rose from £9.2 to £16.7 in Talbot; in Kent the increase was from £10.8 to £16.1 With prices favoring more emphasis on tobacco in Talbot and on wheat in Kent, quite different crop mixes produced similar incomes in the two counties.[26]

The largest slave owners on the Eastern Shore, chiefly members of the merchant-planter class, shifted away from tobacco at a different rate than most of their contemporaries. In Talbot they lagged behind; in Kent they took the lead. Despite the fact that in Talbot tobacco output per worker on the largest plantations was only modest, few merchant-planters were inclined to reduce the land or labor they devoted to the crop. In Kent, on the other hand, the largest slave owners were among the first to diversify, and at least in the 1740s, they received higher gross returns, £18.3 per laborer, than any other farmers.[27]

The picture taken from all of these accounts—those of family farmers as well as of merchant-planters—is of a gradual transition to grain cultivation and a steady rise in income. Initially, diversification could occur without the need for a choice be-

25. Inventories, MHR.
26. Ibid. See note 24 above and prices in the Appendix.
27. Eleven estate inventories of large Talbot County planters and four of wealthy Kent planters survive from the 1740–45 and 1763–72 periods.

Table 25. Output of tobacco and wheat per field hand on
Talbot and Kent farms of slave owners, 1740s and 1760s

	1740s		1760s	
	Number of farms*	Output	Number of farms*	Output
Talbot County				
Tobacco (pounds)	59	1,520	22	880
Wheat (bushels)	12	13	18	54
Number of farms in sample	59	–	22	–
Kent County				
Tobacco (pounds)	38	1,540	16	530
Wheat (bushels)	25	40	53	93
Number of farms in sample	40	–	55	–

*Farms were excluded when total output came to less than 200 pounds of tobacco or 30 bushels of wheat. For example, of the 59 farms in the Talbot inventories from the 1740s, only 12 listed wheat crops of over 30 bushels. On these 12 farms, output per worker averaged 13 bushels. The output figures given here are thus higher than averages for all farms listed elsewhere in this study. The calculation of output per field hand was made by the method described in Table 7. Only farms with fewer than ten field hands were considered.
SOURCE: Inventories, MHR.

tween tobacco and wheat because the intense but brief periods of fieldwork required to sow wheat in the fall and harvest it in the spring left ample time to tend a tobacco crop. Although the returns per laborer were higher for the new staple than for the old, planters could not keep their field hands busy year round without raising more than one crop. Hence as local merchants and Philadelphia traders created marketing networks for Eastern Shore grains, landowners diversified production. Many farmers, however, went further. Especially in Kent, but eventually in Queen Anne's and Talbot as well, farmers shifted from tobacco to grain, and with this decision left behind the agricultural practices that for almost a century had dominated the Eastern Shore economy.[28]

28. Wheat brought considerably better returns per worker than tobacco. Output per field hand in a good crop year averaged around 100 bushels of wheat and 1,600 pounds of tobacco. In 1760s Kent prices, the wheat was worth 1.7 times as much as the tobacco. Relative returns to land are discussed in the text below.

Graph 9. Percentage of income attributable to the three major cash crops on the farms of slave owners in Talbot and Kent counties, 1740s and 1760s

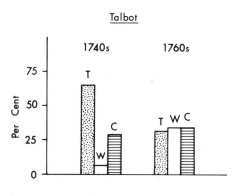

Talbot

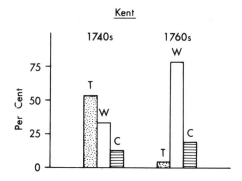

Kent

Note: T = tobacco; W = wheat; C = corn. Farms with more than ten field hands have been excluded.
SOURCE: Inventories, MHR.

We are thus left with two questions: Why was tobacco eventually abandoned? And why first in Kent? To restate the first of these questions: Why, when field hands had sufficient time to tend both wheat and tobacco, did farmers elect to use their laborers solely to raise grains? If labor constraints did not force the decision on Eastern Shore farmers, perhaps the land requirements did.

Over the short run, tobacco needed far less land than wheat: two or three acres per worker per year compared to thirteen to eighteen acres. But when crop-rotation practices are taken into account, the picture changes. If a planter wished to maintain soil fertility, then, after three years of planting tobacco on a plot, the land had to be rested about twenty years. In other words, for each eighth of an acre under production, seven-eighths of an acre had to be held in fallow. With wheat, a much shorter rotation was customarily used, with two harvests of winter wheat followed by one season in fallow. For wheat, then, one-third of an acre was rested for each two-thirds cropped.[29]

Eastern Shore farmers, in essence, balanced the returns to one-eighth of an acre of relatively fertile tobacco land against those to two-thirds of an acre of somewhat depleted wheat land. If tobacco yields were fairly high, around 500 pounds per acre, and wheat yields correspondingly low, about 6 bushels an acre, the returns in 1760s prices were nonetheless 50 percent better for wheat than for tobacco. If wheat yields reached 8 bushels per acre, still not a very impressive figure, returns to land for grain were twice those for tobacco.[30]

Over the course of the eighteenth century, the higher returns to land that wheat gave Eastern Shore farmers took on added importance. Both in absolute terms and relative to other production costs, land prices rose continuously. Planters must have found it increasingly difficult to let tobacco land lie fallow twenty years given the promise of quick wheat profits. The options were to replant tobacco land after shorter rest periods and accept progressively lower yields or to cut back the fallow period even more, hire labor, and convert tobacco pasture to wheat land. By employing landless poor whites or their neighbors' slaves, some

29. On crop yields and rotation practices, see John Beale Bordley, *A Summary View of the Course of Crops and the Husbandry of England and America; with a Comparison of Their Products, and a System of Improved Courses, Proposed for Farms in America* (Philadelphia, 1784), and *Essays and Notes on Husbandry and Rural Affairs* (Philadelphia, 1801); Carl Raymond Woodward, *Ploughs and Politics: Charles Read of New Jersey and His Notes on Agriculture, 1715–1774* (New Brunswick, N.J., 1941); and William Tatham, *An Historical and Practical Essay on the Culture and Commerce of Tobacco* (London, 1800). An excellent summary of the literature is contained in Stiverson, *Poverty in a Land of Plenty*, pp. 85–103. Where possible, I checked the information in these accounts against reports in Virginia plantation diaries.

30. This calculation assumes wheat was at 44 pence per bushel and tobacco at 1.85 pence per pound.

farmers acquired the harvest labor they needed and made the transition to a new staple crop.[31]

Did maximization of wheat production leave any land for tobacco? A single worker supporting two dependents could handle about 15 acres of winter wheat; he had to plant another 4 acres of corn for food, set aside a minimum of 3 acres for the homestead, garden, and orchard, and leave about 9.5 acres in pasture, for a total of 31.5 acres. If he had a 50-acre farm and managed it with extreme care, he had left 18.5 acres for tobacco (2.2 in crop, the rest in fallow). Such a farm could produce 90 bushels of wheat, 48 bushels of corn, 1,110 pounds of tobacco, and some fruits and vegetables—about what small farms in Talbot did produce. In other words, as long as the land–labor ratio remained at about 40:1 or above, maximization of wheat production left land for tobacco. The hiring of labor allowed individual proprietors to shift to wheat, especially in Kent, where marketing the crop was easy, but left an aggregate surplus of land on which some tobacco could be produced.[32]

Yet however feasible farmers found it to persist as tobacco planters, there were compelling reasons to shift their remaining land out of the traditional staple. Devoting this land to wheat, even if it could not increase the number of acres cultivated (because of the labor constraint), could increase the fallow period and raise yields. With fields worn out by constant planting and too extensive to fertilize easily, farmers must have found this an attractive method to improve soil quality and crop output. Perhaps more important, they could shift tobacco land to corn and thereby both expand their marketable grain crop and ensure themselves a food supply if the harvest fell short of expecta-

---

31. See chap. 5 for a discussion of land and labor costs. On hired labor, see Carville V. Earle, "A Staple Interpretation of Slavery and Free Labor," *Geographical Review* 68 (1978): 51–65. On the Eastern Shore, the use of hired labor to harvest wheat became important after the Revolution and was more a consequence than a cause of the shift to wheat.

32. For land use, see note 29. Without knowing more about the amount of land on the Eastern Shore actually suitable for cultivation, it is impossible to calculate the land–labor ratio exactly. In the 1770s, the ratio was no higher than 50:1 (acres/taxable). For a stimulating discussion of the relationship between corn and cotton farming in the antebellum South, see Gavin Wright, *The Political Economy of the Cotton South: Households, Markets, and Wealth in the Nineteenth Century* (New York, 1978), pp. 43–88.

tions. In the end, while the records simply do not allow us to recapture the entire story, it was most likely this dual pressure from corn and wheat that drove tobacco from the Eastern Shore.

This leaves only the question of why tobacco planting disappeared sooner in Kent. Kent had been more slowly settled and was more sparsely populated than Talbot. If land constraints had been the only factor affecting the decision to abandon tobacco, Kent farmers would not have shifted to wheat so early. In Kent, however, wheat brought a better price. Proximity to Philadelphia put Kent farmers in contact with grain merchants and lowered the cost of getting the crop to market. The development of grain marketing in Kent and the persistence of the tobacco trade in Talbot form the final chapter in the story of diversification on the Eastern Shore.[33]

THE CHANGING COMMERCIAL SECTOR OF THE EASTERN SHORE ECONOMY

As long as most agricultural activity on the Eastern Shore remained related to tobacco production, most local commercial activity was dependent on the development of personal and business connections between wealthy planters and London tobacco merchants. The transformation of the agricultural sector of the Eastern Shore's rural market economy, however, both depended on and created changes in the organization of commerce.

To the south, in Talbot County, the story centered on the rise of Oxford. Innkeepers had plied their trade on the eventual site of the town since the 1670s, but not until the mid-1690s, when the royal government temporarily renamed the location Williamstadt and designated it an official port of entry for the Eastern Shore, did Oxford acquire a permanent if small popula-

33. See the Appendix for prices. Three factors affected the price differential between Kent and Talbot: transport costs, the organization of the market, and the quality of wheat (soil). Transport costs are carefully discussed in Earle and Hoffman, "Staple Crops and Urban Development." Below I have emphasized market organization, but I assume that the proximity of Kent to Philadelphia was the most important factor in cutting costs. Soil conditions also mattered. As noted in chap. 2, there was a greater percentage of high-quality wheat acreage in Kent than in Talbot or Queen Anne's.

tion of merchants and artisans. For almost three decades, little changed in the community. As the tempo of the Atlantic tobacco trade picked up, however, the town acquired a limited urban character. The major changes dated from the early 1720s, when Anthony and Thomas Richardson and Samuel Chamberlaine arrived to establish stores for Liverpool merchants Foster Cunliffe and Richard Gildart. Three local retailers of considerable wealth, Benjamin Pemberton, Robert Ungle, and Robert Grundy, also located in the town, handling consignment trade for London merchants. By the 1730s, Oxford could claim ten to twelve permanent homes and shops, several warehouses, three taverns, a ferry, a windmill, and a marketplace, ranking it among the more prominent towns in the northern Chesapeake. Developed lots sold for over 4,000 pounds of tobacco (approximately £25), somewhat more than the cost of a small farm. Then Robert Morris arrived. Morris or a relative had served as a factor for Thomas Johnson of Liverpool during the second decade of the eighteenth century, but had not stayed long in Talbot County. Around 1735 he returned, this time as an agent for Cunliffe, and over the next fifteen years he made Oxford the center of a prosperous trade between Talbot County and Liverpool.[34]

Liverpool tobacco merchants deserved substantial credit for Oxford's prosperity between the 1720s and 1750s. Cunliffe's and Gildart's ships carried off between a third and half of Talbot's tobacco each year, and the ongoing competition in Talbot between their factors and London shippers meant that local tobacco planters profited more than farmers to the north did from the generally improved tobacco prices of the mid-eighteenth

34. On Chamberlaine, see Oswald Tilghman, *History of Talbot County, Maryland, 1661–1861*, 2 vols. (Baltimore, 1915), vol. 1, pp. 531–552. On Richardson, consult Maryland Wills, vol. 21, p. 306; vol. 22, pp. 12, 361, MHR. For the arrival of these factors, see Talbot County Land Records, PF no. 13, pp. 68, 81–85, 245, MHR. Anthony Richardson's partner was Anthony Bacon, whose career has been described in Louis Namier, "Anthony Bacon, M.P.," *Journal of Economic and Business History* 2 (1929–30): 20–70. Chamberlaine's continuing interest in Oxford is discussed in a legal document in the Chamberlaine collection, Gift Collection, G 801, MHR. The settlement of local merchants in Oxford can be traced through the Talbot County Land Records and the Maryland Wills, MHR. For Robert Morris, see the Robert Morris Ledger Book, MHR; Henry Callister Papers, MHS; Oxford Port of Entry Records, MHR; Tilghman, *History of Talbot County*, vol. 1, pp. 66–83; and Tyler, "Foster Cunliffe and Sons."

century. The presence at one time or another of Chamberlaine, the Richardsons, Morris, and at least half a dozen other
Liverpool factors at Oxford forced London traders to rely on
such local merchants as Grundy, Ungle, and Pemberton to ex-
pedite the tobacco business. Morris, in turn, secured Liverpool's position in Talbot by developing a network of stores and
warehouses linked together by sloops that transferred tobacco
from the Wye, St. Michael's, and Great Choptank to Oxford. If
competition made trade more profitable for the planter, it also
worked a major reorganization of the credit structure by giving
small planters a real choice in deciding to turn to the great
merchant-planters, such as Richard Bennett, George Robins,
and Edward Lloyd III, who worked in conjunction with London
consignment merchants, or to the resident factors for Cunliffe
and Gildart. As long as the Liverpool trade continued, grain
production was discouraged and tobacco remained the chief
staple in Talbot's agricultural economy.[35]

Even so, during the middle decades of the eighteenth century
Oxford became a grain port. With warehouses and credit available in the town, merchants could easily store cargoes of grain
for New England shippers. Attracting these shippers was the
first step in connecting Talbot County with distant markets for
corn and wheat. On and off, of course, the great planters built
their own vessels, but only Richard Bennett remained active year
after year in trade with New England and the West Indies. But
seven of the eighteen vessels that cleared Oxford in 1731 belonged to Talbot or Queen Anne's residents, only four of the
twenty-three in 1740, and only five of forty-two in 1760—all not
unusual years. As important as the ownership of coastal vessels
was to the business of Eastern Shore merchant-planters, the sum
total of trading activity conducted by these local shippers was of
limited consequence in expanding grain production. The most
significant contribution Talbot merchants made to the development of the grain economy was their involvement in the growth
of Oxford. As the port grew, Oxford provided an ever more

35. For trade at Oxford, see the sources listed in note 34 above. Credit relationships were determined from the Inventories, MHR.

convenient turnaround point for sloops coming south from Boston, Salem, and Newport in search of corn, wheat, and flour.[36]

Oxford's commercial character changed in the 1760s. During the previous decade, Cunliffe's and Gildart's firms had gradually pulled out, motivated by an overextension of credit during the 1740s and excessive bad debts, and by Robert Morris's death (he was killed by the wadding fired from a ship's cannon during a ceremony in his honor) and the incompetence of his successor. As Liverpool capital was withdrawn and grain prices soared in the 1760s, first local planters and then Glasgow, Philadelphia, and London merchants moved in, devoting energy and money to both tobacco and grains. In the early 1760s, local merchant-planter families (the Lloyds, Skinners, Goldsboroughs, Dickinsons, Ennalls, and Chamberlaines) and several resident merchants (James Seth, Henry Costin, Joshua Clark, and Thomas Noel) made numerous ventures into West Indian commerce. But the Glasgow firm of Spiers, French, Mackie and Company and Philadelphia merchants opened trade with Southern Europe, and except for Edward Lloyd IV, who engaged in direct trade with both England and Portugal, no Talbot merchants put their money into large-scale, long-haul endeavors. If the ultimate result, in the early 1770s, of the influx of outside shippers and capital was to check the development of local trade, the renewed competition for both grains and tobacco among Philadelphia, London, and Glasgow shippers put Oxford merchants in an enviable position and improved the economic security and clout of the Talbot farmer who had diversified.[37]

To the north, Chestertown served Kent and Queen Anne's counties. Begun about 1726 on a plot of farmland along the northern bank of the Chester River, the port continued to grow until the American Revolution. By 1750 the town had over a hundred inhabitants, and among the owners of town lots could be counted eighteen merchants and factors, twenty-three artisans, ten self-styled gentlemen, nine professional people (doctors and lawyers), ten single women, and three innkeepers. By

36. Oxford Port of Entry Records, MHR and MHS.
37. Ibid. On Morris, see Tilghman, *History of Talbot County,* vol. 1, pp. 66–83.

1770 the population had doubled, and stately homes, busy stores and taverns, and numerous warehouses crowded the waterfront.[38]

The town grew step by step with the grain trade. Unlike the situation in Talbot County, little competition developed between London and the outports for the tobacco of the northern Chesapeake, and long after London merchants had modified their tactics elsewhere, they still conducted a river trade on the Chester, dealing on shipboard with planters and taking crops on consignment. The names that dominate the history of the tobacco business on the Chester—John Falconer, John Hyde, and Robert Crookshanks in the early part of the century, John Hanbury, James Buchanan, and William Anderson later— almost all came from the London merchant elite. The year-to-year movement of freight rates left little doubt that even on those rare occasions when Bristol and Bideford merchantmen ventured north of Kent Island, the tobacco trade offered planters in Kent and Queen Anne's counties little bargaining room and left them dependent on English merchants whose financial assets dwarfed those of a typical planter. The rise of Chestertown as a grain port consequently helped both to reorganize the way commerce was conducted on the northern Eastern Shore and to alter local reliance on English credit. Kent farmers never had the option Talbot planters had, of shifting trade at will between outport factors and local agents of London firms. For the farmers who lived along the Chester, the grain trade provided an answer to the insecurity and dependence associated with the traditional staple.[39]

About mid-century, the decline of the tobacco trade at Chestertown and in the Chester River region began. In the earliest settled parts of Kent County, along the bay, the trade held its own in the 1750s, and then, after the boom years 1760–61, ta-

38. Information on residency in Chestertown may be found in the Kent County Land Records, MHR. Also consult the Ringgold letters in the Galloway Papers, Library of Congress, Washington, D.C., and John W. Reps, *Tidewater Towns: City Planning in Colonial Virginia and Maryland* (Charlottesville, Va., 1972).

39. On Chestertown trade, see the Chestertown trade records in the Annapolis Port of Entry Records, MHS; Kent County Tobacco Inspection Records, 1749–68, MHR; and the freight rate listings found throughout the Kent County Land Records, MHR. See also Earle and Hoffman, "Staple Crops and Urban Development."

pered off probably 20 percent or more during the next decade. In the inland areas, whose rapid population growth increasingly provided the economic stimulus for Chestertown and the northern Eastern Shore, some 350 hogsheads of tobacco were cleared during the boom in 1752 (about one-quarter of all the tobacco shipped from Kent County), only 240 hogsheads during 1760, the next boom year, and fewer than 50 hogsheads annually after the middle of the decade. As Chestertown's relative position in the tobacco trade deteriorated, its position in the grain trade pulled even with that of Oxford, surpassed Oxford's in 1769, and presented a challenge to Annapolis by 1774.[40]

Chestertown's grain trade grew under the auspices of local merchants. By their success in the 1760s in extending credit freely, building their own sloops and ships, opening the trade route to Southern Europe, and even dealing in tobacco and slaves, Thomas Smyth, Emory Sudler, Thomas and William Ringgold, and William Flubey captured trade that had previously gone to Annapolis and gave small farmers new markets for their produce. Thomas Ringgold's 130-ton *Chester,* built in 1766, and Smyth and Sudler's 160-ton *Friendship,* completed a year later, each with a carrying capacity of over 7,000 bushels of wheat, were used extensively in commerce with Spain and Portugal, generally making two voyages a year in the late 1760s to Cadiz or Lisbon. Smaller vessels belonging to James and Joseph Hynson, Samuel Wallis, and Richard and Thomas Gresham returned yearly to the Caribbean with cargoes of corn and flour.[41]

As Chestertown's commercial horizons extended in the early 1770s, the virtual monopoly that local shippers enjoyed on the port's economic life in the 1760s disappeared. Philadelphia firms made the chief inroads, taking control of most of the large-scale, long-distance trade in wheat and leaving Chestertown's merchants, the Ringgolds, Smyth, Sudler, and Flubey, firmly in control of the regional credit structure and active as economic mediators between the farming population and the major credit suppliers in Philadelphia. Ironically, the depen-

40. Kent County Tobacco Inspection Records, 1749–68, MHS.
41. Chestertown trade records in the Annapolis Port of Entry Records, MHS; Inventories, MHR.

dence of the planters on London tobacco merchants had simply been exchanged for dependence on Philadelphia merchants, and the role of the great merchant-planters as middlemen in the tobacco trade had been taken in the grain trade by Chestertown merchants. After the Revolutionary War, Chestertown would become little more than a pawn in the struggle between upstart Baltimore and established Philadelphia for control of the Delmarva Peninsula.[42]

Eastern Shore merchants and, to a greater extent, Pennsylvania and New England shippers created the marketing arrangements that brought Talbot, Kent, and Queen Anne's farmers into the Atlantic grain economy. By seizing opportunity, they helped to direct change. Their role, while not a major factor in bringing diversified agriculture to the region, played a necessary part in the process of economic transformation. In particular, their activities both reflect and help to explain the dominance of wheat farming in Kent and the persistence of tobacco planting in Talbot. While the cost factor in getting wheat from the Eastern Shore to Philadelphia best accounts for the higher prices in Kent than in Talbot, the work of Liverpool merchants in creating an efficient, competitive market for tobacco in Talbot may have delayed the movement toward a wheat economy in the Great Choptank region, and the growth of Chestertown may have sped the spread of wheat cultivation to the north.

During the lifetimes of two generations, Eastern Shore planters diversified agricultural production; within one more generation, most planters became wheat farmers. In 1700 a planter's son could expect to spend his life producing tobacco for European consumers. By 1760 the balance of economic activity had shifted toward supplying food for other colonies and Southern Europe. Two factors underlay the region's economic transformation: the first was the expansion of the Atlantic grain market; the second, the growth of population. The expansion of the

42. For a general discussion, look at Hoffman, *Spirit of Dissension,* and Diane Lindstrom, *Economic Change in the Philadelphia Region, 1810–1850* (New York, 1977).

grain market gave planters the opportunity to end their dependence on a single cash crop and subsequently controlled their decision to shift to wheat. The growth of population forced them to make that decision, forced them to choose whether to use their land for diversified agriculture or wheat production.

Tobacco planting left sufficient time to sow and harvest wheat. Nothing kept farmers, as long as they had ample land, from growing both tobacco and grains. Through the mid-eighteenth century, the land–labor ratio remained high enough so that farmers could diversify easily. Thus when Philadelphia merchants, who needed grains to supply the expanding West Indies and New England markets, began turning to the Eastern Shore, local farmers responded by growing more corn and wheat. The only cost was in terms of leisure: planters had to force themselves and their slaves to work harder, but, of course, whites benefited accordingly in productivity and profit. As the amount of land available for each laborer diminished because of population growth, a point was eventually reached where the decision to grow one market crop meant that production of the other had to be cut back. Faced with this dilemma, most planters switched to the crop that brought the greatest profit—wheat. Wheat maintained its advantage over tobacco, despite the improvement of the tobacco market, because of the rapid growth of Southern European demand for food. For individual families, the splitting of an estate among children, the addition of a slave, or a bad year for tobacco may have triggered the decision about land use. For the society as a whole, population pressure and the expansion of the Atlantic grain trade were the critical factors. By the 1770s the Eastern Shore had become part of the rich agricultural hinterland that spread out from Philadelphia across the Delmarva Peninsula.

Conclusion

In the years before the American Revolution, spacious plantation homes along the bayside necks in Talbot, Kent, and Queen Anne's provided eloquent testimony to what many white families had acquired after one hundred years of English settlement on the Eastern Shore. Neatly bricked walls, well-proportioned architecture, and carefully designed interiors distinguished these dwelling places. Curtains hung behind glass windows; silverware was set on tables crafted in England. In adjacent kitchens, smokehouses, and grinding mills, food was stored and prepared. White owners depended on black slaves to do the tiring fieldwork, menial household jobs, and skilled artisanal tasks. Land was properly fenced; tobacco, wheat, and corn crops were periodically rotated; livestock was attentively managed; and orchards and gardens were regularly tended. Inland were smaller farms, as often tenancies as not, somewhat fewer slaves, and more wheat fields than tobacco plots. The mix of livestock and arable husbandry was similar to that on the bayside, and the households, although not so substantial, showed conspicuous signs of affluence. Only well into the backcountry, beyond the Chester and Great Choptank, did frontier conditions exist. There less well-rooted settlers lived in crude log houses, practiced self-sufficiency farming, and still had abundant uncleared land.[1]

The prosperity, inequality, and geographic mobility evident

1. Talbot and Kent County Land Conveyances, Maryland Inventories, the Assessment of 1783, Kent County Guardian Bonds, MHR.

on the Eastern Shore in the 1770s were the products of a history that began in seventeenth-century rural England. The purpose of this study has been to explore that history and to place the process of development, and the particular role of the market in shaping life in Talbot, Queen Anne's, and Kent, in a broader colonial context.

Historians have taken three distinct but related approaches in their efforts to explain colonial development. One approach focuses on the background of the immigrants and emphasizes cultural and structural continuities in the transfer of society from Old World to New. A second concentrates on demographic and generational change and analyzes how such factors as life expectancy, family size, and the land–labor ratio affected colonial society. And a third approach begins with the economy and explores the relationship of the market to the pace of growth and the pattern of development. Each approach is perhaps more applicable to some colonies than others. The continuity of Old World values and behavior seems more evident in the English settlement of Pennsylvania than in the response of adventurers to the physical environment in the Caribbean; and the emphasis on generational change perhaps captures more correctly the essence of the development of New England towns than it describes life in the southern staple colonies. Yet each of these themes has something to tell us about the development of society on Maryland's Eastern Shore.[2]

An emphasis on the character of the original migration is particularly valuable in distinguishing the experiences of settlers in New England and the Chesapeake. The first English people to arrive in Massachusetts were a relatively homogeneous lot. Most came with their families and shared feelings of duty and

---

2. See, for example, the analysis in Philip J. Greven, Jr., *Four Generations: Population, Land, and Family in Colonial Andover, Massachusetts* (Ithaca, N.Y., 1970); James T. Lemon, *The Best Poor Man's Country: A Geographical Study of Early Southeastern Pennsylvania* (Baltimore, 1972); and Richard S. Dunn, *Sugar and Slaves: The Rise of the Planter Class in the English West Indies, 1624–1713* (Chapel Hill, N.C., 1972). Three works on early modern Europe that explicitly deal with the distinctions mentioned in the text are J. D. Chambers, *Population, Economy, and Society in Pre-Industrial England* (London, 1972); Jan de Vries, *The Dutch Rural Economy in the Golden Age, 1500–1700* (New Haven, 1974); and Robert Brenner, "Agrarian Class Structure and Economic Development in Pre-Industrial Europe," *Past & Present*, no. 70 (1976), pp. 30–75.

love toward kin; most were neither wealthy not impoverished. They held the same intense Puritan beliefs and felt the same strong sense of communal obligation. None of these traits was entirely lacking from the immigrant groups that settled the Chesapeake, but there diversity prevailed. Some came as freemen; others were dependent. Some came with wealth and connections; others were penniless and friendless. Puritans came, but so did Anglicans, Catholics, and Quakers. English people originally took up most of the land, but they brought with them Irish servants and African slaves. Migration itself thus laid the foundation for the social stratification and pluralistic culture that distinguished the Chesapeake from New England.[3]

Yet as diverse as these settlers were, at least the English people among them shared a culture that the spread of a market economy had already affected. They lived in an age during which commercial agriculture had encroached on the domain of the rural husbandman, and they left a society in which the circulation of money, the expansion of credit, the growth of trade, and the improvement of farming had removed traditional restraints from individual economic initiative. Familiarity with a market economy did not so much predispose them to a particular way of life as it left them free to change as they confronted new conditions in a new world.[4]

One set of conditions, emphasized in the demographic approach to colonial development, that shaped the lives of English settlers grew out of the relationship of population, land, and family. In any community where population growth occurred on

3. On New England, see Kenneth A. Lockridge, *A New England Town: The First Hundred Years, Dedham, Massachusetts, 1636–1736* (New York, 1970); on the Chesapeake, the best description of the settlement process is in the classic work of Wesley Frank Craven, *The Southern Colonies in the Seventeenth Century, 1607–1689*, 2d ed. (Baton Rouge, 1970).

4. Compare Joyce Oldham Appleby, *Economic Thought and Ideology in Seventeenth-Century England* (Princeton, 1978), pp. 129–157, 242–279; and Edmund S. Morgan, *American Slavery, American Freedom: The Ordeal of Colonial Virginia* (New York, 1975), pp. 44–70. Morgan does not follow other historians in tracing attitudes about labor to the Puritan sense of calling and the Protestant work ethic. Rather than work hard, white Virginians, Morgan argues, often refused to work at all; rather than sustain themselves for the glory of their God, they accumulated as much as possible for their own welfare. To accumulate without working, they brutalized the poor whites, Virginia Indians, and African slaves.

a limited supply of land, family size and inheritance practices decisively affected the social structure through their effect on property distribution. In large families, if estates were divided relatively equally, children began their careers with a small fraction of the property their parents had had. In small families, or in cases where primogeniture was practiced, landholdings were passed on virtually intact from generation to generation. The more family size and inheritance procedures varied within a society, the more extensive the inequality that resulted from estate divisions. At the same time, population growth, regardless of the way one generation redistributed its property to the next, forced down the land–labor ratio. A community had to farm a higher percentage of its land, and after most land was in production, then had to crop its acreage more intensively. In the European version of this process, population pressure often strained resources beyond the breaking point and led to decline in productivity, food shortages, and ultimately famine or plague. In the colonies, children lost the guarantee that they would inherit enough land on which to live, kinship bonds between generations weakened, and the young left.[5]

Colonial development was also shaped by the involvement of immigrants in commercial agriculture and Atlantic trade. In each colony, settlers' response to the Atlantic market depended on the climate and soil conditions they faced and the resources they found at hand. Whatever crops they grew or activities they engaged in, the initiation of trade generally created a boom economy, but the sequence that inevitably followed—rising production, falling prices, and increasing costs—slowed the pace of growth and accelerated the movement toward an unequal and in some places brutal social order. As growth gave way to stagnation, many settlers shifted from commercial agriculture to subsistence farming or left. In some cases, little economic improve-

5. In addition to the works cited in note 2, I found especially beneficial Robert Gallman's "Family Size, Inheritance Systems, and the Distribution of Land in Early Colonial North Carolina," unpublished paper presented to the 1979 Organization of American Historians convention, and P. M. G. Harris's "Integrating Interpretations of Local and Regionwide Change in the Study of Economic Development and Demographic Growth in the Colonial Chesapeake, 1630–1775," *Working Papers from the Regional Economic History Research Center* 1, no. 3 (1978): 35–72.

ment occurred over the remainder of the colonial era. In other cases, the growth of demand for the traditional staple or a new market crop revitalized the commercial economy. When prosperity returned to the society, however, the benefits were not shared as widely as they had been in the earlier boom era.[6]

Neither market nor demographic conditions erased very quickly the differences that initially existed between the close-knit, homogeneous New England communities of husbandmen and that diverse lot of settlers who spread out along the coastline and river banks of Maryland's Eastern Shore and went to work making money from tobacco. New England's development was not, however, unaffected by the market. A substantial number of merchants made their living from the fisheries off Newfoundland and from the fur- and timber-rich forests of western Massachusetts and the Maine coast. Along the Connecticut River, farmers sold surplus flour and meat to shippers engaged in provisioning West Indian planters. But except for the inhabitants of the seaports and the Connecticut Valley, New Englanders had far less contact with Atlantic trade than did residents of the Eastern Shore. The pace and pattern of development depended less on the market in New England than in Talbot and Kent, and the process of social stratification occurred more slowly. In rural Massachusetts towns, the cost of land was not pushed up rapidly (as on the Eastern Shore) by its potential for market production. Instead, early marriages, long life expectancy, and large families gradually made it more difficult for each generation to provide sufficient land for the next. These same demographic conditions tended slowly to create an ever wider range in the amount of property held by various members of the community. Eventually, a point was reached where children no longer had the guarantee that their inheritance would

6. Gary M. Walton and James F. Shepherd, *Shipping, Maritime Trade, and the Economic Development of Colonial North America* (Cambridge, England, 1972), presents a concise, theoretical statement on the role of commerce in colonial economic growth. Harold A. Innis, in *The Fur Trade in Canada: An Introduction to Canadian Economic History,* rev. ed. (Toronto, 1956), was the first to outline carefully the way colonial staple economies operated, but see the arresting critique in Calvin Martin's *Keepers of the Game: Indian–Animal Relationships and the Fur Trade* (Berkeley, 1978).

be enough to live on, and in many cases, they had no choice but to leave the family and community of their birth. The step-by-step spread of the market inland and the slow commercialization of agricultural life late in the colonial era further eroded the homogeneity and stability that had previously characterized New England towns. As a result, by the 1760s rural New Englanders ended up facing a social situation in some ways like that in the northern Chesapeake.[7]

In the Caribbean, the great profitability of sugar production, the relative scarcity of land, and the deadliness of the disease environment created a way of life that was a warped reflection of the way people lived on the Eastern Shore. Those whites who settled early and survived rose rapidly once sugar cultivation began. Using black slaves as well as white servants, planters amassed enormous wealth, and with this wealth bought out smaller landowners. Soaring land values choked off opportunity abruptly. The end of opportunity stopped the immigration of English servants; unhealthy living conditions discouraged women from coming. The first problem planters solved by increasing their importation of slaves; the second problem they never really did solve. The result was that blacks, despite the fact that planters literally worked them to death, outnumbered whites, and men outnumbered women. Family life was limited, and children born in the West Indies often did not reach adulthood. In Barbados, the most prosperous seventeenth-century Caribbean island, the sugar boom finally ended in the 1680s. Soil exhaustion pushed costs up enough and rising production forced prices down enough to begin an exodus of planters to the

7. The best discussion of New England commerce remains Bernard Bailyn's *New England Merchants in the Seventeenth Century* (Cambridge, Mass., 1955). For the population model of New England development, see Greven, *Four Generations,* and Daniel Scott Smith, "Parental Power and Marriage Patterns: An Analysis of Historical Trends in Hingham, Massachusetts," *Journal of Marriage and the Family* 35 (1973): 419–428. Both of these works indicate that before population pressure led to emigration, average age of first marriage rose. On the deepening social crisis in colonial New England, compare Michael Zuckerman, *Peaceable Kingdoms: New England Towns in the Eighteenth Century* (New York, 1970), and Robert A. Gross, *The Minutemen and Their World* (New York, 1976), pp. 68–108 and notes 17 (p. 209), 37 (p. 214), and 38 (p. 215).

mainland colonies. In the eighteenth century, however, the growing demand for sugar (for use with tea) and the development of sugar plantations in the vast, previously unexploited interior of Jamaica brought new riches to West Indian planters.[8]

There is, of course, a parallel in the pattern of boom, stagnation, and revitalization in the West Indies and on Maryland's Eastern Shore. Moreover, with the rise of Talbot's merchant-planters and the spread of slavery in the region, Eastern Shore society moved a little closer to the social order in the plantation colonies to the south. But here the similarities ended. Life in the Caribbean was harsher (through the 1840s there was an excess of deaths over births among Jamaican slaves), the wealth of the white planter class was much larger (the average estate value of a Jamaican planter in the 1770s was over £9,000 sterling), and the dependence on slave labor was far greater (blacks outnumbered whites nine to one) than in Talbot, Queen Anne's, and Kent.[9]

The balance struck in the Chesapeake between the desire for profit and the concern for self-sufficiency was unlike that arrived at by Caribbean adventurers or New England husbandmen. In the Chesapeake as well as the Middle Colonies, family farming and generational changes developed alongside commercial agriculture and market changes. In responding to demographic and economic conditions, white residents of Maryland and Virginia fashioned a society much like the one they had left in rural England. On the Eastern Shore, in particular, the relationship of change occasioned respectively by demographic and economic conditions turned on the fact that permanent English settlement began in 1658. Consequently, the experiences of the first generation of opportunistic immigrant tobacco planters coincided with the last stages of the boom period in Anglo-Chesapeake trade; the first generation of native-born white householders came of age during the years of Atlantic wars and economic stagnation; and the lives of this generation's children

8. Dunn, *Sugar and Slaves,* pp. 3–116.

9. Richard B. Sheridan, "The Wealth of Jamaica in the Eighteenth Century," *EHR* 18 (1965): 292–311, especially pp. 297 (slave population) and 301 (wealth figures); and "The Rise of a Colonial Gentry: A Case Study of Antigua, 1730–1775," *EHR* 13 (1961): 342–357; and Philip D. Curtain, *The Atlantic Slave Trade: A Census* (Madison, Wis., 1969), pp. 29–30, 57–58, 75–77, 80–81.

and grandchildren stretched out over the period of commercial revitalization and market reorganization. This is the story my study has analyzed, and it only remains briefly to draw it together.[10]

English settlement of the Eastern Shore began during the boom period in the Chesapeake tobacco trade. Through the 1680s, tobacco prices remained high enough to bring large numbers of English immigrants to Talbot and Kent. Some paid their own passage, patented land, and quickly set to work growing tobacco and corn. Others, unable to afford the cost of transportation to the New World, agreed to work out a term of service in return for passage and in expectation of eventually becoming independent proprietors. The prosperous state of the market allowed the economy to support an ever growing number of landowners, and their control over the labor of servants (and later slaves) made possible the gradual increase in the wealth of the free settler population. Profit margins, however, shrank. Land costs rose while tobacco prices—as Chesapeake production pushed against inelastic European demand—fell. Each new wave of immigrants, however propitious the boom conditions that brought them, faced a less advantageous situation than had earlier settlers. The society became progressively more unequal; the periodic growth of the dependent labor force and the redistribution of income from servants and slaves to the region's larger landowners only heightened this inequality.

In 1689 the situation facing Eastern Shore planters worsened. With market conditions already very bad, war broke out between England and France, and after the short peace of 1697–1701, fighting continued through 1713. War foreclosed attempts to expand the English tobacco reexport trade and kept Chesapeake crop prices below a penny per pound. White immigration to the Eastern Shore virtually stopped, and except during the boom of 1697–1701, householders had to get by without servant labor and with reduced incomes. Most adjusted by working less at commercial agriculture and more at corn and livestock farming.

The downturn in market conditions coincided with the transi-

---

10. Unless new data are introduced, statements about the Eastern Shore will not be footnoted.

tion on the Eastern Shore from a society of immigrant male tobacco planters to one of second-generation family farmers. The simple parceling up of the bayside land in Talbot and Kent (as well as the rising market value of farms) helped to constrict opportunity and to direct the flow of English immigration to other regions of the Chesapeake and to other colonies. When immigration let up, the sex ratio, which had been as high as three to one, fell, more marriages occurred, and a new social structure emerged. The acquisition of labor became less important; householder status became more important. Marriage between the children of first-generation immigrants cemented bonds that had previously depended only on mutual residency or business associations. With these marriages, natural population growth began; the division of property among the children born of this generation increased the number of landowners in the region, brought more land into production, and raised the value of plantations.

Because family size was somewhat smaller on the Eastern Shore than in New England, estate divisions did not play as important a role in Kent and Talbot as in rural Massachusetts in the creation of inequality. But it is clear that most merchant-planters benefited by being in each case one of the few heirs to one or more family estates amassed in earlier, more prosperous times by immigrant planters. Their parents' wealth allowed the merchant-planters to weather the recession of 1689–1713 in considerably better shape than their neighbors did. They purchased slaves (to replace the servants they could not get) and more than maintained their income despite the price collapse. Their parents' position allowed them to claim provincial offices and the sinecures that went with those posts. Most also acted as middlemen between other residents and English merchants, and a few risked large sums by trading grains, lumber, and meat for rum and sugar in the war-torn Caribbean. Some acquired renters to work the land they could not farm themselves and debtors to earn them interest on the money they could not otherwise invest. This range of activity not only established their dominance of the Eastern Shore's economy but also set them apart from elites in other colonies.

For the poor, this era of low tobacco prices promised little. The immigrant laborer or freed servant could not turn to family or kin for land and could not accumulate through his own labor in less than half a decade enough to buy a fifty-acre tract. In good times, credit was an alternative to savings, but during a recession, few planters would lend money to a person whose only collateral was his anticipated income from tobacco. Most propertyless whites, in fact, had only the hope of leaving, which a great many did after they had made a sufficient amount during the boom of 1697–1701 to acquire a horse and to put together a small stake with which to get started elsewhere. By the first decade of the new century, the social structure of the Eastern Shore—the hierarchy of merchant-planters, householders, poor whites, and slaves—was in place.

The end of Queen Anne's War in 1713 did not alter this social order. But with the end of war came a gradual return to prosperity and the beginning of a fundamental reorganization of economic life. The causes of these changes were rooted in both market and demographic conditions. The expansion of the English tobacco trade with Ireland, Northern Europe, and France slowly increased the price Eastern Shore planters received for their staple crop. Over the course of the eighteenth century, however, a similar growth in demand for grains, first in New England and the Caribbean and later in Southern Europe, offered new marketing opportunities to the region's established planter families. Because planters could not use all their land or time growing tobacco, they were able to introduce cash grains without curtailing production of the traditional staple. As soon as marketing arrangements were established, the shift toward diversified agriculture began.

But population growth eventually changed the planters' situation. In each Eastern Shore county between 1713 and 1776, population grew continuously: at a rate of 1.4 percent annually in Talbot, 1.9 percent in Kent, and 2.2 percent in Queen Anne's. These growth rates brought about a gradual equalization of population density in the region and forced down the land–labor ratio. Planters approached a point where they could bring all of their land into production. Faced with a choice of farming more intensively (and accepting lower yields or using better cropping methods) or of cutting back on one market crop, most began to abandon the least profitable crop, tobacco.[11]

The direct economic benefits to the region's householders from the revitalization of the market economy were twofold: they not only received better returns on the sale of their crops but by mixing wheat and corn growing with tobacco cultivation, they also raised the total output on their farms. Between the 1720s and 1760s, the average income that a planter derived from a field hand climbed from around £5 to about £17; average household income increased from £14 to £47. From around £120 in 1700, the average wealth of a Talbot householder rose to £140 in the 1730s and to £190 in the 1760s. Compared to income and wealth figures for the Caribbean, these estimates are not impressive, but for few other colonies is there such clear evidence of real economic improvement not only for the elite but also for the much larger householder class.[12]

The increase in household income and average wealth not

11. For the years 1713, 1755, and 1776, the population (in thousands) of each county was: 4.3, 8.8, 11.0 (Talbot); 3.2, 10.1, 15.3 (Queen Anne's); and 3.1, 8.3, 11.6 (Kent). Population figures are given in Table 2; in Arthur Karinen, "Numerical and Distributional Aspects of Maryland Population, 1631–1840," Ph.D. dissertation, University of Maryland, 1958, pp. 202–203; and in the Provincial Tax Lists of 1776, MHR. Density figures can be calculated on the basis of 202,000 acres in Talbot, 303,700 in Queen Anne's, and 216,400 in Kent; acreage totals come from the Debt Books, MHR.

12. The 1720 field-hand-income figure is based on the assumption that tobacco was the only market crop; see Table 16. The derivation of the 1760 figure is explained in chap. 6. The 1720 household income figure was obtained by use of the data on production and social structure in chaps. 3 and 5; the 1760 figure is based on the following data:

Merchant-planters	30 hhds	×	19.5fh/hhd	×	£9.5/fh	=	£5,558
Slave owners	370 hhds	×	4.2fh/hhd	×	£16.7/fh	=	£25,952
Other landowners	160 hhds	×	£20.3/hhd			=	£3,248
Other tenants	325 hhds	×	£20.3/hhd			=	£6,598
	885 hhds					£41,356

or approximately £47/hhd, where hhd = household and fh = male field hand (or the equivalent number of female and child workers; see Table 7). These income figures are discussed in chap. 6; the figures for the number of households and the number of field hands per household come from the Provincial Tax Lists of 1776, MHR. The wealth estimates given in the text are discussed in the Appendix.

only reflected better prices and fuller land use, but also the growing flow of income from slaves to masters. Between 1713 and 1776, the number of blacks on the Eastern Shore increased sevenfold and the percentage of slaves in the population climbed from 13 to 40 percent. Some of this increase in the number of Eastern Shore blacks was attributable to the slave trade, but unlike the situation in the Caribbean, in Kent, Queen Anne's, and Talbot, births exceeded deaths. Natural population growth tended to concentrate ownership among the merchant-planters; the slave trade worked to spread ownership more widely (especially during the 1739–42 boom). Both processes enlarged the proportion of blacks in the population and gradually made the control of Afro-American laborers, rather than simple householder status, the most important symbol of having become an established planter.[13]

While bringing prosperity to Eastern Shore householders in general, revitalization of the economy set the residents of Talbot and Kent on divergent courses. In Kent, proximity to the Delaware River, the main link to the Philadelphia grain market, pushed that county's farmers more quickly toward specialization in wheat. In Talbot, lower grain prices and the strength of trading connections between the merchant-planters and English consignment shippers kept the county's inhabitants committed longer to the traditional staple. By the 1760s, planters in the Great Choptank region grew corn and a substantial amount of low-quality tobacco, sent their grain to the West Indies by coastal vessels, and marketed tobacco through Liverpool and Glasgow factors at Oxford. To the north, residents still cultivated a little Oronoco tobacco, which they consigned to London wholesalers, but most householders belonged to the wheat economy that linked Chestertown to Philadelphia, Lisbon, and Oporto. By the era of the American Revolution, Kent had replaced Talbot as

13. Estimates of the size of the slave population are based on data in *AM*, vol. 25, pp. 256–258 (adjusted) and the Provincial Tax Lists of 1776, MHR. By way of comparison, by mid-century blacks comprised about half the non-Indian population in Virginia and two-thirds the non-Indian population in South Carolina; see Gerald W. Mullins, *Flight and Rebellion: Slave Resistance in Eighteenth-Century Virginia* (New York, 1978), pp. 15–16; and Peter H. Wood, *Black Majority: Negroes in Colonial South Carolina from 1670 through the Stono Rebellion* (New York, 1975), pp. 142–155.

the center of economic life on the Eastern Shore, and the average wealth of the white population improved county by county as one moved from south to north.[14]

Probably few other regions of the Chesapeake experienced as substantial a degree of economic growth as did the eighteenth-century Eastern Shore. In the years after 1713, however, there did occur throughout Maryland and Virginia a process of regional economic specialization that paralleled the shift on the Eastern Shore from tobacco to grain and from trade with English shippers to dependence on Philadelphia merchants. At the heart of the Chesapeake economy in 1713 were three major marketing systems, fixed on the James, York, and Patuxent rivers and monopolized by London and Bristol merchants. The impetus for change was provided by west-coast British shippers. Taking advantage of their favorable geographical position, they expanded their reexport trade with Ireland and France and then employed the capital earned in this trade to seize the initiative from consignment merchants, establish Chesapeake stores, and buy tobacco directly from Maryland and Virginia planters. They

14. I estimated Kent and Talbot wealth by using the inventories. The figures, when planters with over £1,000 (in pre-1720 prices) and nonhouseholders are excluded, come to:

Decade	Talbot	Kent
1720s	£114	£111
1740s	153	167
1760s	193	211

These estimates include wealth in slaves but not local debts or land. Unlike the Talbot figures discussed above, these figures were arrived at merely by averaging the individual inventory totals. The assumption was that the bias in the use of inventories to make wealth estimates was the same for both counties; the figures have only comparative value.

Figures for 1782 were derived from the assessment of that year (records at MHR). The data are complete in terms of people but much less comprehensive than the inventories in terms of property evaluated. Eastern Shore figures for householders, land excluded and in 1782 prices, were:

Kent	£183
Queen Anne's	161
Talbot	150
Caroline	111

struck first at the points of least resistance, the Rappahannock and the Eastern Shore, where Liverpool traders already had a foothold, and the Potomac, where few London merchants operated. By the 1740s, Glasgow merchants had begun to challenge London ones directly in the Upper James. The Potomac, Rappahannock, and Upper James regions, the major beneficiaries of the internal migration of population during the mid-eighteenth century, pushed past the counties of the Patuxent and York rivers as the most productive areas in the Chesapeake. Tobacco production in the Rappahannock area, tied chiefly to Liverpool and Whitehaven and the Irish reexport market, faltered after the 1740s, but the Potomac and Upper James trades, linked more closely to the French market, continued to grow until the American Revolution (see Map 4).[15]

At the same time that the expansion and redirection of the reexport trade helped Potomac and James river tobacco planters, the Atlantic economy also offered Chesapeake farmers the option of lessening their dependence on the traditional staple. In Virginia, a coastal trade in corn, pork, and lumber developed slowly in the Accomac and Lower James regions. By the middle of the eighteenth century, the demand of West Indian sugar growers for corn and flour led to substantial increases in grain production in the Lower James region and to the spread of grain cultivation to the Rappahannock and York river tobacco counties. While local production in the Upper James still centered on tobacco, merchants in this part of Virginia handled increasing amounts of wheat obtained by an overland trade with the newly settled counties west of the Blue Ridge Mountains. In Maryland, cash grains were first introduced on the Eastern Shore, but before 1750, as we have seen, the expansion of the tobacco trade played the prime role in the region's economic revitalization. After mid-century, however, with the growth in Southern Euro-

15. Trading patterns were determined from the Virginia Naval Office Records, PRO; Maryland Naval Office Records, PRO; Maryland Port of Entry Records, MHS and MHR; Customs 16/1, PRO; and the Calvert Papers, MS 174, no. 596, MHS. See also Morgan, *American Slavery, American Freedom,* pp. 410–420; and Jacob M. Price, *France and the Chesapeake: A History of the French Tobacco Monopoly, 1674–1791, and of Its Relationship to the British and American Tobacco Trades,* 2 vols. (Ann Arbor, 1973), vol. 1, pp. 649–671.

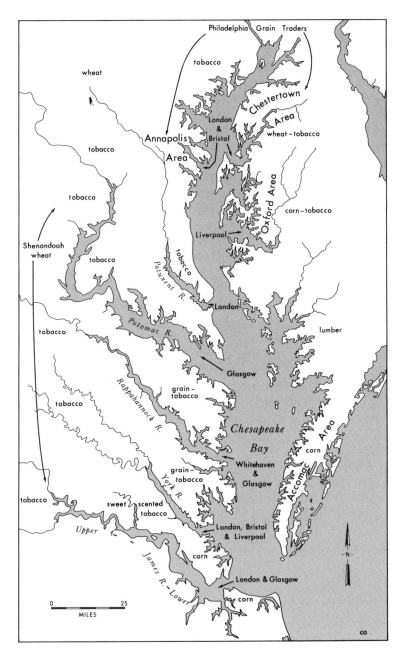

Map 4. Trading regions in the Chesapeake around 1760

pean demand for wheat, more and more farmers adopted grain cultivation, so that by the era of the American Revolution a vast wheat belt existed in the northern Chesapeake, stretching from Kent County on the Eastern Shore through Cecil, at the head of the bay, across Baltimore and newly settled Frederick County to the west, and on to the fertile Shenandoah Valley. By the 1770s, remarkable diversity characterized the Chesapeake economy, and regional specialization had become the pattern in both Maryland and Virginia.[16]

The pattern of development in the northern Chesapeake in general and on the Eastern Shore in particular had important consequences for the subsequent growth of the American economy. The fortunes of the Lloyds, Chamberlaines, Tilghmans, and their kin provided one source of investment capital for regional financial and commercial development. As Talbot merchant-planters and Chestertown wholesalers ended their direct involvement in the shipment of grains, both their businesses and their surplus funds became stakes in the burgeoning rivalry of Philadelphia and Baltimore. But perhaps of even greater importance, the eighteenth century closed with the Eastern Shore still essentially a society of prosperous householders. While not large investors, they were all consumers. The grain they sold and the goods they bargained for in return linked them first to Philadelphia and then to Baltimore and helped to create a market for the wares fashioned in and shipped by way of these urban centers. Throughout the Middle Colonies, this favorable mix of concentrated investment capital and small-scale rural demand provided the basis for nineteenth-century intraregional development.[17]

16. Excellent discussions of the spread of wheat farming may be found in David Klingaman, "The Significance of Grain in the Development of the Tobacco Colonies," *JEH* 29 (1969): 268–278; Ronald Hoffman, *A Spirit of Dissension: Economics, Politics, and the Revolution in Maryland* (Baltimore, 1977); and Robert D. Mitchell, *Commercialism and the Frontier: Perspectives on the Early Shenandoah Valley* (Charlottesville, Va., 1977).

17. Historians have asserted that the concentration of wealth in the hands of a colonial elite helped to provide investment capital for nineteenth-century development. The question is what degree of wealth concentration was most conducive to economic growth. In the 1770s, wealth was least concentrated in the middle colonies (and average wealth, slaves excluded, highest); in this region, local demand probably played a more important role in economic growth than

The development of the Eastern Shore left an even more fundamental legacy, one rooted in the culture itself. White settlers had had to change their behavior frequently in response to market and demographic conditions. In the minds of the poor, the discouragements of staying had been measured against the uncertainties of leaving; in the families of simple householders, spending had been balanced against investment, security against risk, a new cow against a new servant. On the plantations of the rich as well as the farms of humbler whites, land and labor were bought and sold, crops produced, and established trading arrangements dissolved as the market dictated. For the society as a whole, change came slowly; for individuals it was more abrupt. On the aggregate, change was a product of circumstance, of supply and demand; on the individual level— that of John Edmondson purchasing a huge tract for speculation, Robert Goldsborough growing wheat for the first time, Isaac Cox buying some finery for his home, or Edward Lloyd outfitting a 150-ton vessel for direct trade with Southern Europe—change was more a matter of choice. And just as occurred in the colonies to the north, countless such decisions eventually made the market itself a social attitude and engrained more deeply in the culture calculation, consumption, and improvement.[18]

---

elsewhere. For comparative statistics, see Alice Hanson Jones, *American Colonial Wealth: Documents and Materials*, 3 vols., 2d ed. (New York, 1978). Two extremely valuable treatments of intraregional rural demand are in Jan de Vries, "Peasant Demand Patterns and Economic Development, Friesland, 1550-1750," in *European Peasants and Their Markets*, ed. William N. Parker and Eric L. Jones (Princeton, 1975), pp. 205-239; and Diane Lindstrom, *Economic Change in the Philadelphia Region, 1810-1850* (New York, 1977). On Baltimore, see James Weston Livingood. *The Philadelphia–Baltimore Trade Rivalry, 1780-1860* (Harrisburg, Pa., 1947); and George Terry Sharrer, "Flour Milling and the Growth of Baltimore, 1783-1830," Ph.D. dissertation, University of Maryland, 1975.

18. Put differently, white householders in the northern Chesapeake had many of the entrepreneurial traits often associated with the development of the antebellum North of a capitalist culture and manufacturing economy. This fact poses a problem for those who seek an explanation for the nature of antebellum society in the colonial experience or who assert that the future shape of American society was by the 1770s irreversibly embedded in the American character. These contentions are not so much wrong as simplistic (both in their characterization of America and in their failure to deal with the process of change between the 1770s and 1830s). For the outstanding exception to the way in which such

This entrepreneurial legacy, however, was irreparably flawed. For with the culture of the market came a deepening commitment to a repressive social order; and this commitment would ultimately sap from Chesapeake society the energy to respond to changing conditions that had once been the hallmark of its economic life.[19]

---

arguments are generally fashioned, see James A. Henretta, *The Evolution of American Society: An Interdisciplinary Analysis* (Lexington, Mass., 1973), pp. 83–117.

19. There is no study of the profitability of slavery in the antebellum northern Chesapeake. When such a study is done, it will probably demonstrate that the use of slave labor in wheat farming was profitable (the internal rate of return was greater than zero) and that the sustained natural population growth among blacks made slavery an economically viable institution (returns were higher than replacement costs). Nonetheless, the institution built into the Eastern Shore's economy structural restraints that kept whites from moving toward new forms of agricultural organization (greater reliance on tenancy or wage labor) and that limited further development of rural demand. On the first point, see Carville V. Earle, "A Staple Interpretation of Slavery and Free Labor," *Geographical Review* 68 (1978): 51–65; the second point could best be explored in a new comparative study of the causes and consequences of the rise of Philadelphia and Baltimore.

68 (1978): 51–65;

Appendix

Commodity Prices and Wealth Estimates

The data in Table A1, covering Maryland tobacco prices in the seventeenth century, and Tables A2 and A3, showing agricultural commodity prices in Talbot and Kent counties in the seventeenth and eighteenth centuries, come chiefly from inventories of the assets of deceased white residents of Talbot and Kent counties. Inventory prices appear to reflect the actual market values of commodities. To assure accuracy, I did not use listings for trash or debt tobacco or for "sorry" or short corn. Where possible, I checked prices from the inventories against listings in mercantile correspondence and court cases.

Table A1. Maryland tobacco prices, 1660–79 (pence per pound)

Year	Price	Year	Price	Year	Price	Year	Price
1660	1.50*	1665	1.10	1670	1.15*	1675	1.00
1661	1.50	1666	0.90	1671	1.05	1676	1.05
1662	1.60*	1667	1.10	1672	1.00	1677	1.15
1663	1.55*	1668	1.25	1673	1.00	1678	1.15
1664	1.35	1669	1.15	1674	1.00	1679	1.05

*Price based on no more than three observations.
Source: Russell R. Menard, "Farm Price of Maryland Tobacco, 1659–1710," *MHM* 68 (1973): 80–85.

Table A2. Talbot County agricultural commodity prices,
1680-1719 (pence per unit)

Year	Tobacco (pound)*	Wheat (bushel)	Corn (barrel)	Year	Tobacco (pound)*	Wheat (bushel)	Corn (barrel)
1680	1.00†	40†	100†	1700	1.00	44	98
1681	–	39	100†	1701	0.95	47	99
1682	0.60†	43	92	1702	0.85	48	97
1683	–	42	–	1703	0.85	48	95
1684	0.70†	48	86	1704	0.80	43	96
1685	1.05	48	99	1705	0.80	38	94
1686	0.95	43	90	1706	0.85	42	96
1687	0.80	38	78†	1707	0.70	41	91
1688-92	0.70	–	71	1708	0.85	42	95
1693	0.60†	–	60	1709	0.80	39	91
1694	0.55†	36†	59	1710	0.65	36†	90
1695	–	–	75†	1711	0.95	37	81
1696	0.85	38†	72	1712	0.85	44	93
1697	1.05	48†	88	1713	0.80	39†	84
1698	0.95	36†	80†	1714	0.85	41†	93
1699	1.05	39	108	1715	0.95	31	81
				1716	0.95	36	77
				1717	1.05	38	93
				1718	1.25	36†	98
				1719	1.10	38	98

*Rounded to nearest 0.05 pence.
†Price based on no more than three observations.
SOURCES: Inventories and Accounts, MHR; Inventories, MHR.

Table A3. Talbot and Kent county agricultural commodity
prices, 1720-74 (pence per unit)

	Talbot			Kent		
Year	Tobacco (pound)*	Wheat (bushel)	Corn (barrel)	Tobacco (pound)*	Wheat (bushel)	Corn (barrel)
1720	1.00	41	92	1.05	39	99
1721	0.95	43	99	0.90	36†	97
1722	1.00	39	99	1.00	36	98
1723	1.00	40	99	1.00	35	91
1724	1.10	41	95	1.05	36	103
1725	1.60	38	94	1.05	35	104
1726	1.05	37	90	1.00	36	94
1727	1.05	38	90	1.05	34	96
1728	1.05	42	101	1.05	38	103
1729	1.00	41	92	1.00	36	98
1730	1.00	39	96	1.05	36	97
1731	0.95	30	84	1.00†	30	85
1732	0.95	36	88	1.05	32	94
1733	1.05	42	87	1.05	34	98
1734	1.25	38	94	1.05	33	96

	Talbot			Kent		
Year	Tobacco (pound)*	Wheat (bushel)	Corn (barrel)	Tobacco (pound)*	Wheat (bushel)	Corn (barrel)
1735	1.40	38	97	1.10	37	97
1736	1.55	38	95	1.40	38	97
1737	1.50	34	110	1.65	44	112
1738	1.80	42	117	2.05	47	127
1739	1.90	39	100	1.95	40	107
1740	1.85	32	93	1.65	40	104
1741	1.85	51	118	1.80	48	119
1742	1.85	54	135	1.55	49	125
1743	1.65	47	114	1.55	39	112
1744	1.25	36	100	1.30	35	97
1745	1.05	34	94	1.25	34	95
1746	1.15	37	99	1.25	36	95
1747	1.25	39	96	1.15	35	97
1748	1.65	41	115	1.30	39	111
1749	1.95	45	115	1.75	45	106
1750	2.05	41	115	2.30	45	123
1751	2.20	44	124	2.00	43	108
1752	1.80	41	108	1.70	43	95
1753	1.70	45	114	1.70	43	108
1754	1.50	43	104	1.75	46	108
1755	1.45	44	106	1.50	46	106
1756	1.75	42	114	1.85	45	108
1757	1.80	37	93	1.85	37	97
1758	2.40	40	100	1.90	39	88
1759	2.65	41	101	2.75	47	114
1760	2.00	42	115	1.80	49	111
1761	1.90	45	108	2.20	57	97
1762	1.45	46	111	1.75	49	106
1763	1.75	46†	113†	1.70	49	114
1764	1.35	45	106	1.50	43	100
1765	1.65	42	97	1.75	39	115
1766	1.80	44	116	1.85	45	113
1767	2.00	46	115	1.75	50	121
1768	2.40	44	102	2.35	50	99
1769	2.30	44	111	2.25	47	112
1770	2.50	44†	126	2.15	47	123
1771	1.85†	48†	120†	1.95	53	117
1772	2.00†	48†	138	2.15	61	112
1773	–	–	–	1.80	65	117
1774	–	–	–	1.50	63	111

*Rounded to the nearest 0.05 pence.
†Price based on no more than three observations.
SOURCE: Inventories, MHR.

Maryland Price Index

Table A4 allows one to compute prices and inventory wealth totals in real terms relative to seventeenth-century levels by dividing the price or wealth total by the index number. P. M. G. Harris constructed the index for the inventory research of the St. Mary's City Commission. The index measures inflation in the prices of European manufactured goods (pewter and cloth), labor (servants and slaves), and agricultural products (cow and calf, corn, and wheat). I have constructed from less adequate data a commodity price index (excluding labor) for the Eastern Shore. The index indicates that inflation followed a course on the Eastern Shore similar but not identical to that in the rest of Maryland. Ideally, a commodity price index should be used in measuring the growth of *per capita* wealth. Further work may lead to some modification in the figures given in Table A4.

Table A4. Maryland price index, 1660–1774
(1660–1723 = 100)

Year	Index	Year	Index	Year	Index
1660–1723	100	1731	116	1739	134
1724	102	1732	118	1740	136
1725	105	1733	120	1741	139
1726	106	1734	123	1742	141
1727	108	1735	125	1743	144
1728	110	1736	127	1744	146
1729	112	1737	129	1745–74	149
1730	114	1738	132		

Wealth Estimates

In a probate inventory, the administrator of an estate listed a decedent's assets, land excepted, and the value of each asset. About 1,000 pre-1772 Talbot inventories survive, and used cautiously, they can provide estimates of the average wealth of the free white population of the county. Several problems must be solved, however, before inventories are used to estimate wealth. Because the estates of very rich and very poor decedents were often not inventoried, the inventories most accurately reflect the economic status of people in the middle ranges of wealth. Moreover, inasmuch as the decedent population was older and thus probably richer on the average than the general population, the inventories may give a distorted picture of wealth holding. The average estate value derived from inventories, consequently, does not equal the average level of wealth of the white males in the society. Unfortunately, the extent of the bias introduced by the use of inventories to estimate wealth may change from one period to the next.

Put simply, inventory records tend to underrepresent the poor, the very rich, and the young. Two extremely good discussions of these problems can be found in Gloria L. Main, "On the Correction of Biases in Colonial Probate Records," *Historical Methods Newsletter* 8 (1974): 10–28; and Daniel Scott Smith, "Underregistration and Bias in Probate Records: An Analysis of Data from Eighteenth-Century Hingham, Massachusetts," *WMQ* 32 (1975): 100–110. I have taken two steps to adjust inventory estimates for Talbot County planters. First, the estates of men with over £1,000 in inventoried property (in pre-1724 prices) have been excluded. Such estates appear in the records randomly and in small numbers. Leaving these estates in the calculations would make the estimates depend far too much on whether or not a wealthy planter happened to die in a given period of time. Second, wealth estimates have been constructed separately for each of four economic classes: slave owners, other landowners, tenants (other householders, without slaves), and nonhouseholders. The figures below represent averages derived from all inventoried assets except local debts owed to the planter:

Class	1680–89	1704–10	1730–39	1763–72
Slave owners	£292	£232	£360	£442
Other landowners	98	96	107	107
Tenants	53	32	50	92
Nonhouseholders	21	8	18	12

Inventory values have not been adjusted for inflation. I selected time periods for which data on the social structure were available. Problems created by the use of these time periods will be mentioned below.

To average the four figures in a time period, I multiplied each figure by the number of people in the particular economic class. The four products of the multiplication were then added, and the sum was divided by the total number of people in the four economic classes:

Class	1680s	1700s	1730s	1760s
Slave owners	80	145	170	400
Other landowners	320	445	260	160
Tenants	130	185	400	325
Nonhouseholders	270	380	790	545
Total men	800	1,155	1,620	1,430
Average wealth	£84	£74	£76	£161

All figures for the distribution of population by social class are estimates and have been rounded. The 1760s figures are least reliable. These figures indicate an apparent decline in tenancy after the 1730s because some tenants had acquired slaves and are included in the slave-owning category.

The wealth estimates have not been corrected for inflation. Applying deflators calculated from the index numbers in Table A4, I determined the following average wealth figures:

1680s	£84
1700s	74
1730s	61
1760s	108

It is worth the trouble to consider average wealth with the nonhouseholders excluded. The number of nonhouseholders makes a major difference in the calculations. When nonhouseholders left the county (as in the 1704–10 period), the average wealth of the remaining population rose. On the average, whites became richer during recessions because economic conditions forced the poor to abandon Talbot County. The average wealth of the less geographically mobile householding population was:

1680s	£113
1700s	106
1730s	106
1760s	170

These figures reflect the sensitivity of inventory wealth estimates to short-term economic conditions. In light of the general improvement between the 1689–1713 period and mid-century in Talbot's economy, one would expect the wealth figure for the 1700s to be below that for the 1730s. But the former figure is unusually high because of the 1697–1701 boom and the latter figure low because of the recession of the early 1730s. Thus instead of improvement the inventories indicate no change.

Economists generally do not count the value of slaves in wealth estimates because equivalent allowances are not made for other human capital. If the value of slaves is taken out of the wealth averages presented above, the new figures (deflated) are:

Decade	Per white male	Per householder
1680s	£78	£107
1700s	67	96
1730s	51	85
1760s	68	105

In other words, when wealth in slaves and land are excluded, the average wealth of Talbot's white male inhabitants did not increase during the colonial era.

Landholding, however, deserves consideration. Rising land prices characterized the entire period:

Decade	Acres in Talbot	Price per acre
1680s	177,000	£0.17
1700s	293,000	0.27
1730s	202,000	0.46
1760s	202,000	1.22

The average value of land held in Talbot County came to:

Decade	Per white male	Per householder
1680s	£38	£63
1700s	68	102
1730s	57	112
1760s	172	278

Even deflated, these figures suggest that by the 1760s a substantial increase had occurred in the wealth of white males in Talbot.

THE WEALTH OF LARGE SLAVE OWNERS

All of the above calculations have excluded the inventories of the largest slave owners (those with estates in pre-1724 prices of over £1,000). Below is an estimate, derived from the inventories, landowning records, and tax lists, of the number of large planters in specific periods and of their average wealth (deflated):

Decade	Number	Average wealth	Without slaves
1680s	6	£1,480	£1,090
1700s	14	2,030	1,480
1730s	20	3,100	2,420
1760s	30	3,690	2,570

If these figures are included in the estimates of the average wealth (pre-1724 prices, slaves excluded) of householders, then the averages become:

1680s	£118
1700s	120
1730s	141
1760s	189

These averages again show a general improvement during the eighteenth century in the economic position of Talbot householders. Finally, combining the estimates of the average wealth of the richest planters with data on the wealth of other planters, I calculated the percentage of wealth held by the top 10 percent of householders:

1680s	39%
1700s	47
1730s	63
1760s	62

These figures are probably somewhat too high.

Bibliography of Primary Sources

Among printed records on which I relied extensively were William Hand Browne et al., eds., *Archives of Maryland*, 72 vols. (Baltimore, 1883–), and W. N. Sainsbury et al. eds., *Calendar of State Papers, Colonial Series, American and West Indies*, 44 vols. (London, 1860–). The *Archives of Maryland* contain information on population (vol. 25, pp. 255–259), shipowning (vol. 25, pp. 598–601), and tobacco exports (vol. 42, pp. 66–69). Documents in the *Calendar of State Papers* detail conditions in the seventeenth-century tobacco trade.

The listings below note only manuscript sources I used directly in my study. After each source, I have provided a brief description. Where county records are mentioned, the reader may assume that the comments apply to Talbot, Kent, and Queen Anne's County documents. Most Dorchester records have not survived. The collection of the Maryland Hall of Records is indexed and summarized in Morris Radoff, Gust Skordas, and Phebe Jacobsen, *The County Courthouses and Records of Maryland: The Records* (Annapolis, 1963), and in Elizabeth Hartsook and Gust Skordas, *Land Office and Prerogative Court Records of Maryland* (Annapolis, 1940). For the Maryland Historical Society, see Avril Pedley, *The Manuscript Collections of the Maryland Historical Society* (Baltimore, 1968).

Maryland Hall of Records, Annapolis

Assessment of 1783, all counties. List of householders and itemization of wealth (land, slaves, livestock, plate, other).

Commission Book no. 2. Ships built in Maryland in the 1720s and 1730s.

County court records (or judgments). Debt cases, occupations of parties in lawsuits, names of justices of the peace, salary figures, names and ages of newly arrived servants, taxable population figures, and data on taverns, ferries, and bridges.

County land records (or conveyances). Deeds, leases, land prices, descriptions of houses on plantations owned by orphans, boundary-dispute records with names and ages of witnesses, and tobacco freight rates.

Federal direct tax returns of 1798. Descriptions of houses.

Kent County tobacco warehouse inspection records, 1748-70. Exports, hogshead weights, and tobacco prices.

Oxford port-of-entry records, 1742-46, 1753-54. Tobacco and grain exports.

Provincial debt books (by county) from 1733 on. Land listed by owner.

Provincial inventories and accounts. List of decedent's assets (crop, household furnishings, livestock, labor, debts, but not land); names of kin and creditors; exchange rates; commodity prices.

Provincial patents. Boundary, location, acreage, and original grantee of tracts; names of those for whom land was claimed under head-right system.

Provincial rent rolls, by county, from 1733 on. Land listed by tract name.

Provincial tax list of 1776. Listing of the number of people by household, age, sex, and race; various hundreds in Talbot and Queen Anne's.

Provincial wills. Information on inheritance patterns, landowning, kinship, family size, and occupations.

Robert Morris ledger book. Account from 1740s of Liverpool factor.

Maryland Historical Society, Baltimore

Annapolis port-of-entry records, MS 21. Tobacco and grain exports; data for 1756-75 for Annapolis and 1767-75 for Chestertown.

Callister Papers. Letters to a Liverpool merchant from his factor.

Calvert Papers, MS 174. Revenue statistics on tobacco trade.

County 1721-22 tax lists and Talbot 1733 tax list, Scharf Collection, MS 1999. Heads of households and number of taxables by race.

Hollyday account book, MS 1317. Revenue statistics from tobacco trade.

Lloyd Papers, MS 2001. Papers on plantation management; 1706 Talbot County rent roll.

Oxford port-of-entry records, MS 638. Tobacco and grain exports; data for 1731-33, 1740-42, 1759-75.

Myrtle Grove Farm, Easton, Maryland

Robert Goldsborough plantation book. Record of plantation management.

Public Record Office, London (microfilm locations noted below)

Colonial import–export records, Customs 14, 1768–72. Tobacco and grain exports by Chesapeake naval districts (University of Maryland Library).

English port books, E.190. Data on seventeenth-century London, Bristol, and Liverpool trade (University of Virginia Library).

Import–export ledgers, Customs 3, 1697–1775. London and outport imports and exports (University of Maryland Library).

Maryland Naval Office Records, C.O. 5/749, 1689–1700. Tobacco exports (Library of Congress).

Virginia Naval Office Records, C.O. 5/1440–1447, 1700–1752. Tobacco and grain exports (Library of Congress and University of Virginia Library).

Virginia State Library, Richmond

Virginia court order books. See note on Maryland county court records.

Bibliographical Essay on Selected Secondary Sources

The last decade has witnessed a renaissance of Chesapeake studies. Characterized by systematic, detailed research, rigorously defined methodology, and precise, quantitative findings, the new work has addressed itself to the fundamental problem of explaining the two-century-long pattern of development in colonial Maryland and Virginia. As the conclusion to this study indicates, three themes run through the new literature: one, economic; a second, demographic; and a third, cultural. Happily, few scholars have contended for the primacy of any one view. Instead, their attempt has been to isolate and understand the role of each factor in the general process of development.

In the economic model of Chesapeake development, the expansion of European tobacco markets plays the key role. Here our understanding owes much to Jacob M. Price's work, consummated with the publication of his magisterial *France and the Chesapeake: A History of the French Tobacco Monopoly, 1674–1791, and of Its Relationship to the British and American Tobacco Trades,* 2 vols. (Ann Arbor, 1973). Price has demonstrated how the eighteenth-century growth of tobacco reexports to France helped pull the Chesapeake out of the stagnation of 1680–1720. His work ties the periodic infusion of French capital into the tobacco trade to the economic booms in Maryland and Virginia, and shows how French money allowed Glasgow shippers to establish a store system in the Chesapeake that greatly increased the efficiency with which local merchants retailed goods and dispatched tobacco. Moreover, by differentiating English merchants in terms of the markets with which they dealt, the trading strategies they pursued, and the Chesapeake areas from which they secured tobacco, Price has given us a powerful analytical tool for explaining regional variations in the development of Maryland and Virginia.

Complementing Price's work on the post-1670s Chesapeake is an important article on an earlier period by Russell R. Menard: "Secular Trends in the Chesapeake Tobacco Industry, 1617–1710," *Working Papers from the Regional Economic History Research Center* 1, no. 3 (1978): 1–34. Menard has suggested that supply factors—improvements in agricultural techniques and marketing organization—contributed enormously to the extensive economic growth during the Chesapeake's early-seventeenth-century boom period. John Hemphill's unpublished work "Virginia and the English Colonial System, 1689–1733: Studies in the Development and Fluctuation of a Colonial Economy under Imperial Control," Ph.D. dissertation, Princeton University, 1964, also makes an important contribution to the study of the tobacco trade. Hemphill did pioneering research on three indicators of economic activity in the Chesapeake: the exchange rate between Virginia currency and English sterling, the level of tobacco imports in England, and the movement of freight rates for the shipping of tobacco to London. While many of Hemphill's findings have been revised by Price and John J. McCusker (*Money and Exchange in Europe and America, 1660–1775: A Handbook* [Chapel Hill, N.C., 1978]), his discussion of trade cycles and political economy remains extremely valuable. Finally, a more general statement of the relationship between supply and demand factors can be found in Gary M. Walton and James F. Shepherd, *Shipping, Maritime Trade, and the Economic Development of Colonial North America* (Cambridge, England, 1972). Assuming that overseas trade provided most of the opportunities for economic growth, they measured the impact of falling supply costs for distributing colonial produce on the development of the colonial economy. Following Price, they stressed the importance of the outport system of Chesapeake factors and stores in loading tobacco more speedily and thus cutting operating expenses.

While deserving as much attention, the population history of the colonial Chesapeake has proved more difficult to reconstruct than the story of the market. No comprehensive model relating population, land, and family has been worked out along the lines suggested by Philip J. Greven, Jr., and Kenneth A. Lockridge (see citations below) for colonial New England towns. Until recently, in fact, few scholars thought that the demographic history of the Chesapeake could be written because few detailed birth, marriage, and death records survived there as they did in New England. The early work of Arthur Karinen, "Numerical and Distributional Aspects of Maryland Population, 1631–1840," Ph.D. dissertation, University of Maryland, 1958, is thus all the more impressive, and the innovative methodology of Russell R. Menard and Lorena S. Walsh, "Death in the Chesapeake: Two Life Tables for Men in Early Colonial Maryland," *MHM* 69 (1974): 211–227, all the more important. Since these works were written, several other fine studies have appeared: Darrett B. Rutman and Anita H. Rutman, "Of Agues and Fevers: Malaria in the Early Chesapeake," *WMQ* 33 (1976): 31–60; Allan Kulikoff, "A 'Prolifick' People: Black Population Growth in the Chesapeake Colonies, 1700–1790," *Southern Studies* 16 (1977): 391–428; and Daniel Blake Smith, "Mortality and Family in the Colonial Chesapeake," *Journal of Interdisciplinary History* 8 (1978): 403–427. These studies point to the contrast between the high death rates in Maryland and the relatively low ones in colonial New England and explore the shift in the Chesapeake from an immigrant to a native-born population.

Much of the most exciting work on the Chesapeake has combined economic and demographic analysis. This approach has been used especially by the scholars on the St. Mary's City Commission (SMCC). The commission, established to conduct an archaeological and historical investigation of St. Mary's City, Maryland (the colony's first capital and oldest tobacco port), has undertaken as well a systematic study of economy and society in the lower western shore counties surrounding St. Mary's. Among the most important essays to result from this work are Russell R. Menard, "From Servants to Slaves: The Transformation of the Chesapeake Labor System," *Southern Studies* 16 (1977): 355–390; Lois Green Carr and Lorena S. Walsh, "Changing Life Styles in Colonial St. Mary's County," *Working Papers from the Regional Economic History Research Center* 1, no. 3 (1978):

72–118; and Lois Green Carr and Russell R. Menard, "Servants and Freedmen in Early Colonial Maryland," in *Essays on the Seventeenth-Century Chesapeake,* ed. Thad W. Tate and David L. Ammerman (Chapel Hill, N.C., forthcoming). Each of these studies is characterized by an attempt to relate market and demographic factors to wealth accumulation, social stratification, and economic opportunity. My own work along these lines first appeared in "The Settlement and Growth of Maryland's Eastern Shore during the English Restoration," *Maryland Historian* 5 (1974): 63–78, and "Economy and Society on Maryland's Eastern Shore, 1689–1733," in *Law, Society, and Politics in Early Maryland,* ed. Aubrey Land, Lois Green Carr, and Edward C. Papenfuse (Baltimore, 1977), pp. 153–170. A preliminary overview of the smcc's work, suggesting the general relationship between the growth of population and the economy, has been presented in P. M. G. Harris, "Integrating Interpretations of Local and Regionwide Change in the Study of Economic Development and Demographic Growth in the Colonial Chesapeake, 1630–1775," *Working Papers from the Regional Economic History Research Center* 1, no. 3 (1978): 35–72.

The cultural approach to Chesapeake history has been presented compellingly in Edmund Morgan's *American Slavery, American Freedom: The Ordeal of Colonial Virginia* (New York, 1975). Morgan tells how Englishmen left behind a fragmented, oppressive society only to be thrust into an even more unruly, exploitive world in Virginia. In this new world, subsequent generations eventually fashioned a prosperous, stable social order based on slavery and republican values. While he examines the impact that market and demographic conditions had on this transition from disorder to stability, Morgan subtly weaves into his story another theme: that of the endurance of a hierarchical social structure. The analysis of this social structure and of the belief system that helped to create and sustain it form the core of his book.

Morgan's special concern is to demonstrate the role of slavery in fulfilling the desires and eliminating the fears of Virginia whites. Adoption of the system transformed economic tensions into racial hatreds, propped up the economic structure by justifying the exploitation of the poor, and provided a basis for community solidarity around the ideology of white freedom. If Morgan overemphasizes the disorder in the seventeenth-century Chesapeake and pictures eighteenth-century Virginia society as more homogeneous than it was (see Rhys Isaac, "Evangelical Revolt: The Nature of the Baptists' Challenge to the Traditional Order in Virginia, 1765 to 1775," *WMQ* 31 (1974): 345–368), there is in his work a challenge to all those who assert the primacy of market and demographic factors over considerations of class and culture. It is to be hoped that Morgan's work will engender new debate about the relationship of the colonial and antebellum South.

Where Morgan's discussion of slavery ends, the work of Gerald W. Mullin and Allan Kulikoff begins. Both scholars, blending history and anthropology, have attempted to bring increased accuracy to the portrayal of eighteenth-century Chesapeake society by taking into account the lives of black slaves. While Mullin in *Flight and Rebellion: Slave Resistance in Eighteenth-Century Virginia* (New York, 1972) concentrates on the adjustment of individual blacks to white culture, Kulikoff in "The Beginnings of the Afro-American Family in Maryland," *Law, Society, and Politics,* ed. Land et al., pp. 171–196, and "The Origins of Afro-American Society in Tidewater Maryland and Virginia, 1700 to 1790," *WMQ* 35 (1978): 226–259, emphasizes the way demographic and locational factors affected efforts of black families to create an indigenous culture. Though Mullin's and Kulikoff's interpretations differ, both illuminate the social relations on which the viability of plantation agriculture rested.

The eighteenth-century Chesapeake, as virtually every historian agrees, differed significantly from Maryland and Virginia in the seventeenth century. In addition to the three general models of Chesapeake development cited here, scholars have advanced two explanations of change that are particularly applicable to the Eastern Shore. The first deals with the entrepreneurial initiative of Chesapeake planters. This is the theme of Aubrey Land's pathbreaking study, "Economic Base and Social Structure: The Northern Chesapeake in the Eighteenth Century," *JEH* 25 (1965): 639–654. Beginning his essay with a discussion of Richard Bennett of Queen Anne's County, Land argues convincingly for the nonagricultural source of many of the greatest fortunes in Maryland. Land was among the first to use inventory wealth records, which allowed him to picture the full range of economic activity in which Chesapeake planters engaged. Edward C. Papenfuse's *In Pursuit of Profit: The Annapolis Merchants in the Era of the American Revolution, 1763–1805* (Baltimore, 1975) provided evidence of the growing role that local capital played in encouraging trade and urban development along the northern western shore, a picture duplicated in Kent County during the 1760s.

Second, several scholars have done important work on the causes and consequences of agricultural diversification. For both its detail and its breadth, L. C. Gray's classic *History of Agriculture in the Southern United States to 1860*, 2 vols. (Washington, D.C., 1932) is the obvious starting point. Gray correctly emphasized the profitability of slavery, the mixed character of Virginia agriculture, and regional differences in the Chesapeake's economy, but he gave less attention than scholars have recently paid to the social and demographic contexts of agricultural change. Gray's work should be read in conjunction with Gregory A. Stiverson's *Poverty in a Land of Plenty: Tenancy in Eighteenth-Century Maryland* (Baltimore, 1977), which contains an excellent discussion of the agricultural practices of Maryland wheat farmers and tobacco planters. My study "The Operation of an Eighteenth-Century Chesapeake Tobacco Plantation," *Agricultural History* 49 (1975): 517–531, by stressing the profitability of tobacco production, raised the question of why planters shifted to wheat farming.

Ronald Hoffman, in his book *A Spirit of Dissension: Economics, Politics, and the Revolution in Maryland* (Baltimore, 1973), was the first to explore systematically the significance of diversified agriculture in Maryland. He linked the spread of grain culture to the development of trade between the northern Chesapeake and Philadelphia, and he demonstrated that the switch to diversified farming, while it ended the planters' complete dependence on English tobacco merchants, also made them more vulnerable to market fluctuations. In a more recent study, "Staple Crops and Urban Development in the Eighteenth-Century South," *Perspectives in American History* 10 (1976): 7–80, Hoffman and Carville Earle have looked at the relationship of tobacco and grain economies to urban development. Earle began this analysis in *Evolution of a Tidewater Settlement System: All Hallow's Parish, Maryland, 1650–1783,* University of Chicago Department of Geography Research Paper no. 170 (Chicago, 1970). Some of his more arresting conclusions—that the inspection act of 1747 drastically affected the tobacco trade, and that during recessions in the staple economy, planters tended to increase their wealth—seem untrue of the Eastern Shore. Both points, however, form part of a persuasive argument about the way planters adjusted their use of land and labor in response to the market. Earle has carefully portrayed how economic conditions affected the balance most planters kept between market agriculture on the one hand and self-sufficiency farming and home industry on the other. In a recent article, "A Staple Interpretation of Slavery and Free Labor," *Geographical Review* 68 (1978): 51–65, Earle has raised the question of whether the switch to wheat farming made slavery in the northern Chesapeake less profitable than wage labor. The competition between tobacco and wheat in Virginia and the impact that the marketing of these crops had on population distribution and urban development have been treated by Robert D. Mitchell in *Commercialism and Frontier: Perspectives on the Early Shenandoah Valley* (Charlottesville, Va., 1977).

The ongoing reinterpretation of Chesapeake history owes much to historians who have worked on other regions. Particularly valuable for a comparative perspective are Kenneth A. Lockridge, *A New England Town, the First Hundred Years: Dedham, Massachusetts, 1636–1736* (New York, 1970), and Philip J. Greven, Jr., *Four Generations: Population, Land, and Family in Colonial Andover, Massachusetts* (Ithaca, N.Y., 1970). The emphasis in these works on population growth and family values should be contrasted with the focus on economic growth and market values in Charles S. Grant, *Democracy in the Connecticut Frontier Town of Kent* (New York, 1961), and Richard L. Bushman, *From Puritan to Yankee: Character and Social Order in Connecticut, 1690–1765* (Cambridge, Mass., 1967). Comparative analysis provides the theme of Gloria L. Main's "Inequality in Early America: The Evidence from Probate Records of Massachusetts and Maryland," *Journal of Interdisciplinary History* 7 (1977): 559–581.

Richard S. Dunn, in *Sugar and Slaves: The Rise of the Planter Class in the English West Indies, 1624–1713* (Chapel Hill, N.C., 1972), has woven together economic, demographic, and cultural history and brillantly portrayed a society that was an exaggerated mirror image of the Chesapeake. In the Caribbean, mortality rates were high, white women and children were few, and family life was fragile. Plantations were larger, the exploitation of blacks was more brutal and systematic, and the fortunes made from staple agriculture were greater. On the Middle Colonies, James T. Lemon's *The Best Poor Man's Country: A Geographical Study of Early Southeastern Pennsylvania* (Baltimore, 1972) and Sung Bok Kim's *Landlord and Tenant in Colonial New York: Manorial Society, 1664–1775* (Chapel Hill, N.C., 1978) treat the small family farmers whose arable husbandry was the backbone of the economy. Lemon's book is notable for his contention that these farming endeavors were infused with liberal (market) values, while Kim's study is important because he asserts that landlords and tenants both profited from the New York manor system.

Finally, several studies should be noted because they provide a picture of the larger world of which the Eastern Shore was a part. Among those that deal most explicitly with market and demographic conditions are James A. Henretta, *The Evolution of American Society, 1700–1815: An Interdisciplinary Analysis* (Lexington, Mass., 1973); Joan Thirsk, ed., *The Agrarian History of England and Wales, 1500–1640* (Cambridge, England, 1967), vol. 4; and Jan de Vries, *The Economy of Europe in an Age of Crisis, 1600–1750* (Cambridge, England, 1976).

Index

A

Accomack County, Va., 26n, 219
Amsterdam, Neth., 37–38, 166
Anderson, William, 124, 128, 202
Annapolis, Md., 170–171, 174, 176–177, 203
Anne Arundel County, Md., 177
Artisans, 51, 90–92, 105, 107, 201

B

Bacon, Anthony, 199n
Baltic trade, 38, 58
Baltimore, Md., 174, 204
Barbados. *See* West Indies.
Bennett, Edward, 121
Bennett, Richard I, 121–122, 125
Bennett, Richard II, 122, 128
Bennett, Richard III, 121–124, 126, 128, 200
Bennett, Robert, 122
Bermuda, 34, 176
Bideford, Eng., 113, 202
Blacks, 144–145. *See also* Slaves.
Bollingbroke Hundred, Talbot County, Md., 162–163
Bowden, Peter, 89
Brazil, 58
Bremen, Ger., 166
Bristol, Eng., merchants of, 22, 36, 48, 59, 75, 114, 218
Buchanan, James, 202

C

Carter, Landon, 184–186
Carter, Robert "King," 184
Cecil County, Md., 60, 67, 177
Chamberlaine, James, 128
Chamberlaine, Samuel, 126–129, 131, 134, 199–200
Chamberlaine, Thomas, 128
Chester River, 26, 44–45, 73, 206
  trade on, 92, 95, 170, 172, 201–202
Chestertown, Md., 45, 178, 201–204, 217
Clark, Joshua, 201
Climate, 43
Corn, 47, 82–83, 173, 184. *See also* Grain production.
Costin, Henry, 201
Covington, Sarah, 128, 131
Cox, Isaac, 136–138, 222
Credit, 39, 55n, 117–118, 202–204
Cromwell, Oliver, 122
Crookshanks, Robert, 202
Cunliffe, Foster, 124, 127, 199–201

D

Delaware, 45, 54, 57
Diversified farming, 22–23, 183–198
Dorchester County, Md., 20, 26, 47, 66, 73, 75–76
Dublin, 166
Dutch trade, 37–38, 58
Dutch wars, 49, 52

245

The Atlantic Economy
and Colonial Maryland's
Eastern Shore

Designed by G. T. Whipple, Jr.
Composed by The Composing Room of Michigan, Inc.
in 10 point VIP Baskerville, 2 points leaded,
with display lines in Baskerville
Printed offset by Thomson/Shore, Inc.
on Warren's Number 66 text, 50 pound basis.
Bound by John H. Dekker & Sons, Inc.
in Holliston book cloth
and stamped in All Purpose foil.

Library of Congress Cataloging in Publication Data

Clemens, Paul G. E. 1947–
    The Atlantic economy and Colonial
    Maryland's Eastern Shore
    Bibliography: p.
    Includes index.
    1. Eastern Shore, Md.—Economic conditions. I. Title.
HC107.M32E323   330.9′752′1   79-26181
ISBN 0-8014-1251-X